Social Justice, Education and Identity

This book answers key questions regarding social justice in education. Its central theme is how the education system, through its organisation and practices, is implicated in the realisation of just or unjust social outcomes. In particular, the writers examine the ways in which the identities of individuals and groups are formed and transformed in schools, colleges and universities.

The book contains examples drawn from early years through to higher education. It has a dual focus, addressing:

- theoretical debates in social justice, including how the concept of social justice can be understood, and theoretical issues around social capital, and class and gender reproduction;
- the formation of learner identities, focusing on how these are differentiated by class, ethnicity, gender, sexuality and (dis)ability.

Carol Vincent has assembled a wide-ranging collection of lucidly argued essays by a panel of internationally respected contributors. The authors draw on their current and recent research to inform their writing, and so theory is balanced with extensive empirical evidence. Therefore the debates contained here have implications for policy and practice, as well as being theoretically and analytically rich.

This book will provide unrivalled coverage of the subject for researchers, academics, practitioners and policymakers in education.

Carol Vincent is Senior Lecturer in Education Policy at the University of London's Institute of Education.

Social Justice, Education and Identity

Edited by Carol Vincent

 RoutledgeFalmer
Taylor & Francis Group

LONDON AND NEW YORK

First published 2003
by RoutledgeFalmer
11 New Fetter Lane, London EC4P 4EE

Simultaneously published in the USA and Canada
by RoutledgeFalmer
29 West 35th Street, New York, NY 10001

RoutledgeFalmer is an imprint of the Taylor & Francis Group

Selection and editorial matter © 2003 Carol Vincent;
individual chapters © their authors

Typeset in Times by GreenGate Publishing Services
Printed and bound in Great Britain by MPG Books Ltd, Bodmin

British Library Cataloguing in Publication Data
A catalogue record for this book is available from the British Library

Library of Congress Cataloging in Publication Data
Social justice, education, and identity / [edited by] Carol Vincent.
    p. cm.
    Includes bibliographical references and index.
    1. Educational sociology. 2. Social justice–Study and teaching. 3. Identity
    (Philosophical concept) I. Vincent, Carol, 1963–

    LC191.S6564 2003
    370.11'5–dc21

                                                        2003043204

ISBN 0-415-29695-1 (Hbk)
ISBN 0-415-29696-X (Pbk)

Contents

Illustrations

Figures

Tables

Notes on contributors

Madeleine Arnot is Reader in Sociology of Education and Fellow of Jesus College at the University of Cambridge. She has published extensively on gender, race and class relations in education and has been actively involved in promoting equality policies and citizenship education. Her recent books include: *Challenging Democracy: International Perspectives on Gender, Education and Citizenship* (edited by J. Dillabough, RoutledgeFalmer 2000) and *Reproducing Gender? Essays on Educational Theory and Feminist Politics* (RoutledgeFalmer 2002).

Stephen J. Ball is Karl Mannheim Professor of Sociology of Education and Director of the Education Policy Research Unit at the University of London Institute of Education. His work is mainly focused on social class and education policy. His new book is *Class Strategies and the Education Market: the Middle Class and Social Advantage* (RoutledgeFalmer 2003).

Ghazala Bhatti is a lecturer at the University of Reading. Her research focuses on the impact of ethnicity, social class and gender on the educational experiences of children and adults. She is also interested in expoloring parents' participation in their children's education. She is a convenor of the network on Social Justice and Intercultural Education for the ECER (European Conference on Educational Research).

Paul Connolly is Senior Lecturer in Sociology at the University of Ulster. His publications include: *Racism, Gender Identities and Young Children* (Routledge) and *Researching Racism in Education* (Open University Press), the latter with Barry Troyna. He is currently completing a major research study of sectarianism and children in Northern Ireland and is also working on a book on boys and schooling in the early years.

Alan Cribb is Senior Lecturer in Ethics and Education and member of the Centre for Public Policy Research at King's College London. He has a particular interest in the interface between public policy and professional ethics and has published widely on this theme and related issues in applied ethics.

Debbie Epstein is Professor of Education at Goldsmiths College, University of London. She has published widely on sexuality, gender and race. Her recent books include *Schooling Sexualities* (with Richard Johnson, 1998), *Failing Boys? Issues in Gender and Achievement* (with Jannette Elwood, Valerie Hey and Janet Maw, 1998) and *A Dangerous Knowing: Sexuality, Pedagogy and Popular Culture* (with James T. Sears, 1999) and *Silenced Sexualities in Schools and Universities* (with Sarah O'Flynn and David Telford, 2003).

Eva Gamarnikow is Lecturer in Sociology and Human Rights at the Institute of Education, University of London. She has a strong interest in social policy and social justice, and the role of social capital theory in current policy thinking. Together with Anthony Green she has written about various aspects of New Labour education policy and social capital.

Sharon Gewirtz is Professor of Education and a member of the Centre for Public Policy Research at King's College London. Her research, which embraces both empirical and theoretical work, is in the sociology of education. Her latest book is *The Managerial School: Post-Welfarism and Social Justice in Education* (Routledge, 2002).

Anthony Green is a Lecturer in Sociology of Education at the Institute of Education, University of London. He has an ongoing interest in theoretical, conceptual and methodological aspects of researching equity issues in education policies and practices. Together with Eva Gamarnikow he has written about various aspects of New Labour education policy and social capital.

Roger Hewitt is a Senior Research Associate in the Centre for Urban and Community Research, Goldsmiths College, University of London. His research has been concerned with issues of racism and the social contexts of adolescent racial violence. More recently he has been working on the effects of asylum seeker dispersal and 'community relations'. His published work includes *White Talk Black Talk: Inter-racial Friendship and Communication Amongst Adolescents* (1986) and *Routes of Racism* (1993). He is currently working on a book for Cambridge University Press to be called *Racism and the White Backlash*.

Diana Leonard is Professor of Sociology of Education and Gender and Head of the Centre for Research in Education and Gender at the Institute of Education, University of London. Diana's current research interests include: women and doctoral studies; changes in doctoral studies globally; assessment of the PhD (especially the viva); and International students in the UK. She has also researched extensively on issues of gender in schooling, in particular: gender, violence and education; gender and special educational needs; gendered learning styles. She has published widely on these subjects and on feminist theory. Her most recent book is *A Woman's Guide to Doctoral Studies*. Previous books include: *Sex in Question: French Feminism* (with

Lisa Adkins); *Familiar Exploitation: A New Analysis of Marriage in Contemporary Western Societies* (with Christine Delphy); and *The Politics of Gender and Education.*

Melanie Mauthner is Lecturer in Social Policy in the Faculty of Social Sciences at the Open University. Her research explores cultures of friendship and kinship, especially among siblings, an area she is researching for the Joseph Rowntree Foundation, and she has written *Sistering: Power and Change in Female Relationships* (Palgrave 2002). She has co-edited *Ethics in Qualitative Research* with Maxine Birch, Julie Jessop and Tina Miller (Sage 2002), and *The Politics of Gender and Education: Critical Perspectives* with Suki Ali and Shereen Benjamin (Palgrave 2003).

Carrie Paechter is Reader in Education at Goldsmiths College, University of London. Her research centres around the intersection of gender, power and knowledge, the construction of gendered, spatialised and embodied identities, and the processes of curriculum negotiation. Her most recent books are *Educating the Other: Gender, Power and Schooling* (Falmer Press 1998) and *Changing School Subjects: Power, Gender and Curriculum* (Open University Press 2000).

Diane Reay is a researcher at London Metropolitan University. She has researched widely in the area of social injustice and has written over 80 articles which address inequalitites of social class, race and gender.

Michael J. Reiss is Professor of Science Education and Head of the School of Mathematics, Science and Technology at the Institute of Education, University of London. He works in the fields of science education, bioethics and sex education. For further details see www.reiss.tc

Sheila Riddell worked as a teacher of English in a comprehensive school for seven years before doing a PhD in the sociology of education at Bristol University. She moved to Scotland in 1988 and since then has researched and written extensively on special educational needs and disability policy. She is currently Director of the Strathclyde Centre for Disability Research at the University of Glasgow.

Lyn Tett is Professor of Community Education and Lifelong Learning at the University of Edinburgh. Her research interests lie within the broad area of community-based learning and education. Her latest book is *Community Education, Lifelong Learning and Social Inclusion* (Dunedin Academic Press 2002).

Carol Vincent is a senior lecturer in education policy at the Institute of Education, University of London. She has written and researched widely on parents' relationships with the education system, and her last book was *Including Parents?: Education, Citizenship and Parental Agency* (Open University Press 2000). She is currently directing a project exploring parental choice of early years childcare.

Chris Watkins has been a teacher in a large secondary school, a teacher in charge of a unit for pupils whose effect on school was disruptive, and a trained school counsellor. He is now a reader in education at the University of London Institute of Education, where his current areas of work include effective learning in classrooms and school, and school behaviour. Recent research projects include 'The violence-resilient school' (detailed in Chapter 7). He has been an executive member of the National Association for Pastoral Care in Education since 1982. His project as an educator is to support schools in helping young people compose a life and make a difference, and to help teachers learn and grow in a healthy school environment.

Acknowledgements

When I remarked to colleagues that I was editing a book, the most common reaction was a dry laugh and an assurance that this was a thankless task. This has made me greatly appreciate the contributors to this book. They have responded to my various queries and comments with great thoughtfulness, incisiveness, courtesy (however they actually felt!) and promptness. It has been a pleasure to work with them. I would also like to thank Hywel Evans, then at RoutledgeFalmer, for his support of this project. And finally, thanks go, as ever, to Ian, Madi and Daniel, my family.

Carol Vincent
December 2002

Introduction

Carol Vincent

This book is a collection of writings on the theme of social justice, education and identity by researchers who are members of the British Educational Research Association's (BERA) Special Interest Group (SIG) in Social Justice. The authors seek to theorise the concept of social justice, inquire into its presence or absence in various sites and explore how the education system, through its organisation and practices, is implicated in the realisation of just or unjust social outcomes (Dehli 2002, personal communication). A particular theme is how the identities of individuals and groups are formed and transformed in schools, colleges and universities.

These are the kind of concerns that have sustained the SIG since its inception. I convened the group – a loose network of researchers and practitioners with a theoretical and practical interest in social justice – in 1997. The impetus, a very sad one, was the untimely death of Professor Barry Troyna from cancer the previous year. Barry had written extensively on race and education, and also on methodology. Questions of social justice were always to the fore in his work, and we hoped that the SIG would provide a forum in which to carry forward the issues which were of concern to him. The original rationale for the SIG set out the following aims:

• To focus on the changing nature of the relationship between social justice and education in the light of the recent restructuring of the education system.
• To focus on the concept of social justice itself, and to ask with Harvey (1993) 'which theory of social justice is the most socially just'. What are the definitions of social justice which are useful to apply to a study of education?
• To consider the processes by which academic critique can or should influence political agendas.

The title of this book, the linking of social justice and identity, may need some explanation. Social justice has traditionally been discussed in economic terms. However, distributive justice, as it is often referred to, overlooks the cultural and relational aspects of social justice. In the 1970s and early 1980s, in the study of education and other social science disciplines, class-based analyses occupied a prime position. As a result, the structuring of experience that resulted from other dimensions of identity – belonging to a particular gender, ethnic, racial and/or religious grouping for example – received less attention. The current focus on difference, the 'politics of recognition', is a response to that. Hence the bringing together here of social justice and identity. Our understanding of who we are, the others with whom we identify and those with whom we do not, how the social groupings to which we belong are perceived, these factors are now understood to be key in understanding and interrogating the concept of social justice. Education, because of its crucial role in the production and reproduction of particular identities and social positionings, is a particularly fruitful site in which to consider the playing out, or the performance, of social justice and identity issues. In the next two sections, I will briefly explore some of the main debates pertaining to understandings of both social justice and identity.

Social justice

Over the years, contributors to the SIG have tackled in particular the issue of how to understand social justice; how to make sense out of, how to develop and apply that most amorphous of concepts. As Morwenna Griffiths (1998: 90) points out, social justice has a temporal and spatial dimension. That is, what is considered as just at one juncture in history, or in one place, or amongst one social group, is not necessarily considered so in another. Ways of thinking characteristic to our own time, although not hegemonic, stress contingency, fluidity, subjectivity, 'situated knowledge' (Haraway 1991), ways of thinking which we broadly label postmodernist. Applying such filters to social justice leaves us with two dilemmas. The first is that postmodernism's emphasis on relativity has been seen by some critics as neutralising the possibility of political action and change (Skeggs 1991, Cole and Hill 1995). The second dilemma is that we are left, amongst 'the lived muddle of justice ethics' (Seddon 2003), with little 'hope of finding a dominant perspective and metanarrative of justice which will guide us,' (Griffiths 1998: 90). On the first point, several commentators have argued that, on the contrary, postmodernist perspectives invite change, and create the necessary intellectual conditions by rendering the familiar strange (as Ball (1990) points out with reference to mass education). As Elizabeth Atkinson puts it, 'far from being mere word play, the deconstruction of [policy] texts that claim to liberate, to educate, to emancipate, offers a powerful way forward in opposing the status quo' (2002: 83). And also, I would suggest, such deconstruction offers a way forward in interrogating and challenging particular models and conceptions of social justice. For example, the current UK government's approach to social justice contains a particular 'spin' which some would question. Jordan highlights the values and beliefs inherent in New Labour's conception of social policy, an emphasis shared by other centre-left governments:

> The strongest appeal of the new politics of welfare is to a set of ethical principles that will reconcile social justice with efficiency … The prize is a society

that combines prosperity and fairness. The explicit appeal is to a set of values – hard work, thrift, community, family, solidarity and respect for authority.

(Jordan 1998: 24)

Here we can see the influence of New Labour's 'something for something' policy imperative, the emphasis on community regeneration, social inclusion, building networks of social capital; emphases that require, not macro systemic change, but micro change, in the form of family and community improvement, and the isolation and amelioration of deficiencies in family and community organisation, relationships, values and outlooks. Briefly, Jordan describes this understanding of socially just welfare policies as one which 'deals in moral categories such as "genuine need" and "reciprocity" that stand as proxies for "deserving" and "belonging"' (Ibid. 206). Those situated outside these categories – as neither deserving nor belonging, the most obvious example in the context of the UK being asylum seekers – are largely excluded from the benefits open to other better placed individuals. Social justice here is partial, exclusionary and tied to particular ways of behaving and particular attitudes. Jordan's account also reveals the way in which social justice is still most commonly used to mean distributive justice, issues of benefits and resources and 'who gets what'. At this point, we return to the second dilemma noted above: the difficulties of defining a 'grand narrative' of social justice, meaningful to all. As an introduction to debates in this area, I have found useful the work of Iris Marion Young (1990, 1996, 1997). She argues that the distributive paradigm is limited, because it assumes

a single model of justice for all analyses of justice: all situations in which justice is at issue are analogous to the situation of persons dividing a stock of goods and comparing the size of the portions individuals have. Such a model implicitly assumes that individuals or other agents [are]. as nodes, points in the social field, among whom larger or smaller bundles of social goods are assigned.

(Young 1990: 18)

This paradigm has obscured consideration of broader questions about 'the social structure and institutional context that often help determine distributive patterns' (1990:15). Young is interested in conceptions of justice in relation to heterogeneous and differentiated communities. Her argument is that differentiation by class, gender, age, disability, sexuality, ethnicity and perceived racial group generate distinct versions of what 'justice' looks like. But distributive justice alone is insufficient to engage with this cultural complexity. Accordingly Young maintains that concepts of domination and oppression, not just the concept of distribution, should be the starting point for a politics of social justice. This means giving centre stage to an analysis of social structures and institutional contexts which influence the nature of distribution. Her conception of 'five faces of oppression' (exploitation, marginalisation, powerlessness, cultural imperialism and violence

(Young 1990)) combines distributional *and* cultural or relational dimensions of social justice, thus producing a framework for a 'political-economic analysis of social life' (Gewirtz 1998: 477). Writing specifically about education, Connell makes a similar case arguing that 'education is a social process in which the 'how much' cannot be separated from the 'what'. There is an inescapable link between distribution and content' (Connell 1993:18).

Young – like others such as Nancy Fraser (1997), Sylvie Benhabib (1992, 1996a, b) and Ann Phillips (1993, 1995, 1999) – places difference and diversity at the centre of her theorising. Many of these writers have been influenced by and have contributed to the focusing of attention on gender, racial, and/or cultural differentiation – what has become known, as I noted above, as 'the politics of recognition'. Such a focus has had many benefits and has resulted in a sense of collective identity amongst many minority groups which has been articulated in the public sphere. However, some commentators ask whether the shift in attention away from social class inequalities has resulted in the politics of recognition, important and beneficial though it is, 'crowding out' older issues of economic equality (Phillips 1999). Nancy Fraser pursues similar questions and argues that if we are to increase social justice, we need to develop strategies that maintain both economic redistribution and cultural recognition – a task easier stated than acted upon. Alan Cribb and Sharon Gewirtz in this volume discuss the tensions which arise from clashes between demands for distribution and recognition.

Young argues that 'the realisation of a politics of difference' requires 'an institutional and ideological means for recognising and affirming diverse social groups by giving political representation to these groups and celebrating their distinctive characteristics and cultures' (1990: 240, also Yeatman 1994). Young sees this potential being realised through what Cribb and Gewirtz (this volume) refer to as 'associational justice'. Her specific proposals are 'regional governments, composed of representatives from neighbourhood assemblies, which hold those representatives accountable' (ibid. 252, see also Troyna and Vincent 1995 for comment). Radical conceptions of citizenship, such as Young's, emphasise a re-working of the concept, starting from the contested nature of public purposes and the citizenry's diverse cultural and political identities and values. Through a process of public dialogue, rival positions reach compromises, temporary settlements, if not consensus (Vincent 2000: 15–16, Martin and Vincent 1999).

The problems associated with such proposals are well known. They may prove to be little more than 'romantic localism' (Rizvi 1993: 155), as there is no guarantee that public dialogue, whether it takes place in regional government or even local neighbourhood forums will automatically lead to the reconstitution of existing power relations in ways which further social justice. The uneven spread of those citizens oriented towards participation in formalised arrangements within representative democracies is likely to lead to citizen forums with homogeneous rather than diverse social representation. Then there is the problem of relativism where everything and anything goes. Local citizen forums may take decisions others regard as intolerant or self-serving. Third, talk of negotiating difference, working with diversity, deliberative dialogue, sounds grand in abstract, but the lived reality is often of sheer hard labour and effort, schisms and alliances, frustration and alienation. It is for this reason that social movements often work best if they are single issue, offering one focus of concern to which all can sign up regardless of other differences (Vincent 2000). Most of us are not and do not expect to be involved in any type of collective action around public-sector services such as education. The explanation for this lack of faith in the possibility or utility of collective action can be framed simply: we live in a passive, although perhaps increasingly cynical, polity where the politics of 'domestication, containment and boundary drawing' (Benhabib 1996a: 7) predominate (see Vincent 2000 for an elaboration of this argument). However contributors to this book reveal the range of sites and points of intervention and engagement where social justice concerns can be identified. Their analyses emphasise (degrees of) space, agency and the contestation of dominant educational discourses and practices.

Identity

Much of the current work on identity does not emphasise political identities or the relationship between the individual and the polity. It is however particularly valuable in helping us to understand how educational subjectivities are constructed. Recent empirical and theoretical work in this area argues for an understanding of identity as fluid, not fixed; multiple, not single; and transforming, not static. As Stuart Hall observes:

> Cultural identities come from somewhere, have histories. But … far from being eternally fixed in some essentialist past, they are subject to the continual play of history, culture and power … identities are the names we give to the different ways we are positioned by, and position ourselves within, the narratives of the past.
>
> (Hall 1993: 394, cited in Rassool 1997)

Hall draws attention to the fact that we are both assigned social identities and create our own sense of identity, our self-image. When there are tensions between assigned social identity and self-image, people work to resolve the tensions in different ways (Woods and Jeffrey 2002: 90). As several contributors to this volume note (Arnot, Epstein, Reay, Riddell), the effect of structural forces and individual agency combine to shape identities. 'People may "make themselves" … but they do so (to misquote Marx) in conditions not of their own choosing' (Epstein, this volume). One example is provided by the primary school teachers in a recent study by Woods and Jeffrey (2002). The teachers have to re-position themselves in relation to a social identity now defined by performance targets and outputs. These mid-career teachers generally reacted by learning to generate a public social identity of a teacher competent in performance when faced with the demands of inspection, but this identity hid another self which maintained their original professional values about the purposes of their teaching, and rejected the requirements and regulation of a performative culture.

Bakare-Yusuf (1997) provides another very different example of identity work in her account of young black women involved in the 1980s raregroove scene. For these aspirational women, participating in a multiracial, largely privileged social milieu, and one that was not seen as traditionally 'black', allowed them to express their self-image as black, non-traditional, upwardly mobile, young women. Taste in music (and Bakare-Yusuf cites Bourdieu (1986) on taste as the basis for social distinctions) is used by these women as part of their struggle to 'articulate the plurality of their identities, cultural ethnicity, cultural capital and experience against the backdrop of some "essentialising past" which attempts to homogenise the (re-)presentation and experience of the black female subject' (Bakare-Yusuf 1997: 83). Thus their taste in music allowed them to move beyond what they perceived to be the limits of their assigned social identities.

As Madeleine Arnot points out (this volume), creativity is a key factor in processes of 'identity constructions, identifications and alliances'. This recognition highlights a problematic aspect of identity politics, the politics of recognition. For such an approach, as Bakare-Yusuf's respondents recognised, risks imposing fixed definitions of particular groups, what it means to be, say, a black woman, a working-class mother, a lesbian, what attitudes, what values, what priorities to hold. Such a politics can be both a basis for and a constant barrier to social justice (Ball 2002, personal communication), as it generates a binary divide between us and others (Leonard 1997: 157; also Walkerdine *et al.* 2001).

Of course defining 'us' and 'them' is a major occupation of children and young people, as they experiment with and learn about the social world. Compulsory education in particular is uniquely bound up with processes of identity formation. Just as we are learning what it is to be a member of a particular social group, we enter a system which provides a running commentary on the development of our skills and abilities, our behaviour and attitudes, our families and their lifestyles. This can be affirming for some, but very disabling for others (see Arnot, Ball, Bhatti, Epstein, Paecheter, Reay, this volume). In a recent paper, Elaine Unterhalter (2001) commenting on Sen's writing about the development of human capabilities, notes that there is considerable empirical evidence that education, or at least formal schooling in particular contexts, 'may as much be a case of capability *deprivation* as of human capability in development'.

Bev Skeggs's (1997) study of a group of young women enrolled in caring courses in an FE college shows how the curriculum functions to affect individual subjectivities. The caring courses occupy a position of low status within the college hierarchy, 'this organisation also generates a network of subject positions in relation to these hierarchies ... it defines what it is to be cultivated and clever against what it is to be practical and useful and responsible' (1997: 60). The women students invest in the latter characteristics, particularly valued in their work placement settings, in an attempt to invert the usual academic/practical distinctions (see also Arnot, this volume). Again constraint and creativity work together to form identities.

Of course education can also be enormously liberating, opening up perspectives, attitudes, skills, bodies of knowledge that can enhance lives. But alongside such enhancement may come difficult transitions. Education for some is a process of 'border crossing'. I am thinking here of Raymond Williams' book *Border Country* (1960) where the protagonist, supposedly based on Williams himself, journeys into and away from a small village in Wales near the border with England. The village was where he had grown up, but he lived a very different adult life in London. Like Williams, some people feel that as a result of their educational experiences they 'leave' a particular 'structure of feeling' (to use Williams' term), that is a set of shared cultural assumptions, beliefs and orientations, that they are required to exchange a known lifestyle and a known identity for another (Reay, Bhatti, this volume). But of course the places where we started from can never be entirely left, and the disjunction between the old and the new can provide pain (Walkerdine *et al.* 2001) but also possibilities of establishing cultural identities that are transgressive of old boundaries and categories (Kohli 1993).

Conclusion

Even these few brief notes on social justice and identity suggest the tenacity of apparently irreconcilable issues. Thus it is unsurprising that policies in education and other public-sector areas typically fail to engage with the tangle of issues involved here, falling back instead on apparently uncontested understandings of social justice or its current watered-down version – social inclusion, within which education is returned to the status of an unproblematic meritocratic vehicle. As Harry Brighouse notes (2001), whilst educational policy implications cannot be simply read off from theorising at the level of generality of Fraser, Young, *et al.*, paying attention to the implications of such theorising can direct our attention towards previously unquestioned assumptions and help us make judgements between 'good' and 'bad' education policy – that is, those policies that further socially just outcomes for all pupils and those that do not. For, as Barry Troyna noted, the task of education research should not stop at 'deconstructing the obvious', unpacking 'reality', but should also produce analyses 'which possess a particular strategic edge … to identify those elements which have the potential to change or resist the "social reality" as it is articulated through the current educational reforms' (1994: 82).

The structure of the book

The following chapters of this book discuss and extend various concepts of social justice and identity and their articulation with education at various stages (early years, school, higher and adult education) and in various localities. The book moves, with some overlap between themes, from theorising conceptions of social justice (Alan Cribb and Sharon Gewirtz) to explorations of identity formation and instances of socially just/unjust practices. After Cribb and Gewirtz come five chapters discussing class identities, their formation, transformation and reproduction (Stephen Ball, Diane Reay, Ghazala Bhatti, Lyn Tett and Madeleine Arnot). Gendered and sexual identities are the particular focus of three chapters (Madeleine Arnot, Debbie Epstein and Carrie Paechter). Areas of the curriculum are considered in two chapters (Carrie Paechter on PE and Michael Reiss on science education). The final three chapters address the formation of ethnic identities (Paul Connolly), the identities available to parents and professionals working within and around local special education policy frameworks (Sheila Riddell), and, continuing the policy focus, the social justice implications of the current UK government policy of diversification and specialisation of schools (Eva Gamarnikow and Tony Green).

Alan Cribb and Sharon Gewirtz set the theoretical scene by developing and refining plural conceptions of social justice. Their emphasis on social justice as being about more than distribution, as including issues of cultural justice and opportunities to participate in decision making are shared by other contributors to this volume. They argue that closer attention should be paid to the tensions that may arise between these different aspects of social justice and, echoing Barry Troyna, that critical researchers are obliged not 'to contract out of the messy business of day-to-day problems' (Willis 1997: 186, quoted in Arnot, this volume). To this end they cite some 'real-world' examples where engagement with different facets of social justice has resulted in valuable practice.

An additional note concerning the relationship between research and researchers, policy and practice may be useful here. It is clearly a highly complex and contested issue (see for example Hammersley 2002 for a critique of the idea that the role of research is to inform policy). I decided against requesting that all contributors include recommendations directly addressing the policy implications of their analyses (although a number do so). This was for two reasons. First, such a request may have resulted in artificial lists of policy 'solutions'. The relationship between the empirical work presented here, and the 'so what?' of policy has, I believe, an organic and perhaps more attenuated nature. Policy implications cannot be read off from every single paper, but can instead result from critical reflection on a body of work from a single researcher or research team, or, perhaps preferably, from debate between several. Second, Gerald Grace's (1995) use of Fay's (1975) policy science and policy scholarship distinction draws attention to the need for researchers to resist the immediate concerns and agendas of policy makers, to focus on what Marginson (1993) calls self-controlled rather than policy-controlled research (cited in Ozga 2000). Theory, as Stephen Ball argues, has a particular role here.

Theory provides this possibility, the possibility of dis-identification – the effect of working 'on and against' prevailing practices of ideological subjection.

The point of theory … should be, in Foucault's words, 'to sap power', to engage in struggle to reveal and undermine what is most invisible and insidious in prevailing practices (Troyna 1994). This is very much a 'practical' concern addressed directly to the practices and interests of educational workers.

(1994: 269)

How we as researchers can best communicate with educational workers (practitioners and policy makers), how we translate critique into material that is meaningful and of practical value beyond the academy is an issue far from being resolved. I hope that this is a theme that members of the social justice SIG will further consider.

Stephen Ball's chapter drawn from his research on the strategies used by middle class families in the education marketplace, considers the decision-making processes of families deciding between state and private secondary schooling. He demonstrates that families called on both public principles and also private interests in order to make their choice. Particular families reached different forms of accommodation with these interests. Ball concludes that families did indeed put first what they saw as the interests of their children even when they had principled objections to private schooling. In cases where a decision to send children to state school was taken, parents were clear that it was their access to a state school that they deemed acceptable which allowed them to make such a choice.

Diane Reay focuses on student choice of higher education institution (HEI), arguing that for working-class applicants 'there is no easy transition, no seamless process'. Instead these students struggled with anxiety, insecurity, a lack of knowledge around the field of HE, and in particular for those who had the possibility of going to an 'elite' university confused ideas and images of self. A concern to find an institution where they felt that they would fit in sat uneasily alongside concerns that an HEI which appeared to attract large numbers of working-class and/or minority ethnic students apparently like themselves was not a 'good' place to go. Her chapter points to the production of segregated and hierarchical student identities and experiences.

Similar themes are taken up by Ghazala Bhatti. She focuses on the experiences of working-class white and Asian-origin students in and after HE. The white mature male students on a Community and Youth course transgressed norms of student behaviour and student–tutor relationships, but experienced their course as a positive experience which allowed them to get jobs, mostly in their own localities working with the communities there. The Asian-origin young women had less successful experiences, as they found themselves with degrees which did not enable them to find employment. Bhatti concludes that for working-class students to be successful they must be instrumental in their choice of course and institution. The account demonstrates that initiatives to widen access and participation to HE will be limited if their effect is to produce graduates who find that they have simply delayed unemployment and the accompanying feelings of waste and alienation.

Lyn Tett gives an account of a health education course for adults which has run in Scotland. The course is underpinned by the belief that ill-health is often the result of damaging socio-economic conditions which can be ameliorated by individuals and communities operating for mutual support. The chapter gives several examples of individuals gaining a greater sense of agency and self-esteem as well as better health through coming together to identify their own health needs, question official discourses which put the blame for ill-health on self-chosen deficiencies in lifestyle, and work for the improvement of health and social services locally.

Madeleine Arnot's chapter is a critical consideration of Paul Willis's (1977) study of working-class boys, *Learning to Labour*. She argues that Willis's text is highly relevant today especially in the area of critical research methodologies and the study of gender and class identity formation. However, she also considers feminist critiques of Willis's portrayal of 'the lads', demonstrating how little consideration was given by Willis to the role of their families, especially their mothers, in the development of their classed and gendered identities. Arnot concludes with a consideration of contemporary 'ladism' and what it tells us of boys' attempts at meaning-making as they engage with school, family and peer culture.

Debbie Epstein, Roger Hewitt, Diana Leonard, Melanie Mauthner and Chris Watkins also understand identity formation as an amalgam of structural forces and individual agency (see also Arnot and Reay). They consider public (in this instance, school) policies and how they contribute to the formation of identity amongst pupils. They focus in particular on the lack of school policies around homophobia. Their chapter demonstrates the prevalence of homophobic attitudes in schools (although not always recognised as such by staff), and the way in which 'emphatic masculinities' make use of homophobia in the process of identity formation, by crudely dis-identifying from any perceived homosexual behaviour and attitudes. Epstein *et al.* conclude that schools have a responsibility to develop practices and policies which challenge homophobia, in order to create a less violent atmosphere for all pupils.

Carrie Paechter takes up the issue of school responsibility in her analysis of how school PE contributes to the formation and perpetuation of localised communities of masculine and feminine practice. PE and sport are particularly salient sites for identity formation for both girls and boys, but whereas participation in sport signifies a legitimate masculine practice, dominant teenage femininities often involve a rejection of sport. Moreover school PE itself positions different activities, and as a result different bodily forms, as suitable for boys and girls. As a result, the congruence between PE and dominant teenage practices of masculinity and femininity restrict the possibilities open to both boys and girls. Paechter concludes by suggesting directions for possible action for change.

Michael Reiss' chapter focuses on another area of the school curriculum: science. He argues for a broader view of science education, one that locates it firmly within a socio-political context, which can be valuably exploited to demonstrate diversity and encourage pupils to engage in value-driven conversations around scientific activity in the wider world. He concludes that one effect of such activities would be to encourage pupils to consider the social justice implications of the lifestyles adopted by those in affluent countries on others far from them in terms of distance, time (intergenerational issues) and even species (interspecific issues). Reiss' chapter includes schemes of work for various age groups.

Paul Connolly's chapter explores the development of ethnic awareness and identities in young children in Northern Ireland, a country where ethnic divisions and distinctions are particularly strong despite the absence of any physical markers. His data collection in one study was based on showing young children images clearly associated with either Catholics or Protestants in Northern Ireland. The research as a whole reveals that ethnic identity formation is apparent in some children as young as three, and grows quickly, accompanied in some cases by prejudice, as children progress through primary school. Connolly concludes his chapter with a discussion of the issues that intervention in and engagement with ethnic prejudice raises for early years practitioners and other adults.

Sheila Riddell's chapter focuses on policy, discussing the findings of a study into the policies and procedures used to administer special educational needs provision in local authorities in England and Scotland. She identifies six normative models of procedural justice – bureaucracy, professionalism, legality, managerialism, consumerism and markets – and interrogates the subject positions open to both parents and professionals under these various frameworks. Individual cases within an English and a Scottish authority are compared in order to demonstrate how local policy frameworks and cultures position parents and professionals differently. The space available to parents and the resources they require to negotiate a different identity are also discussed. She concludes that a scarcity of resources creates a motive for professionals to discourage most parents from active engagement with and challenge to the system.

Eva Gamarnikow and Tony Green continue the focus on policy in their account of New Labour's promotion of a programme of specialisation and diversification in UK secondary schooling. They employ social capital theory to consider how the specialist and beacon status awarded to some secondary schools will and is impacting upon local education markets. According to national policy objectives, such diversity in institutional identity will be accompanied by 'social capitalist professionalist' networks of teachers exchanging specialised knowledge and skills which will improve weak schools in a locality and thereby achieve parity of esteem between institutions. However, Gamarnikow and Green conclude that specialisation/beaconisation policies will rationalise the existing system of educational hierarchy, but that the unequal outcomes will be disguised as process of organic diversity and specialisation.

Acknowledgement

I would like to thank Stephen Ball for his (as usual) helpful and incisive comments on an earlier draft of this introduction.

References

Atkinson, E. (2002) 'The responsible anarchist: postmodernism and social change', *British Journal of Sociology of Education*, 23, 1:73–82

Bakare-Yusuf, B. (1997) 'Raregrooves and raregroovers: a matter of taste, difference and identity' in Mirza, H. (ed.) *Black British Feminism*, London: Routledge

Ball, S.J. (1990) *Politics and Policymaking in Euducation*, London: Routledge

Ball, S. J. (1997) 'Policy sociology and critical social research: a personal review of recent education policy and policy research', *British Educational Research Journal*, 23, 3: 257–274

Benhabib, S. (1992) *Situating the Self*, London: Routledge

Benhabib, S. (1996a) 'The democratic moment and the problem of difference' in Benhabib, S. (ed.) *Democracy and Difference: Contesting the Boundaries of the Political*, Princeton, NJ: Princeton University Press

Benhabib, S. (1996b) 'Towards a deliberative mode of democratic legitimacy', in Benhabib, S. (ed.) *Democracy and Difference: Contesting the Boundaries of the Political*, Princeton, NJ: Princeton University Press

Bourdieu, P. (1986) *Distinction*, London: Routledge

Brighouse, H. (2001) 'Egalitarian Liberalism and Justice in Education.' Inaugural Professorial Lecture, Institute of Education

Cole, M. and Hill, D. (1995) 'Games of despair and rhetorics of resistance: postmodernism, education and reaction', *British Journal of Sociology of Education*, 45, 2: 165–182

Cole, M., Hill, D. and Rikowski, G. (1997) 'Between postmodernism and nowhere: the predicament of the postmodernist', *British Journal of Educational Studies*, 45, 2: 187–200

Connell, R. (1993) *Schools and Social Justice*, Philadelphia: Temple University Press

Fraser, N. (1997) *Justice Interruptus*, London: Routledge

Gewirtz, S. (1998) 'Conceptualising social justice in education: mapping the territory', *Journal of Education Policy*, 13, 4: 469–484

Grace, G. (1995) *School Leadership: Beyond Educational Management*. London, Falmer Press

Griffiths, M. (1998) *Educational Research for Social Justice*, Buckingham: Open University Press

Hall, S. (1993) 'Cultural identity and diaspora' in Williams, P. and Chrisman, L. (eds) *Colonial Discourse and Post Colonial Theory: A Reader*, London: Harvester Wheatsheaf

Hammersley, M. (2002) *Educational Rsearch, Policymaking and Practice*, London: Paul Chapman

Haraway, D. (1991) *Simians, Cyborgs and Women: the Reinvention of Nature*, London: Free Association Press

Harvey, D. (1993) 'Class relations, social justice and the politics of difference' in Squires, J. (ed.) *Principled Positions,* London: Lawrence & Wishart

Jordan, B. (1998) *The New Politics of Welfare*, London: Sage

Kohli, W. (1993) 'Raymond Williams, affective ideology and counter-hegemonic practices' in education' in Dworkin, D. and Roman, L. (eds) *Views Beyond the Border Country: Raymond Williams and Cultural Politics*, London: Routledge

Leonard, P. (1997) *Postmodern Welfare*, London: Sage

Marginson, S. (1993) 'Education research and education policy', *Review of Australian Research in Education*, 2: 15–29

Martin, J. and Vincent, C. (1999) 'Parental voice: an exploration', *International Studies in Sociology of Education*, 9, 3: 231–252

Ozga, J. (2000) *Policy Research in Educational Settings*, Buckingham: Open University Press

Phillips, A. (1993) *Democracy and Difference*, Cambridge: Cambridge University Press

Phillips, A. (1995) *The Politics of Presence*, Oxford: Oxford University Press

Phillips, A. (1999) *Which Equalities Matter?*, Cambridge: Polity Press

Rassool, N. (1997) 'Fractured or flexible identities? Life histories of black diasporic women in Britain', in Mirza H. (ed.) *Black British Feminism*, London: Routledge

Rizvi, F. (1993) 'Williams on democracy and the governance of education' in Dworkin, D. and Roman, L. (eds) *Views Beyond the Border Country: Raymond Williams and Cultural Politics*, London: Routledge

Seddon, T. (2003, forthcoming) 'Framing justice: challenges for research', *Journal of Education Policy*

Skeggs, B. (1991) 'Postmodernism: what is all the fuss about?', *British Journal of Sociology of Education*, 12, 2: 255–79

Skeggs, B. (1997) *Formations of Class and Gender*, London: Sage

Troyna, B. and Vincent, C. (1995) 'The discourses of social justice in education', *Discourse*, 16, 2: 149–166

Troyna, B. (1994) 'Critical social research and education policy', *British Journal of Educational Studies*, 42, 1: 70–84

Unterhalter, E. (2001) 'The capabilities approach and gendered education: An examination of South African complexities.' Paper delivered at conference on Justice and Poverty, Cambridge, June

Vincent, C. (2000) *Including Parents? Education, Citizenship and Parental Agency*, Buckingham: Open University Press

Walkerdine, V., Lucey, H. and Melody, J. (2001) *Growing Up Girl*, Basingstoke: Palgrave

Williams, R. (1960, rpt. 1988) *Border Country*, London: Hogarth Press

Woods, P. and Jeffrey, B. (2002) 'The reconstruction of primary teachers' identities', *British Journal of Sociology of Education*, 23, 1: 89–106

Yeatman, A. (1994) *Postmodern Revisionings of the Political*, London: Routledge

Young, I. M. (1990) *Justice and the Politics of Difference*, Princeton, NJ: Princeton University Press

Young, I. M. (1996) 'Communication and the other: beyond deliberative democracy', in Benhabib, S. (ed.) *Democracy and Difference: Contesting the Boundaries of the Political*, Princeton, NJ: Princeton University Press

Young, I. M. (1997) 'Unruly categories: a critique of Nancy Fraser's dual systems theory', *New Left Review*, 222: 147–60

Chapter 1

Towards a sociology of just practices

An analysis of plural conceptions of justice

Alan Cribb and Sharon Gewirtz

Introduction

Much current writing on social justice or social justice-related issues in policy sociology is based on a conception of social justice as plural. In other words social justice is viewed as having a variety of facets. For example, it is viewed as simultaneously concerning the distribution of goods and resources on the one hand and the valorisation of a range of social collectivities and cultural identities on the other. Whilst we want to welcome the use of such plural conceptions of social justice, there is, we want to suggest, a failure in much of this work to appreciate fully the implications for sociological analysis of such plural notions of justice. This is reflected in two tendencies about which we have some concern.

The first tendency is a common failure to engage adequately with the tensions that may arise between different facets of or claims to social justice (although there are, of course, exceptions, for example, Carspecken 1991). Thus, for example, participative models of education governance are often advocated concurrently with a curriculum which fosters respect for and recognition of diverse cultural identities. Yet potential conflicts between the two positions are often either ignored or glossed over so that there is a failure to address the question of what happens when, for example, participative models of governance produce curriculum policies which either fail to recognise or which disparage particular cultural identities. This is just one example of a tension that might arise between different facets of justice. There are of course many others which are similarly ignored or glossed over in many instances.

The second tendency is what we call 'critique from above'. This is the tendency to treat the work of sociological analysis as something which takes place at a distance from or above the realm of practice. From this perspective, the role of the analyst is to offer a critical account of educational policies and practices from outside the education system. In so far as such analysts view their work as informing practice, this is limited to pointing out to practitioners the social, economic and political contexts which shape or constrain their work or the mechanisms of social reproduction to which they are often presented as contributing. Those engaged in 'critique from above' do not think it is part of their job to consider how the practical difficulties that teachers have to face in trying to implement socially just practices, particularly within a hostile context, might be resolved or accommodated. Critique from above is often linked to a political position that Michael Apple has described as fatalistic – the idea that 'it is impossible to change schools unless the social and economic relations of wider society are transformed first' (Apple 1996: 107). However this position is not very helpful for those who are struggling in schools to, for example,

> create an education that highlights and opposes in practice social inequalities of many kinds, helps students to investigate how their world and their lives have come to be what they are, and seriously considers what might be done to bring about substantial alterations to this.
>
> (Apple 1996: 108)

In this chapter we want to argue that if we take seriously the plural nature of social justice then we need to find ways of adequately engaging with the tensions between different facets of and claims to social justice in ways which help to inform the work of those struggling in and around schools to create more socially just educational policies and practices.

We begin by explaining what we mean by the plural nature of social justice. We then look at some of the implications of plural conceptions of justice for socio-logical analysis. Finally we consider what can be done about these implications. Our aim is to contribute to the development of a mode of analysis which enables sociologists to provide a critical perspective on educational policies and practices whilst at the same time taking seriously and helping to inform the work of those involved in creating those policies and practices.

Table 1.1 Plural models of justice – dimensions of pluralism

Monism	Pluralism
Unified conceptions of justice (e.g. distributive OR procedural etc.)	Justice as multi-dimensional (e.g. distributive AND cultural AND associational)
A single currency of relevant goods	Different, possibly incommensurable, kinds of good
Single account of the relevant criteria for claims to justice (e.g. needs OR desert OR ability to benefit)	'Pluralistic' model of relevant claims (e.g. needs AND desert AND ability to benefit etc.)
Trans-contextual model of justice (i.e. one model of justice for all goods and settings)	Context-dependent model – model depends on nature of good and setting
Universal model – 'recipients' of justice treated the same	Differentiated models – differences between recipients are relevant for justice
Centralised model of justice – a central agent with responsibility for arbitration and 'dispensing' of justice	Diffused and centralised model – i.e. agency and responsibility shared between all, including centre and periphery

In Table 1.1 we bring together and briefly summarise six dimensions of pluralism in models of social justice. The column on the left represents the tendency towards monism and that on the right the tendency towards pluralism. We are not pretending to synthesise these different dimensions into a single theory or model; here we are merely listing the dimensions and thereby indicating some of the complexities in the field. The first row relates to the *kind of concern* represented by social justice. Is it treated as a single kind of concern – for example, a concern with the distribution of goods (or alternatively with fair procedures for exchange of goods), or does justice relate to a non-reducible set of concerns including distribution of goods but also encompassing contexts and processes of social relations and political association? The second, and closely connected, row relates to the *kind of good* included within models of social justice. Are goods treated as if they form a single currency captured by labels such as 'material goods' or 'primary goods', or do we proceed as if a range of different, and sometimes competing, kinds of goods have to be considered together? The third row relates to the *kind of claim* which underlies models of justice. Do we fasten upon a single relevant criterion for justice claims, such as needs, or do we recognise that a number of different, and sometimes incompatible, criteria for claims may all have relevance for justice? The fourth row – again closely connected to the others – relates to the *scope of models of justice*, in particular whether the relevant criteria for justice, or the appropriate model of justice is context-dependent. Is one model of justice adequate for every sector and every kind of good, or should models shift between contexts and related goods? The fifth row, which we might call the *scope of allocative principles*, raises the familiar distinction between tendencies towards universalism and differentiation with regard to the beneficiaries of justice. The sixth and final row raises the perhaps less familiar, but equally important, question of the *scope of responsibility*. Do our models assume the existence of some real or hypothetical central agent (such as the state) bearing the responsibility for arbitrating and meeting claims of social justice, or is this responsibility diffused across a plurality of agents?

Implications of plural conceptions of social justice for sociological analysis

It seems to us that there are at least three significant implications of plural conceptions of justice for sociological analysis: first, the social justice agenda is enlarged; second, tensions within and between different facets of justice need to be acknowledged and responded to; and third, the distinction between evaluation and action collapses.

The social justice agenda is enlarged

Plural models of justice substantially enlarge the agenda of evaluation. Many things which might traditionally have been treated as falling outside the scope of a concern for justice come to be seen as falling within it. This raises the question of whether these more 'comprehensive' models of justice are sufficient in themselves – i.e. would an adequately constructed model of 'comprehensive justice' be the only necessary axis against which critical educators need evaluate things, or are there other morally relevant considerations which fall outside social justice? We will not pursue this question further here but simply offer a summary account of social justice which indicates what, for the purposes of this discussion, we take to be its broad scope and parameters: a concern with social justice is a concern with the principles and norms of social organisation and relationships necessary to achieve, and act upon, equal consideration of all people in their commonalities and differences.[1]

Tensions within and between different facets of justice need to be acknowledged and responded to

If we accept that social justice has a variety of facets, then we must also accept that these facets might sometimes be in tension with one another. Whilst there are many ways of conceptualising what are the significant categories of social justice, we want to use an analytic framework here which one of us has used in the past (Gewirtz 2000, Power and Gewirtz 2001, Gewirtz 2002). This framework, which draws upon but extends the models developed by Nancy Fraser (1997) and Iris Marion Young (1990), identifies three concerns of justice/injustice – distributive, cultural and associational.

Distributive justice refers to the principles by which goods are distributed in society. This is the conventional conception of justice, defined by Rawls (1972: 7) as concerning 'the way in which the major social institutions ... distribute fundamental rights and duties and determine the distribution of advantages from social cooperation'. Distributive justice includes concerns about what Fraser calls economic justice, defined as the absence of the following:

- Exploitation (having the fruits of one's labour appropriated for the benefit of others)
- Economic marginalisation (being confined to undesirable, poorly paid work or having access to none)
- Deprivation (being denied an adequate material standard of living)

(1997: 13)

But it also can include concerns about the distribution of cultural and social resources (or in Bourdieuan terms cultural and social capital).[2]

The second form of justice, cultural justice, is defined by Fraser in terms of the absence of the following:

- Cultural domination (being subjected to patterns of interpretation and communication that are associated with another culture and are alien and/or hostile to one's own)

- Non-recognition (being rendered invisible by means of … authoritative representational, communicative, and interpretative practices …)
- Disrespect (being routinely maligned or disparaged in stereotypic public cultural representations and/or in everyday life situations)

(1997: 14)

Fraser argues that, where there are injustices of distribution, a politics of redistribution, aimed at producing a more equal distribution of goods, is required. Whilst for cultural injustices, a politics of recognition, aimed at producing respect for and a positive affirmation of the cultural practices and identities of oppressed groups, is necessary. Fraser also argues that the politics of redistribution and the politics of recognition can have contradictory aims. For example, in the case of material inequalities, redistribution remedies often call for the elimination of the 'economic arrangements that underpin group specificity' (1997: 16) and are therefore aimed at undermining group differentiation. Recognition remedies, on the other hand 'often take the form of calling attention to, if not performatively creating, the putative specificity of some group and then of affirming its value. Thus, they tend to promote group differentiation' (Fraser 1997: 16).

For groups that suffer from distributive and cultural injustices, for example groups subordinated by sexist or racist practices, the two different kinds of remedies can work in opposite directions producing what Fraser calls a 'redistribution–recognition dilemma' (Fraser 1997: 23). We return to this dilemma below, but first we want to introduce the third form of justice in this framework – associational justice.

Associational justice can be defined by the absence of

patterns of association amongst individuals and amongst groups which prevent some people from participating fully in decisions which affect the conditions within which they live and act.

(Power and Gewirtz 2001: 41)

Associational justice can be viewed as both an end in itself and as a means to the ends of distributive and cultural justice. That is, for distributive and cultural justice to be achieved it is necessary for previously subordinated groups to participate fully in decisions about how the principles of distribution and recognition should be defined and implemented. However, it is important to acknowledge that it is far from straightforward in practice for subordinated groups to become involved in decision making, even when the opportunities are there, given the history of these groups' exposure to distributive and cultural injustices.

Much work in policy sociology operates implicitly with an understanding of social justice as having all three facets. However, attempts to engage adequately either implicitly or explicitly with the tensions between these are rare. At best the tensions are acknowledged but attempts to engage with their practical consequences are few and far between. Thus, for example, whilst the conflict that Fraser identifies between a politics of redistribution and a politics of recognition might be accepted as valid, there seems to be a reluctance to grapple with how such tensions might be resolved or accommodated in practice. There are however some notable exceptions and we look below at some examples of work that takes seriously these tensions. One example we consider is from the work of Ken Jones and Anton Franks on progressive approaches to English teaching which implicitly attempts to resolve tensions between distributive and cultural injustices. Another example is an article by Luis Gandin and Michael Apple (2002) which grapples with the tensions that inhabit an educational programme being implemented in Porto Alegre, Brazil; a programme which is attempting simultaneously to promote economic, cultural and associational forms of justice. But, first, to illustrate the kind of tensions we are talking about, we want to use a third example, from the work of Alastair Bonnet and Bruce Carrington on ethnic monitoring and classification.

The decision of whether or not to support and implement policies of ethnic monitoring is problematic for those who are committed to challenging both distributive and cultural injustice. From the perspective of distributive justice, ethnic monitoring can be viewed as having a vital role to play in providing the information needed to combat discrimination on the basis of 'race'. Thus in education it has historically been supported by those concerned about the over-representation of minority ethnic groups in some educational settings, for example, schools for the 'educationally subnormal', and the under-representation of minority ethnic groups in other settings, for example, universities (Bonnett and Carrington 2000: 491). From this perspective

> policies to widen access and achieve more balanced student intakes, to improve pastoral care provision or to increase equal opportunities in staffing should be informed by reliable data rather than anecdote or hunch.
> (Bonnett and Carrington 2000: 499)

From a cultural justice perspective, however, ethnic monitoring can be viewed as problematic. From this position, which often draws on Foucauldian-inspired concerns about governmentality and the production and use of statistics, ethnic monitoring is to be discouraged because it operates as a normalising, racialising and essentialising form of classification or discourse:

> The collection of statistics and the proliferation of inscriptions, with their technologies for classifying and enumerating, become effective techniques of governmentality, allowing civil domains to be rendered visible, calculable and, therefore, governable .... [E]numeration requires categorisation, and [the] defining [of] new classes of people for the purpose of statistics has consequences for the way in which we conceive of others and think of our own possibilities and potentialities.
> (Hacking 1990: 6, cited in Bonnett and Carrington 2000: 489)

"'Counting" leads to the articulation of "norms" whereby people are considered "normal" if in their characteristics they conform to the central tendencies or statistical laws; those that do not are considered "pathological"' (Murdoch and Ward 1997: 312, cited in Bonnett and Carrington 2000: 489).

Whilst Bonnett and Carrington do not articulate the issues around ethnic monitoring in terms of conflicting facets of justice – or, more specifically, what Fraser calls the redistribution–recognition dilemma – this is the key issue that they are grappling with.[3] They conclude from their analysis that ethnic monitoring is a 'problematic necessity' and that there is a need to develop approaches to monitoring which avoid the worst excesses of essentialism. Building on their research on students' attitudes to ethnic monitoring, they make some constructive recommendations on how systems of ethnic monitoring might be improved.

The distinction between evaluation and action collapses

As we have noted above, one of the implications of accepting that social justice has cultural and associational facets as well as a redistributive one, is that responsibility for social justice is diffused. The promotion of social justice can no longer be viewed as the state's responsibility alone. If we accept, for example, that social justice demands the recognition of diverse identities and modes of association that include rather than marginalise, then we are all responsible for the promotion of social justice. For in our everyday lives we must struggle to ensure that our personal relations with others are informed by principles of social justice and that the institutions in which we operate take social justice concerns seriously. This has consequences for the work of sociologists. If we are all responsible for promoting social justice, then we can not evade engaging in a constructive way with the practical dilemmas faced by those struggling for social justice in and around educational sites. In other words, the position of critique from above that we identified in the introduction to this chapter becomes untenable. It is not enough simply to identify tensions or dilemmas that are embedded within the work of practitioners, or contextual factors which shape or constrain what they do, or to document processes of social and cultural reproduction. If we take plural conceptions of justice seriously, then we need to try and ensure that our work is of practical help to those struggling to do their best to advance the cause of social justice in challenging circumstances. This is the position adopted within certain traditions of cultural studies and feminist academic praxis. This is also the position implicitly adopted by Bonnet and Carrington in relation to their research on ethnic monitoring that we alluded to above.

To the extent that we take plural conceptions of social justice seriously, we must shift our empirical focus away from an overriding concern with mechanisms of social and cultural reproduction. Rather we need to embrace a 'cultural politics' perspective, exemplified, amongst others, by the work of Ken Jones and Michael Apple, some of which we discuss below. This perspective concerns itself not only with documenting and explaining social and cultural reproduction but with documenting, analysing and contributing to struggles that are concerned to challenge and interrupt these processes. This is in part because, if we focus only on examples of reproduction and injustice, this can itself act to inhibit the cause of justice by presenting reproduction as somehow inevitable. But it is also because it is only by analysing examples of practices aimed at promoting social justice that we can explore how tensions and conflicts might be overcome or accommodated in reality.

The remainder of this chapter is concerned to open up as a field of investigation the task of bringing together an evaluative sociological perspective with a practical one. In other words, how can sociologists of education achieve a form of sociological analysis which takes seriously and helps to inform local struggles for social justice, whilst at the same time offering a critical perspective on the context in which those struggles take place?

Moving forwards

The method we are recommending, and drawing upon in this chapter, is analogous to the method that philosophers call 'reflective equilibrium' following Rawls' (1972) account of ethical reasoning. Reflective equilibrium is the systematic attempt to move 'back and forth' between our putative ethical theories and our considered intuitions in matters of practice. The object is to 'test' the principles against the particular intuitive judgements and vice versa and, as far as possible, to revise both until the greatest possible coherence is achieved between them (coherence being one aspect of rigour in ethical theory). What we are interested in is the same move between the general and the particular – in this case between plural models of justice and the complex tensions and judgements inherent in 'just practices'. The underlying rationale for this style of working is the recognition that there are advantages and disadvantages in the epistemological perspectives of both theory and practice – in both abstract analysis and embodied forms of expertise. This epistemological shift, therefore, reflects the shifts towards more plural conceptions of justice. The tidiness of abstract distinctions is helpful but becomes insufficient to the extent that justice is plural, diffused and differentiated. Abstract distinctions need to be complemented by a more grounded understanding of the possibilities of enacting justice.

We can illustrate the inadequacy of an exclusive reliance on abstract distinctions by considering Nancy Fraser's discussion of the 'redistribution–recognition dilemma'. In order to explore and try to resolve the tensions between a politics of redistribution and a politics of recognition, Fraser takes some examples of what she calls 'real-world applications that concern different cases of oppressed groups'. One of these 'real-world' applications is the case of working-class non-professionals. She argues that this is an affinity group based on the shared experience of powerlessness and non-respectability and that this group would not survive as a group if economic oppression were solved by redistribution:

Suppose, for example, that the division of labour between task-defining work and task-executing work were abolished. In that case, all jobs would encompass both sorts of work, and the class division between professionals and non-professionals would be abolished. Cultural affinities that differentiate professionals from non-professionals would probably wither away as well, since they appear to have no other basis of existence. Thus, a politics of redistribution that successfully combated the political-economic oppression of powerlessness would effectively destroy this group as a group ... [T]he politics of difference, in contrast, would not foster the overcoming of oppression in this case. On the contrary, by entrenching the very specificities that redistribution would eliminate, it would work against the overcoming of oppression.

(Fraser 1997: 200–1)

However, as one of us has argued before, Fraser is operating here with a reductionist and economistic notion of class culture:

Indeed, Fraser admits as much in a footnote, when she argues that she is 'conceiving class in a highly stylized, orthodox, and theoretical way in order to sharpen the contrast to the other ideal-typical kinds of collectivity' she discusses. She goes on to argue that she herself prefers 'a less economistic interpretation, one that gives more weight to the kind of cultural, historical and discursive dimensions of class emphasised by such writers as E. P. Thompson' (p. 34, n.15). But Fraser's appreciation of the complexity of class culture appears to be confined to that footnote. It does not emerge in her discussion of class in the 'real world'.

... The weakness in Fraser's economistic interpretation of class culture becomes apparent when one attempts to apply her analysis to the site of education. The logic of Fraser's argument is that the education system, teachers and schools should not celebrate or affirm working-class cultural affinities because this would interfere with a politics of redistribution. If working-class identities can really be reduced to a sense of powerlessness and non-respectability, as Fraser suggests, then indeed it would be inappropriate for curricula and pedagogies to affirm them. However, there are few who would accept this negative and narrow characterization of working-class cultural affinities, and there are clearly dimensions of working-class subjectivities which could be affirmed and celebrated without interfering with a politics of redistribution.

(Gewirtz 1998: 483 n., 481)

So how would we approach the 'redistribution–recognition dilemma' from our modified 'reflective equilibrium' perspective? Our approach is based on the view that tensions between different facets of social justice need to be *understood* concretely and *managed* concretely; that is, they cannot be resolved simply at the *a priori* level or at a high level of abstraction. Thus we have to move between a discussion of principles and real real-world examples (as opposed to the kind of pretend or idealised real-world examples that Fraser uses in the example identified above).

We want to begin to illustrate our approach by looking at the real examples of pedagogic practice given by Ken Jones in an article written with Anton Franks which critiques aspects of the official English of the 1990s (Jones with Franks 1999). Although not explicitly presented as such, Jones and Franks are describing, using real 'real-world' examples, an approach to English teaching which reconciles the demands of distributive and cultural justice – a form of reconciliation, the possibility and importance of which Fraser perhaps underestimates. This approach is based on what Jones and Franks call a Brechtian approach to teaching. One aspect of this approach is the view that

> art forms should make audiences more aware that larger social arrangements … can be transformed: these arrangements do not last for ever, and purposeful human activity can change them … At the core of [Brecht's] project is the belief in members of the audience as producers of meaning and agents of social change … [T]he purpose of such a project is clear – to develop the kind of knowledge of the world which allows a sense of its transformability, and to develop the skills which enable people to participate in such change.
>
> (Jones with Franks 1999: 43, 45)

Translated into teaching, this approach involves a redistribution of the cultural tools needed to decode and critically engage with dominant cultural forms. At the same time 'the immediate experience and social interests of learners are permitted to sit beside, or stand against, familiar and "official" cultural forms – the recommended texts of the National Curriculum' (ibid. 50). Thus this approach to teaching is based on a politics of recognition as well as redistribution. It places learners in 'powerful positions', because

> it affirms their knowledge and experience, and at the same time asks that they question it, in the process of making sense of and responding to a particular text. It draws from experience, but does not hesitate to cross its boundaries.
>
> (Jones with Franks 1999: 53)

To provide a sense of what Brechtian pedagogy looks like in practice, we reproduce here extracts from Jones and Franks' discussion of a classroom activity involving a class of 15-year-old boys in a London comprehensive school studying a GCSE examination text, Arthur Miller's *A View from the Bridge*. The activity, as Jones and Franks point out, was a relatively conventional one, which involved the boys devising their own trial scene. But it exemplifies an approach to teaching which enables students to draw on their own cultural resources in order to develop the skills of textual interpretation and critical analysis. Alongside figures from Miller's play, the boys had devised their own characters consisting of lawyers, a judge and a jury:

> [T]he occasion was impressively theatrical. The lawyers spoke in measured, formal tones, probing with questions, summarizing and evaluating the responses. The witnesses were thoughtful, upset and indignant; the boys playing Beatrice and Catherine wept without embarrassment and without raising a giggle; the jury exchanged whispered comments and earnestly discussed their response to the evidence. The 'play' lasted over an hour, and as the students left the classroom they were still discussing it.
>
> (Jones with Franks 1999: 52)

According to Jones and Franks, the lesson enabled the boys not only to practise the skills of textual analysis of the kind required for GCSE success, 'but it also achieved much more' (ibid. 52). The boys had used their own cultural knowledge to create an original play which, like Miller's, used language and action to explore issues of power, conflict and control:

> Throughout, the boys were bringing to bear more than their knowledge of the play: they were drawing also from what they knew of courtrooms and legal processes, experiences which were gathered from life and from television and film. The pleasure of the activity lay in the process of exploration – of coming to understand a social order that extended beyond the boundaries of the play itself. This process was not a simple one. The attitudes of many students to the courtroom were affected by their experience within migrant communities and youth sub-cultures – they were not uncritical observers of the legal scene, and did not always accept the frames it offered for understanding and judging the actions of the characters. As their value systems changed, so the language they used shifted from classroom vernacular to courtroom formality, and back again.
>
> (Jones with Franks 1999: 52–3)

Hence, the activity was a vehicle for students to deploy insights from their own experience and cultural resources in the development of a critical response to the text and associated issues of power, language and contested perceptions of 'the truth'.

This is one of three learning activities Jones and Franks use to exemplify the Brechtian approach, all of which work to reconcile two of the three facets of justice described above; that is they recognise and value students' own cultural knowledge whilst building the cultural capital necessary for those students to be able to engage confidently with high culture and the skills of critical analysis. As we have already indicated, however, there can be further tensions between the two facets of justice that they seek to reconcile (redistribution and recognition) and the facet of associational justice. Associational justice calls for a consideration of the social and political context within which schooling takes place and of the possibilities of building higher levels of participation within these contexts. It is by no means clear that greater participation from parents and students in curriculum construction would lead to the Brechtian approach advocated by Jones and Franks, and if it did not, the just practices they advocate could be impeded. Reconciling all three facets of justice – redistribution, recognition and association – is the challenge faced by those engaged in the policy reforms which constitute our next example.

This concerns the educational policies, currently being developed and implemented in the city of Porto Alegre, which are described and analysed in an article by Luis Gandin and Michael Apple (2002). Porto Alegre is the capital of the state of Rio Grande do Sul in southern Brazil which is governed by a coalition of leftist parties led by the Workers' Party. The city administration has, since coming to power in 1989, instituted redistributive policies which have resulted in 'significant material improvements to the most impoverished citizens of the city' including wider coverage of basic sanitation services and education (Gandin and Apple 2002: 261). The principles of redistribution have been governed by a system of participatory budgeting which has enabled 'active popular participation and deliberation in the decision-making process for the allocation of resources for investment in the city' (ibid. 261).

At the same time an educational project for the city is being implemented in the form of the Citizen School. The Citizen School is explicitly aimed at social transformation. According to a former mayor of the city cited by Gandin and Apple, it 'institutes the possibility for citizens to recognise themselves as bearers of dignity, to rebel against the commodification of life' (Silva 1999: 10, cited in Gandin and Apple 2002: 263).

We do not have the space here to go into detail about the operation of the Citizen School, but simply to draw attention to four key aspects of the policy. First, the organisation and management of the schools and the construction of policies and the curriculum are all based on strongly participative and democratic modes of decision making. The school councils which are responsible for establishing the schools' goals and priorities include representation from teachers, students and parents who are also provided with opportunities to learn the skills of participation. The principal is directly elected by all members of the school.

Second, the schools are financially autonomous and able to manage their resources 'according to the goals and priorities established by the School Council' (ibid. 269). In other words accountability as well as financial responsibility is devolved: 'In this sense, what the Popular Administration is avoiding is a common practice in Brazil and many other countries where power is devolved to local units but these are held accountable by criteria not based on democratic decisions' (Gandin and Apple 2002: 272).

Third, one of the organising aspirations is to structure the organisation of learning in a way that eliminates 'the mechanisms in schools that perpetuate exclusion, failure and dropouts' (Gandin and Apple 2002: 266).

Fourth, the curriculum which is constructed as a consequence of these processes, echoes the Brechtian model described by Jones and Franks:

> The starting point for the construction of curricular knowledge is the culture(s) of the communities themselves, not only in terms of content but in perspective as well ... The students are not studying history or social or cultural studies through books that never address the real problems and interests they have ... the students learn history by beginning with the historical experience of their families. They study important social and cultural content by focusing on and valorizing their own cultural manifestations. A real shift is occurring because the focus is not on the 'core/official' knowledge organized around dominant class and race visions of the world, but on the real problems and interests of the students and the community. It is important to note that these students will ultimately still learn the history of Brazil and the world, 'high' culture, etc., but this will be seen through different lenses. Their culture will not be forgotten in order for them to learn 'high status' culture. Rather, by understanding their situation and their culture and valuing it, these students will be able to simultaneously learn and will have the chance to transform their situation of exclusion.
>
> (Gandin and Apple 2002: 267–8)

Gandin and Apple report a remarkable story of a concern with, and relative success at, reconciling the implementation of different facets of social justice. But they also point up the need for continual evaluation and rethinking, and areas of potential concern.

For example, one problem they identify is the possibility that one of the policies designed to eliminate the mechanisms in schools that perpetuate failure – the creation of 'progression groups' where students who have experienced multiple failures in the past are given close attention – might risk 'creating a "second-class" group of students'. This problem emanates from the possible collision of distributive and recognitional concerns. Another example of a potential problem that Gandin and Apple discuss is the concern that race- and gender-based oppression might be viewed within the schools as of lesser significance than class oppression. A final problem they raise is the possible danger that the more powerful groups might dominate the deliberative processes. However, they also indicate that there is no evidence of this to date. The authors conclude by stating that, in spite of these potential problems, they 'are optimistic about the lasting impact of [the Citizen School's] democratizing initiatives and its construction of a more diverse and inclusive education' (ibid. 277–8).

It seems to us that the lesson of Gandin and Apple's research is that in order to take just practices seriously it is necessary both to celebrate what has been and can be done and at the same time theoretically to interrogate practice with a view to refining those practices. In a sense, Gandin and Apple's analytic approach is a model of the method we are advocating here.

Conclusion

We strongly suggest that the focus upon concrete attempts at enacting social justice in and around educational sites is important for future policy sociology. We have only been able to illustrate this potential briefly, and in general terms, in this chapter. But we have attempted to articulate the substantive and methodological basis for taking this focus seriously. Sociology has an important and powerful critical role, but there is a danger that this criticality leads to an equally powerful 'distancing' role – whereby the sociological perspective is seen as inherently other than that of the practical actor. In the case of social justice this leads to the possibility of sociological work embracing the plural and contested constructions of justice at an analytical level whilst at the same time implicitly relying on a 'have it all' evaluative stance. This possibility is denied to the teacher or educational administrator who simply has to find the best available means of managing the tensions we have considered. Asking about socially just educational practices requires policy sociology to combine action-oriented and critical perspectives. It demands a respect for practice and a willingness to see educational practices as sites of justice not merely injustice. It also requires sociologists to see their own educational practices as not merely embodying particular conceptions of justice, but also as having direct effects on the possibility of these conceptions being realised.

Acknowledgement

An earlier version of this chapter was published in the *Journal of Education Policy*, 17 (5), 2002. Thanks to Carol Vincent for her constructive advice and enthusiastic encouragement.

Notes

1 This account is not offered as anything other than a relatively inclusive and open-ended 'definition', and one that will be interpreted very differently by different people. For example, for some 'equal consideration' will be understood as requiring equal outcomes, for others it will be interpreted more conservatively.
2 We are open to the suggestion that the distributive conception of social justice might be constructed in such a way that it also encompasses what we are delineating here as the other facets of justice. Our concern here is less with the labels than with the different facets that the labels denote.
3 It is important to acknowledge that such tensions are not only displayed or articulated within sociological analysis, but also that these articulations are reflections of debates that have taken place within black communities since the 1970s.

References

Apple, M. (1996) *Cultural Politics and Education*, Buckingham: Open University Press

Bonnett, A. and Carrington, B. (2000) 'Fitting into categories or falling between them? Rethinking ethnic classification', *British Journal of Sociology of Education*, 21, 4: 487–500

Carspecken, P. (1991) 'Parental choice, participation and working-class culture: an analysis of power and secondary schooling', in Birmingham Education Group II, *Education Limited: Schooling and Training and the New Right since 1979*, London: Unwin Hyman

Fraser, N. (1997) *Justice Interruptus: Critical Reflections on the 'Postsocialist' Condition*, New York and London: Routledge

Gandin, L and Apple, M. (2002) 'Challenging neo-liberalism, building democracy: creating the Citizen School in Porto Alegre, Brazil', *Journal of Education Policy*, 17, 2: 259–280

Gewirtz, S. (1998) 'Conceptualizing social justice: mapping the territory', *Journal of Education Policy*, 13, 4: 469–484

Gewirtz, S. (2000) 'Bringing the politics back in: a critical analysis of quality discourses in education', *British Journal of Educational Studies*, 48, 4: 352–370

Gewirtz, S. (2002) *The Managerial School: Post-welfarism and Social Justice in Education*, London: Routledge

Hacking, I. (1990) *The Taming of Chance*, Cambridge: Cambridge University Press

Jones, K. with Franks, A. (1999) 'English', in Hill, D. and Cole, M. (eds) *Promoting Equality in Secondary Schools*, London: Cassell

Murdoch, J. and Ward, N. (1997) 'Governmentality and territoriality: the statistical manufacture of Britain's "national farm"', *Political Geography*, 16: 307–324

Power, S. and Gewirtz, S. (2001) 'Reading Education Action Zones', *Journal of Education Policy*, 16, 1: 39–51

Rawls, J. (1972) *A Theory of Justice*, Oxford: Clarendon Press

Silva, L. H. (ed.) (1999) *Escola Cidadã: Teoria e Prática*, Petrópolis: Vozes

Young, I. M. (1990) *Justice and the Politics of Difference*, Princeton, NJ: Princeton University Press

Chapter 2

Social justice in the head

Are we all libertarians now?

Stephen J. Ball

Introduction

Issues of social justice are normally conceived of and dealt with in terms of the effects of policies or institutional practices or the application of abstract principles. Individuals are typically only brought into play as the bearers or perpetrators of injustice – as racists for example – or as the victims of injustice. Here I want to position individuals somewhat differently. I want to look at middle-class parents as the bearers of principles of justice and as actors producing aggregate social effects through the playing out of the relationships between their principles and their actions. Within this I shall consider the way in which principles and actions are, for some, part of a 'liberal' social identity – a way they think about themselves and present themselves to others, that is their relation to the social world. At points my deliberations touch upon some well-worn debates around the issues of liberalism and communitarianism (Kymlicka 1989).

This chapter is drawn from a broader and more general analysis of the strategies of middle-class families in the education market place (Ball 2003). It is also a greatly attenuated version of a more extended discussion of the values, principles and actions of parents in this context. Here the emphasis is upon discussion rather than data, but some extracts from interviews and case studies of two families are deployed to ground and illustrate aspects of the discussion.

Overwhelmingly the existing literature on parents and school choice either excludes consideration of values and principles altogether, or relegates these to a subordinate role. In a sense this is one of a number of ways in which this literature is 'captured by the discourse' (Bowe, Ball *et al.* 1994) it seeks to explain. Both advocates of choice and choice theories tend to rely on narrow rational and utilitarian conceptualisations of the chooser and choice researchers tend to take these on board in an unreflexive way (see Hatcher's (1998) critique of Goldthorpe's work). Altogether little attention is given to values in research into choice and this is part of a more general neglect of the ethical dimensions of social arrangements such as the market within social research – Bottery (1992) being a notable exception. Morgan's (1989: 29) point bears re-iteration, that an over-emphasis on rational calculation can lead to a 'diminishment of our moral understanding of human agency'. As Jordan, Redley and James (1994: 4) suggest, the 'denizen of the marketplace – homo economicus – is somewhat emaciated'. Attention to the role of values and principles in real decision-making settings almost inevitably disturbs the neat simplicities of 'homo economicus'.

The personal aims, interests and desires of individuals are, as Nagel (1991: 14) puts it, 'the raw material from which ethics begins'. This chapter works with some of that raw material and is about the ethics of the education marketplace as enacted through the principles and practices of middle-class families as they attempt to realise their desires for their children in the present and for the future. In previous work I began to explore how the education market 'calls up' and legitimates a certain sort of ethics in the practices and perspectives of education providers (Ball 1997, 1998, Ball, Maguire *et al.* 1997). I argued that a shift is 'taking place in schools and colleges from ... "professional" values or the values of "professional community" (Grace 1995) to the values of the market' (see also Gewirtz *et al.* 1993). That is, where there is competition to recruit, non-market values and professional ethics are being devalued and displaced by the 'need' to 'sell' schools and colleges and make and manage 'image' in the competitive education marketplace. The discourses of policy which animate and infuse the market work to provide a climate of legitimation and vocabulary of motives which make new ways of action thinkable, possible and acceptable and 'old' ways seem less appropriate. Thus, within the educational context the pedagogy of the market 'teaches' and disseminates 'a new morality' (Ball 1998). One part of this shift, I suggest, is the articulation of a market ontology producing new kinds of moral subjects and changing the ways in 'which we think ourselves, the criteria and norms we use to judge ourselves' (Rose 1992: 161). The result may be 'an attenuated creature' (Cohen 1992: 183). This chapter asks just how attenuated that market creature might be.

However, the education market does not invent or import an entirely new values system; rather it draws upon classical liberal views underpinned by political and economic individualism. These individualisms hail and celebrate independent and rational beings 'who are the sole generators of their own wants and preferences and the best judges of their own interests' (Lukes 1974: 79). Choice then is a key concept in the political articulation of these beings. These values both interrupt the fragile discourse of welfare, wherein the state represents collective interests, supports universalism and manages politics to support all members of the citizen-community, and reaffirms the deeply entrenched tenets of bourgeois individualism which had predominated in UK society before the welfare state. These values are given new impetus and a new kind of discursive validity within our contemporary 'market society' – 'the horizon within which more and more people live ever-larger parts of their lives' (Slater and Tonkiss 2001: 203). This market society entails ' ... the privatist dissipation of normative self-obligations and institutional ties' and displays 'unmistakable tendencies towards social closure' (Berking 1966: 190). Thus, 'social protectionism' presents itself 'as a promising strategy in the competitive struggle for material and symbolic advantage – all of these phenomena conjure up the image of a society whose assets in solidarity and legitimacy are exhausted' (Berking 1966: 190). Bourdieu addresses these changes in a rather oblique way when he refers to a transformation in the mode of social reproduction, which means that 'scholastic errors tend to count more than moral errors, with academic anxiety, previously a more male concern, replacing ethical anxiety' (1986: 369).

However, the ethics of the market are not, as I hope to show, hegemonic. They are contested or struggled over 'in the head' or at least in some heads, in the 'profound complexity and disparity' (Cohen 1992: 184) of what Cohen calls 'empirical pragmatics' (183). Here I want to extend my previous examination to focus on the 'consumer' in the education market. Here in particular, the decision making related to choice between state and private schooling provides a rich nexus of personal conflicts within which ethical positions are formulated or tested in relation to practice. This draws attention to the themes of individualism, responsibility and guilt, and in relation to these the contradictory role of the middle-class collectivity, what Jordan, Redley and James (1994: 77) call the 'microcommunities of mutual commitment' – the 'other side' of privatism.

There are, embedded in the literatures on class and on choice, two distinct themes; one which portrays middle-class families as, *sui generis*, decidedly self-interested and calculating, the other, reinforcing this, points up the various effects and consequences of the market ethic as contributing to the destruction of collective social relations and commitments. In other words, the generation of a 'consumer ethic' which 'produces consumers who are isolated' and therefore 'untrammelled by the constraints and brakes imposed by collective memories and expectations' (Bourdieu 1986: 371). This literature is supported more generally by recent work on individuation within high modernity (e.g. Beck, Giddens *et al.* 1994, Giddens 1991).

Nonetheless, I suggest this is only half of the story: the individualism of the school consumer *is*, in particular locations, mediated and encouraged through collective and familial memories and expectations. I will explore this further. I want also to consider how it is that middle-class families 'prioritise their commitments to others, how they reconcile conflicting demands arising from these priorities, and the extent to which they recognise the wider social relevance of their actions' (Jordan, Redley and James 1994: 4). Jordan, Redley and James (12) drawing on their interviews with middle-class families are unequivocal, they find that 'when there was a clash between their political principles and the best interests of their children, they should put the family first'. The picture here is not quite so clear cut, and perhaps the simplest and best position from which to start is Pahl and Wallace's (1985: 106) point that family choices and strategies may well be invested with 'a mixture of rationalities'.

I suggest that strategies of social closure are both informed and driven by a degree of reflexive knowingness but also firmly shaped by the dispositions and practical sense and inventions of habitus. The question is, whether that knowingness extends to an awareness of the effects and consequences of their actions, or whether we should simply accept the dictum offered by Dreyfus and Rabinow

(1983: 189) that 'people know what they do; they frequently know why they do what they do: but [very often] they don't know what what they do does'. In the simplest and maybe, on this occasion, the most useful sense, we need to slip away from the binary, either/or, position. That is, it is neither the case that middle-class families are cynical individualists who recognise that they contribute to and indeed are motivated by, the creation of social inequalities; nor that they are merely trying to do the best for their own children and have no real sense that their individual actions might have larger social consequences. Rather, that we all act within unclear and contradictory values systems which are complexly and unevenly related to our social practices. Our ethics are situated and realised within a variety of material and discursive contexts. In other words, 'We see things from here' as Nagel (1991: 10) puts it, from an individual point of view, or more appropriately for our purposes, from the point of view of the family. Set over and against this is the challenge of seeing that what is true for us is also 'true of others' (10): the problem of recognising others as ourselves. Class and race identities rip across this possibility. Running through the processes of schooling and choice for middle-class families is a strong sense of boundaries between 'us' and 'others' – a sense of 'other' families as not 'normal', as not intelligible in terms of 'our' values, attitudes and behaviour. The whole point is that these 'others' are not easily recognisable or understood, what is there for 'us' does not seem to be true for 'them'. Nonetheless, principles have their part to play within the liberal social identities which these families claim for themselves. They are people who have concerns about the general social good. Within all of this, in making decisions about the schooling of their children, the families represented here are engaged in complex cobbling together of public and private values, all a part of what van Zanten and Veleda (2001) call 'ethical bricolage', although the value of 'putting the family first', in one way or another, remains the centrepiece of this decision-making. In philosophical and commonsense terms this is all very proper. Morally parents have a right, even a duty perhaps, to do their best to get an adequate education for their children. Action taken to benefit a child is not strictly self-interested. We are not required to treat our intimates in the same ways as we treat or think about others. These are 'sound motives' (McLaughlin 1994). In philosophical terms there are actions we are entitled to take even though they may not lead to the best of all possible overall outcomes. It would be difficult to lead a normal life otherwise. However, clearly for some parents their concerns go beyond adequacy to a commitment to achieve maximal positional advantage for their child. This is not easy to defend on moral grounds, particularly as it involves an explicit awareness of, and in effect a condoning of, inequalities of provision. However, Jonathan (1989: 334) does suggest that arguments can be made that parents have a duty to secure the interests of their child 'even (or especially) in circumstances where they are in competition with the interests of children in general'.[1] There is a further difficulty enmeshed in all of this; that is, how do we know what is the best for the child? Is it simply what parents say it is? Is 'best' a singular notion? In particular is what is best now the same as what might be best for their child in the future? This is the basis of deferred gratification. It also raises the question of the child's role in deciding what is in their best interests. All of this means that within the interviews considered here the parents are frequently engaged in sophisticated processes of re-working, recovery and *post hoc* legitimation of a tenuous liberal social identity. Let us see!

I want to run three arguments together here. First, that middle-class values privilege certain sorts of selfish, or at least short-sighted individualism. Second, that the market feeds and exacerbates this to produce 'attenuated beings'. Third, neither of the previous are adequate in all cases to account for the complex, situated values which are involved in decision making about schooling. In effect this is a story that can be told in more than one way – more or less sympathetically or cynically. Should I emphasise the complexity of contradictory value systems and the dilemmas of love as against the social good or the use of *post hoc* rationalisations to legitimate selfish behaviour? At times my tone, and my analytic stance is ambiguous, and not unintentionally so.

Choosing schools

The dilemmas and values within school choice are pointed up particularly well, and particularly sharply, as I have suggested above, when it comes to choosing between state and private schools. I will use this as a focus for the major part of this chapter. I shall employ two different presentational and interpretational devices to 'get at', illustrate and develop the issues adumbrated above. First, I will pick out some aspects from an heuristic model or map of choice which attends specifically to values issues. I will then work through two 'case studies' of values and choice – the Wilkinsons and the Simpsons.

I want to propose a map which will allow us to look at the ethical dilemmas of choice in an orderly way. This map is drawn from and based upon the analysis of parents' accounts of their choice-making. It is a dynamic relational model: the elements are not free-standing categories, they are interacting dimensions in the empirical pragmatics of choice. Only rarely does one element predominate, more typically they interplay to produce analytic complexity and individual doubt and confusion. However, there are particular interpretational difficulties embedded in this kind of analysis and discussion, more than is usually the case when working with qualitative data. How far can we accept these accounts and the motives and rationales presented at face value? To what extent can we read-off or read-into these accounts value rationalities? Indeed to what extent are these respondents ever clear themselves of the reasons for their choices when values are set in relation to other sorts of more practical concerns? What I would suggest here is that rather than seeing the examination of values-in-use as indictments or critical accounts of individuals or families, they are regarded as different possible 'types' of decision-making; although, as we shall see there are some examples where the role of values in relation to choice seems absolutely clear cut. Also the narratives vary in the extent of reflexivity that they display.

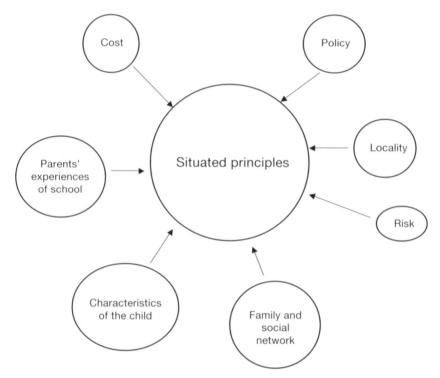

Figure 2.1 A heuristic map of choice and values

While some aspects of the map may seem straightforward, overall I want to stress the messiness and the difficulties which are involved in plotting the work done by values rather than come to any clear-cut resolutions.

For the moment I want to concentrate on just one aspect of the map, that is the way in which the families' principles are 'situated'. As Jordan, Redley and James (1994: 146) found, the 'carefully reasoned' accounts of choice offered by parents work as 'generalised guidelines, and that actual decisions are often taken in the wake of events or developments that are inherently unpredictable'. These parents do not intend to be taken by surprise. There are very few examples of clear-cut, once and for all, principles at work in these parents' accounts. Mrs Brown (see below) believes 'passionately' in comprehensive education. Nonetheless she also recognises that not all comprehensives are the same and that therefore not just any comprehensive will do for her children. School choice is a social mechanism which enables her to put her commitments into practice. Generally, choice is one way of retaining middle-class commitment to the state sector. Principles, like those of Mrs Brown, are thus 'situated' in a particular way within policy. And in stark contrast to other parents, even if the academic progress of her children is not what she would wish, she sees other social benefits of a comprehensive schooling.

On the whole, parents' expectations of schools are primarily utilitarian although issues of social mixing, the relationships between school and the 'real world', are of importance for a small minority of parents.

> ... really that's a lot to do with my politics and my husband's politics, that I passionately believe in comprehensive education, or in state education ... and I think it holds a lot of very good things for children, I wouldn't want them to be closeted away from the real world, I'd rather they went out and saw ... what life was really like for a lot of people ... and understood it. I can see there are faults in it, I think the first two years at the school they wasted their time ... both of my two elder ones. They back-pedalled a lot ... and they didn't get on with work, but I still wouldn't change my mind, I still would want them to go to a comprehensive school, even knowing that ... when it came to the time to send Toby there ... knowing that he would probably back-pedal for a couple of years, I still saw advantages. We had two things very strongly on our mind, one was we wanted co-ed for him, because again three sons ... and so I do believe that boys benefit from being taught alongside girls ... and we both very strongly believe in comprehensive education, so we wanted a comprehensive school ... co-educational school. And there wasn't an awful lot of choice in Northwark in those days. There was a school which in fact was nearer to us, which now I probably would have sent them to, because it's changing, it's getting a good reputation, it has a strong head, and its reputation is improving a lot, but in those days it was a pretty grim place, with a lot of fights outside the school and ... a not very attractive building, so that was off the list. I think we looked at an all boys school, just so that we didn't make our decision without at least having looked at something else, and that absolutely horrified me, it was just like a seething bed of aggression, I didn't like it at all.

There is a further dimension to this situated aspect of principles and values. Principles are situated in relation to the realisation of the comprehensive ideal, as parents saw it. That is, there were a number of parents for whom comprehensive education would be a real choice, in the best possible of all schooling worlds. That is, if comprehensives were what they were 'supposed to be'; although what they were supposed to be was not always clear. And whether if they were what they were 'supposed to be' they would be comprehensive is also unclear. Part of this non-realisation is brought out by the existence of the private sector and its creaming-off of other children like their own, thus creating a social and academic mix in the comprehensive school which is deemed unacceptable. Here we can see some glimpses of a link between individual choices and a more general social good. Here principles are suspended until circumstances change. They do not come into play because the circumstances in which they would or should operate do not pertain. Here government policy towards private schools creates a situation which discourages choice of state school, but the effects of policy arise from the aggregate of individual choices.

Principles are situated in a second sense. As several of the parents made clear, it was possible to take up particular principled stances towards the schooling of their child, given the sorts of schools available to them in their locality, and in relation to the 'sort' of child involved. Some respondents were frank enough to indicate that their principles might not have operated in the same way in a different locality; 'the effects of our actions are altered by the context and because we ourselves are transformed by our place in it' (Nagel 1991: 17). This is also linked in some of the accounts to the targeting of a particular locality when house-hunting. This is the point often made by critics of allocative school systems – that some parents can use their financial capital to 'choose' a state school by buying a house in the catchment area of their preferred school.

> … we knew about Overbury secondary school obviously because it's just across the road from here, so you can't actually miss it … it was something that we had sort of thought about, but neither of the boys had even started school then, they were only 3 and 18 months when we came here … and we had thought probably then that they would go on to St Botolph's and then after St Botolph's, that's when we thought … that's when we might go private, if we went private. And from here there are quite a lot of private schools, so we thought we're sort of getting the best of both worlds really.
>
> (Mr Smith)

As it turned out, as Mr Smith explained, choosing a state school from where he lives was 'easy', dilemmas of principle are avoided. He also suggests that the costs of a mortgage can be seen as an alternative to the costs of private schooling. This is a useful reminder of the argument made by Savage, Barlow, Dickens and Fielding (1992: 59) that 'property costs … are becoming more integrally tied to processes of middle-class formation. We suggest that increasing numbers of the middle-class can draw upon both property and cultural assets'.

> St Vincent's, is a very odd area, cos what happens is … people move into it, and then they start to have children … they like the local schools, and then you find that where they might have moved out they tend to stay and really only move within the area, to stay within the state sector because they either find that they've got a large mortgage so they can't afford to pay the fees … for private education or they want to support state education and actually it's very easy if you live here. You know it's easy to really support state education because if you look at the results they're pretty good … and having said that … the type of parents that live in Riverway and Tideway … they should be good. I mean I think everybody that I know have got a degree.

Values and principles are situated in a third sense. That is, values systems are constructed, or influenced, or inflected within families, social networks and local communities. They become part of the taken-for-granted response to decisions, what people like us, in this place, do. This is where collectivity comes back in, and is a basis for the values of individualism, the putting of the family first. These social contexts constitute a moral community within which the necessity of an attitude, towards family, schooling and parenting, is formed and maintained. Specific versions of the good parent circulate within this community which both provide a repertoire of meanings through which to account for actions and operate to constrain or judge those actions. 'That's the way it is here ... everybody who can afford to sends their children to independent schools, especially in this particular part of the borough' (Mr Curry).

> ... from the way the family operates it will probably be the line of least resistance which is ... if we can afford it then you go to Alleyns as well ... yes, I mean ... or we will afford it somehow and he will go to Alleyns as well.
>
> (Mrs Laidlaw)

As a model of good parenting the actions of the Blairs (Gewirtz 2001) would suggest that paying for private tutoring to underwrite your child's school performance (*Evening Standard* 4.07.02: 1 and 5) is what good parents do. This was certainly the norm in Riverway.

Primary school events and social activities and the school-gate network of mothers, together with children's own reporting back to parents, are all influential in establishing a sense of normal trajectories for children like 'ours' and appropriate choices for parents like 'us'. Norms and expectations circulate through networks of talk, and specifically questions and comparisons related to choice-making, and become embedded over time in particular parental cultures.

The Wilkinsons and the Simpsons

I now want to take a slightly different analytical tack and get even closer to the work of 'ethical bricolage' by taking two families as case studies of choice and ethics in practice. Now you might well wonder why it is that both these case studies are of families who end up choosing state schools rather than private. There are two main reasons. First, they serve particularly well to illustrate the complexity and dilemmas of choice. Second, in contrast to the majority of private school choosers they go beyond the obviousness of choice in their narratives. First there are the Wilkinsons and then the Simpsons. Mr Wilkinson is a senior civil servant and Mrs Wilkinson is a teacher in a private secondary school, they both attended grammar schools and a high status university, and they have three sons, at the time of interview aged 3, 7 and 11.

The Wilkinsons started out thinking about their children's schooling in terms of sending them to private school. However, Mr Wilkinson presents two 'reasons' for eventually choosing state schools for all three sons. The first reason displays careful rational calculation, in the literal sense. The costs are too high, at least that is the opportunity costs. Nonetheless, the Wilkinsons' thinking displays strategic care. The family's material capital will be deployed to fund an educative infra-structure within the home and to provide back-ups and interventions in order to assure success and insure against failure.

> A long time ago we put Toby's name down for St Peter's school ... because St Peter's is the local school ... a private school, of very high standard ... very very expensive, and when we had two children we wondered whether to put the second one down and when it was the possibility of three boys going to a private school, because if you add the fees up, and income ... we could just about afford it, but when we had three, we realised that we had no intention of sending them, we would be spending a fortune ... so on the basis of finance we thought it would need to be a pretty special school that would require us to give up as much as we would have to give up; and in terms of making any financial decision you should look at what else you could buy with that same amount of money ... and we decided that we could do more for our children by spending on computers and books and ... other resources at home, and if necessary later on ... buy coaching and remedial teaching, if that was neces-sary ... than by committing to the private system from the start ... and so we didn't take up the invitation from St Peter's to send Toby along for the tests at age seven, and we've no intention of trying at age 13. So that would be the first reason.

The Wilkinsons' second reason for choosing the state sector is articulated in a dif-ferent discourse and Mr Wilkinson displays a considerable degree of reflexivity in relation to the 'strength' of the family's principles. There are two related elements to these principles. One, identified previously, expresses a belief in educating their children in a setting which reflects the social diversity of the world at large. This includes a rejection of single-sex education and the studied traditionalism of a grammar school. Neither are considered relevant to 'today's' world. The other indicates a link between the family's choice and the general social consequences of choice. This was not common in the data set as a whole. Here what is acknowl-edged is the 'creaming' effect in the state sector which results from choice of private school.

The issue of diversity or mix crops up again below and has an interesting and rather complicated relationship to the issues of boundary and closure which also run through my more general analysis of middle-class strategies. If I can indulge for a moment at least in the safe simplicities of binarism, the families who are referred to in this paper display either one of two tendencies, a preference for absolute or relative closure. In other words, they draw the social boundaries of schooling in different places, on different sides of the state/private boundary. For some, the absolute division of private from state schooling is inescapably neces-sary. For others, like the Wilkinsons, a more fuzzy social division somewhere inside the state system is acceptable but will require careful vigilance and polic-ing, and sometimes pressure to maintain.

The second reason for not going for private education was really on a matter of principle ... everybody's principles I think have a certain degree of strength, and I'm not sure how strong ours would ultimately be, my wife has taught for 10 years in the private sector, and she therefore has an awareness of what qualities there are in a private school as distinct from the qualities you get in a state school ... and we all have to live our lives in a world with a mixture of all sorts of other societies around us ... with other people in society around us ... and I think that's probably what ... on a matter of principle ... would persuade us not to use a private school now ... and because we see in this area how much quality is already being deprived of the comprehensive schools, by the number of children who are driven off each day to the private schools around, and we would prefer not to contribute to that, but to bring up our children in something which represents a small slice of the world that they're going to have to live ... I had forgotten what it was like in an all boys school, and when I got there I remembered what it was like in an all boys school, and for the reasons I gave in not choosing private education, I don't actually think you get a cross section of society ... in a single-sex school, and I would like Toby to grow up in a society which was peopled almost equally by women, and so the last thing to do is to cut all his experience of the opposite sex out ... during his school years. That was ... I think one of my reasons for rejecting Tiffins [grammar]. The other reason was that it was just so old-fashioned. It reminded me of what education was like 25 years ago. I don't want to put Toby through that, I want to put Toby through the education of today ... I'm sure that education has to be very different today than it was when I was at school.

While the Wilkinsons knew what they would be getting in the private sector they were much less sure about 'quality' within the state sector. They believe that having chosen to remain in the state sector, they will have to take the choice of a particular school very seriously indeed. They end up comparing two comprehensive schools and somewhat less seriously a state grammar school, and they develop a checklist of indicators they consider important. These mainly concern the quality of teaching and the subjects and activities on offer, in effect both the instrumental and expressive order. The result is a messy calculus of issues, of very different sorts, both 'big' and 'small', more or less important, resting on both instrumental and expressive values. For example, the Wilkinsons, unlike other families, are not willing to send their sons long distances to find the 'right' school. Like the working-class families reported in Gewirtz, Ball and Bowe (1995) the idea of the school being an extension of the local community is important to them. They are also impressed by the traditional connotations of Latin being offered, and, in contrast, the modern connotations of IT provision.

... we also have set down a checklist I suppose, because we found it very difficult to make a final decision as to which school to opt for. The quality of the staff is a very difficult thing to judge, but I think is actually one of the critical things … how much the teachers are going to stimulate the children to want to learn … and … in every subject it's quite difficult because there are so many subjects that you can't start to get a grasp of … so we … have … at both Fletcher and at Chiswick … been to the open evening when you can go round and look at the school facilities … talk to the staff, talk about how teaching is done in particular subjects, and we've also been on a tour of the schools … looking at the schools in normal working hours. So we've been looking primarily for the quality of the teaching and the choice of subjects offered and taught. So one of the factors for example that makes Chiswick particularly interesting is that they offer a slightly wider choice of subjects that are taught, they don't for example … group all the humanities together quite as much as they do at Fletcher … They offer the option of doing Latin should a child want to do that. Toby probably won't want to do that but nevertheless it's nice to be in a school where you know that that choice is available. Another factor which has influenced us is the quality of the IT equipment on display and the IT which is apparently used in teaching. The reason for this is that we believe that schools which are using IT in this way are more likely to be up to date with other aspects of teaching too, so that we would judge those schools to be up to date, reflecting the current requirements and understanding about subjects taught … Another factor I think is the sports facilities … in particular because Toby loves playing football and neither Sarah nor I were at all sporty when we were at school … and we want to encourage him to be what we weren't, because when you come to be part of a team in any organisation, I think it's extremely valuable that you've been part of a team in some sort of sporting activity; so we've been very keen to encourage Toby in that, and so we've looked at sports facilities … but not only sports facilities, but the encouragement of children to take part, and so therefore we've been impressed by the range of clubs, extra-curricular activities, the sorts of things that children can opt into. So I think those were the key things that we were looking for. Another thing that's very important to us … is that the school should be accessible to where we live … in some ways I rather regret that there is a choice of school at all … because we've sent Toby and Jacob to the local primary school, because it's the nearest school and because we felt it would offer a satisfactory service. There's an awful lot of time and energy wasted in bussing children to schools that are some distance away … both in the private sector and in the state sector, and so what we were looking for was a school to which Toby could walk, a school at which other people would be going from this neighbourhood to that school … in other words a neighbourhood or a community school, and that's why we haven't looked at schools further away from us in this borough, even though they might offer a perfectly adequate product. And in some ways we realised that that could leave us vulnerable, because we know nothing about the other schools in the borough and should we fail to get Toby into Fletcher, we would have no basis on which to judge whether what we were being offered was at all satisfactory.

The Wilkinsons are also influenced by things they did not expect to find, that is impressions which they accumulated during their visits to schools: the effects of how the schools looked, as well as how they presented themselves – impressions 'given' and 'given off'. The third and final source of choice data is the 'objective' cold knowledge provided by school results. Here the Wilkinsons are able to deploy a considerable range of skills and judgements. They see these data as 'requiring' interpretation, both in terms of the intakes of the schools and their current, as opposed to previous, policies and practices. They also find the schools' own interpretation and presentation of results to be 'confusing'.

> The results and presentation of the school ... I haven't mentioned, partly because they require a great deal of interpretation ... the way in which the government statistics were recently received gives a good indication. We were quite surprised ... well we were not surprised, because we were already aware that the results at Chiswick school are nowhere near as good at the moment as the results at Fletcher school, nevertheless we believe the quality of the teaching there that's being offered there at the bottom of the school and the product when those years come through to taking their exams will be very different from what they have now and that's partly because the school has turned itself around and become very much more successful. And so ... in looking at the results ... everyone wants to present their results in their best light. In fact the results were presented in an extremely confusing light, and I think it's actually very difficult indeed to judge how effective a school is, and in particular ... I think it's difficult because you have no idea what the quality of the intake was that the output should really be compared with, you can't work out the added value. But ... we felt with Chiswick that the setting that was available and the choice of subjects ... indicated that the school was now much more interested in catering for the more academic pupils ... and setting does not take place in Fletcher except in maths and so if we go to Fletcher we won't get quite the same ... ability ... the feeling that Toby will be taught in a group of children who want to learn. Both Sarah and I are suspicious about mixed ability teaching, which is what the majority of teaching at Fletcher is. And then ... I realise I'm adding a number of ... supplementary points but ... there is a difference that Fletcher is a school that effectively caters for first to fifth years, there is no sixth form. There are no sixth forms in any Riverway schools, but Chiswick school is a school which includes a sixth form and again we felt that that would influence the quality of staff, because with a teacher in the house, we know that staff are more interested in going to schools where there is a sixth form, so that they get a share of the most challenging teaching, as well as the ability to influence children right at the bottom of the school, and perhaps steer them towards the specialisms at the top of the school.[2]

Grouping practices are viewed as being of major significance in providing contexts for 'more academic pupils', those 'who want to learn'. In other words, there
are lines to be drawn within social diversity and there are limits to community and
social mixing. These are not matters of principle in the general sense, and they are
not seen as such by the Wilkinsons. These are matters of necessity, which make
choice of a state school possible. What this highlights is the way in which different things become issues of principle for different families, and the different
points at which principles give way to practicalities or the embedded values
involved in putting the family first. This also indicates something of the effectiveness or accuracy of New Labour's opinion testing; although it is difficult to know
to what extent the government's overt commitment to setting reflects or moulds
opinion.

The Simpsons are a 'mixed' couple in the sense that Mrs Simpson is a public
sector professional, a speech therapist, and her husband a private sector professional, a civil engineer, who had been made redundant a couple of weeks prior to
the interview. Both parents had been privately schooled. Neither enjoyed or rated
very highly their own school experience.

> He didn't enjoy his education at all, he didn't think it was a very good educa-
> tion. I went to an all girls private day school and didn't enjoy my education at
> all, either. Having said that we both went to university so, if you like, it gave
> us whatever that required. But I felt that my education was very unchalleng-
> ing … very very unchallenging, very dull, and I had so much to learn when I
> left school and went to college. I had to learn to live …

Again here the private system is seen as unworldly, as not offering a proper preparation for the 'real' world. For the Simpsons this real world is a social world. For
parents who choose private school, it is often because it *does* prepare their children
for the 'real' world. But this real world is an economic or utilitarian one. The
Simpsons also have a clear-cut principled position toward private schooling. But
they also recognise the tension between public principles and private pragmatics
and did look at and consider private primary schools. They found these schools
inappropriate for their son. Like almost all of the middle-class parents interviewed,
proper, serious choice-making and being a good parent meant considering, for
their child, all possible options, including private schools. Mrs Simpson also points
up a set of tensions between an educational, child-centred and principled decision-
making ensemble and a more socially instrumental set of concerns. There are
compromises to be made on either side: either choosing the guarantees offered by
the private sector but forms of teaching and learning inappropriate to the child, or
going for state school which is deemed more appropriate, in a variety of ways, but
which does not offer the same guarantees.

> … both of us are very pro state schools. And I have a lot of problems philo-
> sophically with even coping with the fact that independent schools exist. I do

feel that every child has the right to a good education, and I really don't think you should get it just because you've got more money than Joe Bloggs next door. Having said that, when it comes to your child, we did go and have a look ... we looked at actually at every level, we looked at the infant level and did not like at all what they were doing, it was far too heavy ... far too formal ... and then we looked at junior school level and felt that Shavell was better actually than any of the private schools we went to look at ... depending on what you're wanting. If you want them to go to Westminster you have to send them to a prep school, but that's not what we wanted anyway. Ridley particularly is the sort of child ... who doesn't necessarily go down that formal road ... he learns in a very erratic sense ... and there was no room for that sort of ingenuity and individuality I felt, within the prep school system ... you either did A, B and C and you came out with D or you didn't make it. So I felt that that would actually totally inhibit him. And we did go and have a look at Hampton grammar, which is the independent ... but in fact ... the only reason I would have really considered it was because of ensuring ... if you like, like an insurance policy, that if he went there, he was very likely to come out with good results. And I suppose when you send your child to a comprehensive, which is not the system that we knew as children, you have less of a guarantee. However, I would have found it very difficult to make that decision, given my own thoughts about state education, and all of that.

Bernstein's analysis of the new middle classes suggests that these tensions, dilemmas and contradictions are representative of the structural ambiguities embedded in the positioning and perspectives of the new middle-class. He says: 'The contemporary new middle-class is unique, for in the socialisation of its young [there is] a sharp and penetrating contradiction between a subjective personal identity and an objective privatized identity; between the release of the person and the hierarchy of class' (1990: 136). This is also a further aspect of individualism and what Jordan, Redley and James (1994: 94) refer to as 'the discourses of a developmental self'. While perhaps not an ideal-typical new middle-class woman, Mrs Simpson seems very aware of this contradiction and she chooses release rather than hierarchy. She chooses between the particularities of her child and the trajectory of advantages offered by private schooling. However, the alignments between principles, person and advantage differ from case to case, as we have seen.

The son's own preferences play a key role here but are set over and against the expectations and pressures of the extended family. Choice of state school involves taking a stand against norms strongly embedded within history and practices of the family. Brantlinger, Majd-Jabbari et al. (1996: 589) suggest that when it comes to the relationship between liberal principles and practice that mothers' role as 'status maintainers' puts them 'in a contradictory or dissonant position'. In other words, mothers are frequently at the focal point of responsibility for ensuring both the well-being of their children and the reproduction through education and through the children of the social and class position of the family. In some circumstances, personal principles, the child's interests and the expectations of the extended family may be misaligned.

> He said he'd pay us back his pocket money every week, if we promised him we wouldn't send him to an all boys school where you pay fees, and that rather clinched the deal. Also I said would he like to take the exam just in case, now maybe that was just a reassurance for me to say, well alright, he would have a place in grammar school, he's bright enough for that, but we turned it down … and he said, if I don't want to go there, I don't think I'm going to be trying terribly hard in the exam, so I might fail, so I can't see any point in sitting it … and I'm really not sorry. But equally, because he's in contact with both my brother's children, and my husband's children [from a previous marriage] are both at independent schools, both very expensive independent schools … and so we very much had to strike out on our own … and to put this whole conversation in context … it has caused me a huge amount of personal anguish … going down the road that we go, and we've come under huge pressure from parents and in-laws and the rest of the family. And a lot of persuasion that we ought to be sending our children to private school …

In contrast to the Wilkinsons, the Simpsons' account does not touch upon the more general social consequences of their decisions. Their principles come across as primarily abstract and personal rather than grounded in any strong sense of a common good. Even so, though different, neither of these families are simply 'unencumbered', asocial individuals, nor entirely 'separate self-contained, motivated by the pursuit of private desires' (Sandel 1982, quoted in Martin and Vincent 1999: 233). There are some faint glimpses here of what Rikowski (2001) calls 'the class struggle within the human' or the *psychology of class* (15), a 'clash of forces and drives' which recur 'in and through our everyday lives' (15).

So what?

So what, if anything, can we conclude from this examination of the values and principles of the middle-class. I have tried to avoid a one-sidedly grim picture, a dystopic view of a more general de-socialisation and de-moralisation of society (Fevre 2000). I have not sought to overemphasise the role of bourgeois individualism and ignore the growth of what Berking (1966) calls solidary individualism.[3] Berking puts forward a balanced view, wherein the tendencies of individualisation in modern society also involve 'learning, at all levels of social intercourse, to deal with paradoxical demands on one's behaviour, controlling one's affects without ceasing to be natural, utilising the chances offered by an increasing informalisation without casting conventions to the winds, demanding authenticity, and steering clear of the constraints of depersonalisation' (195). In fact, this is a reasonable rendition of the sorts of tensions and dilemmas of 'between-ness' that I want to capture as a common, although not universal, element of the perspectives and orientations of these families. They feel responsible for their children but still recognise themselves as living in a complex and diverse social world, within and towards which they also have some sort of responsibility. Although again it is tempting to want to produce a binary here – a separation between those more clearly typified by bourgeois individualism and those who might be said to be solidary individualists. These are not simply calculating, uncaring people. They are very desperate to do the best for their children. They typically work within and make decisions in a mass of contradictions which set pragmatism and love against principles and the impersonal standpoint. Nonetheless, the outcomes of these decisions may give some support to Goldthorpe's conception of the service class as 'essentially conservative in outlook' (1982: 180).

It is not the individual choices of particular families that create social divisions and inequalities, it is the aggregate, the pattern of choices, the hidden hand of class thinking, if you like, the repetition of certain decisions, views, perspectives and actions – that is, what Bourdieu would call 'a system of dispositions to a certain practice ... the regularity of modes of practice' (1990: 79). Where dilemmas are recognised, these dilemmas capture 'the dialectic between alternative views, values, beliefs in persons and in society' (Berlak and Berlak 1981: 124), but what we see is a particular 'pattern of resolution' (132), or 'dominant modes of resolution' (133). Certainly these families see themselves as autonomous decision makers in a contradictory but all too 'real' world, their sense of responsibility, and of an uncertain future loom large. This sometimes means having to privilege 'necessary' interests over public principles. When it comes down to it 'commitments to the welfare of others ... were not part of the respondents' primary accountability' (Jordan, Redley and James 1994: 197), putting the family first was. Then again we must also realise that people, and circumstances, change. These are not fixed moral subjects and as Kymlicka (1989: 11) suggests, 'we may regret our decisions even when things have gone as planned'. I have tried to present the case that impersonal values do play a part in school choice for the middle-class, that these are not simply attenuated individuals, and indeed there are some families for whom principle is more important than simple advantage. This is not a simple story of self-loathing. Nonetheless, the material presented and discussed here does confirm Jordan's account of the predominance of the 'personal standpoint'. Where it exists, the support of these families for or willingness to trust their children to comprehensive education rests upon being able to find comprehensive settings in which certain kinds of social relations and forms of distinction are available to them. For others, the risks to their child or the imperatives of social advantage make any kind of comprehensive education unthinkable. Ethical considerations do impinge upon the calculus of school choice but are subordinated to both calculation and the values of individualism. That is to say, most families regard the choice between public and private school as having ethical connotations but principles are not adequate in themselves as guides to action. 'Without any ill-will toward others, the logic of their choices must always tend towards giving their offspring a headstart ... ' (Jordan, Redley and James 1994: 222). Nonetheless, these risks are also 'felt' and articulated in terms of safety, and the child's physical and emotional well-being.

A final point on the 'social arrangements' of the education market and social justice. Nagel argues that political theories and the 'social arrangements' to which they give rise require of us a particular kind of relation between the personal and impersonal standpoints. He goes on to assert that 'I believe that any political theory that merits respect has to offer us an escape from the self-protective blocking out of the importance of others ... ' (Nagel 1991: 19). Neither choice theory specifically nor Thatcherite social theory more generally pass Nagel's test of being worthy of respect. However, what Nagel had not anticipated or taken account of is the reinvention of political theories and social arrangements which operate in such a way as to 'externalize the demands of the personal standpoint' (5), rather than the impersonal. The current approach to the management of the public sector in the UK and increasingly elsewhere does take up what Cohen (1992: 183) calls a Thatcherite theory, or rather the colonising legacy of the 'discourse of Thatcherism' (Phillips 1996: 236), and its 'assumption of a grotesquely simplistic notion of causality' with a 'depiction of the individual whose self-direction has been beaten into dust by the reflex hammer of self-gratification', as Cohen (1992: 183)[4] picturesquely puts it. In classical liberal terms this is the rejection of any conception of a public good over and above the sum of individual ends. The values and incentives of market policies give legitimation and impetus to certain actions and values and inhibit and de-legitimise others. The material conditions of the late modern, global economy also play their part in generating certain 'necessities' and making other things seem dangerous or frivolous. In other words, values only ever partly float free of their social context.

Nonetheless, embedded within these situated pragmatics there are several of the essential features of classical liberalism. In particular the central issue here is that of choice, but choice has a variety of functions within liberalism. It is not simply a matter of the exercise of political rights but is also key to the articulation or production of identity. The idea, as Bauman (1993: 4) puts it, is of individuals with 'identities not-yet-given' which in their construction over time involve the making of choices. This is very much to the fore in the relationship between parents' commitments to their child and their commitments to the principle of school choice. That is, some parents seem to believe that they can only enable their child to realise personhood by exercising their freedom to choose an exclusive educational environment, and that their child's particular selfhood might not be realised elsewhere. As against this other parents choose to expose their children to social diversity as part of their self-formation and perhaps in a sense extend for them the possibilities of choice; although the point is that for some parents, such choices may not be welcome. However, as I have suggested and tried to demonstrate, these notions of the choice of what is good for the child are themselves embedded in social attachments and communal values. Here the liberal 'asocial self' is socially validated. For some parents these attachments produce or reinforce a coherence between private principles and social identity (Sandel 1982) which are given further credibility by dominant political models, as noted above. They are clear about what it means to be a 'good' parent. For others, however, things are not so clear cut and they find themselves torn between very different sorts of social identities and values, and thus confront the possibility of being a 'good parent and a bad citizen' (White 1994: 83). For these parents the distinction between public and private spheres, between individualism and communitarianism, is not clear cut. Politics, identity and social justice (in the head, and in effect) are tightly bound and beset by tensions in these messy knots of values, and perhaps we are not all libertarians, yet!

Notes

1 She goes on to assert that 'this places society in general – or its policy-making representatives – in a considerable dilemma' (334).
2 There is an interesting difference in register and tone between Mr Wilkinson's highly rational dissection of school choice-making and the more emotional accounts provided by most respondent mothers.
3 Williams (1959: 325) defines bourgeoisie individualism as resting on 'an idea of society as a neutral area within which each individual is free to pursue his own development and his own advantage as a natural right'.
4 On the other hand, Crewe (1989) reflecting on an analysis of the British Social Attitudes Survey concludes that the 'Thatcher crusade for values change' has failed.

References

Ball, S. J. (1997) 'Markets, equity and values in education', in Pring, R. and Walford, G. (eds) *Affirming the Comprehensive Ideal*, London: Falmer
Ball, S. J. (1998) 'Ethics, self-interest and the market form in education' in Cribb, A. (ed.) *Markets, Managers and Public Service? Occasional Paper No. 1*, London, Centre for Public Policy Research: King's College London
Ball, S. J. (2003) *Class Strategies and the Education Market: the Middle Class and Social Advantage*, London: RoutledgeFalmer
Ball, S. J., Maguire, M. and Macrae, S. (1997) *The Post-16 Education Market: Ethics, Interests and Survival*, BERA Annual Conference: University of York
Bauman, Z. (1993) *Postmodern Ethics*, Oxford: Blackwell
Beck, U., Giddens, A. and Lash, S. (1994) *Reflexive Modernization: Politics, Tradition and Aesthetics in the Modern Social Order*, Cambridge: Polity Press
Berking, H. (1966) 'Solidary individualism: the moral impact of cultural modernisation in late modernity', in Lash, C., Szersynski, B. and Wynne, B. (eds) *Risk, Environment and Modernity: Towards a New Ecology*, London: Sage
Berlak, A. and Berlak, H. (1981) *Dilemmas of Schooling: Teaching and Social Change*, London: Methuen
Bernstein, B. (1990) *The Structuring of Pedagogic Discourse*, London: Routledge
Bottery, M. (1992) *The Ethics of Educational Management*, London: Cassell
Bourdieu, P. (1986) *Distinction: a Social Critique of the Judgement of Taste*, London: Routledge

Bourdieu, P. (1990) *The Logic of Practice*, Cambridge: Polity Press

Bowe, R., Ball, S. J. and Gerwirtz, S. (1994) 'Captured by the discourse? Issues and concerns in researching "Parental Choice"', *British Journal of Sociology of Education*, 15, 1: 63–78

Brantlinger, E., Majd-Jabbari, M. and Guskin, S. L. (1996) 'Self-interest and liberal educational discourse: how ideology works for middle-class mothers', *American Educational Research Journal* 33: 571–597

Cohen, A. P. (1992) 'A personal right to identity: a polemic on the self in the enterprise culture', in Heelas, P. and Morris, P. (eds) *The Values of the Enterprise Culture*, London: Routledge

Dreyfus, H. L. and Rabinow, P. (1983) *Michel Foucault: Beyond Structuralism and Hermeneutics*, Chicago: University of Chicago Press

Fevre, R. W. (2000) *The Demoralization of Western Culture: Social Theory and the Dilemmas of Modern Living*, London: Continuum

Gewirtz, S. (2001) 'Cloning the Blairs: New Labour's programme for the re-socialization of working class parents', *Journal of Education Policy* 16, 4: 365–378

Gewirtz, S., Ball, S. J. and Bowe, R. (1993) 'Values and ethics in the marketplace: the case of Northwark Park', *International Journal of Sociology of Education* 3, 2: 233–253

Gewirtz, S., Ball, S. J. and Bowe, R. (1995) *Markets, Choice and Equity in Education*, Buckingham: Open University Press

Giddens, A. (1991) *Modernity and Self-Identity*, Cambridge: Polity Press

Giddens, A. and Mackenzie, G. (eds) *Classes and the Division of Labour: Essays in Honour of Ilya Neustadt*, Cambridge: Cambridge University Press

Goldthorpe, J. (1982) 'On the service class, its formation and future', in Giddens, A. and Mackenzie, G. (eds) *Classes and the Division of Labour: Essays in Honour of Ilya Neustadt*, Cambridge: Cambridge University Press

Grace, G. (1995) *School Leadership: Beyond Education Management: an Essay in Policy Scholarship*, London: Falmer

Hatcher, R. (1998) 'Class differentiation in education: rational choices?', *British Journal of Sociology of Education* 19, 1: 5–24

Jonathan, R. (1989) 'Choice and control in education: parents' rights, individual liberties and social justice', *British Journal of Educational Studies* 37, 4: 321–338

Jordan, B., Redley, M. and James, R. (1994) *Putting the Family First: Identities, Decisions and Citizenship*, London: UCL Press

Kymlicka, W. (1989) *Liberalism, Community and Culture*, Oxford: Clarendon

Lukes, S. (1974) *Power: a Radical View*, London: Macmillan

Martin, J. and Vincent, C. (1999) 'Parental voice: an exploration', *International Studies in Sociology of Education* 9, 2: 231–252

McLaughlin, T. (1994) 'The scope of parents' educational rights', in Halstead, M. J. (ed.) *Parental Choice and Education: Principles, Policy and Practice*, London: Kogan Page

Morgan, D. (1989) 'Strategies and sociologists: a comment on Crow', *Sociology* 23, 1: 25–29

Nagel, T. (1991) *Equality and Partiality*, Oxford: Oxford University Press

Pahl, R. E. and Wallace, C. D. (1985) 'Forms of work and privatisation on the Isle of Sheppey' in Roberts, B., Finnegan, R. and Gallie, D. (eds) *New Approaches to Economic Life*, Manchester: Manchester University Press

Phillips, L. (1996) 'Rhetoric and the spread of the discourse of Thatcherism', *Discourse and Society* 7, 2: 209–241

Rikowski, G. (2001) 'After the Manuscript Broke Off: Thoughts on Marx, Social Class and Education.' Paper presented at the BSA, Sociology of Education Study Group, King's College London

Rose, N. (1992) 'Governing the enterprising self', in Heelas, P. and Morris, P. (eds) *The Values of the Enterprise Culture*, London: Routledge

Sandel, M. (1982) *Liberalism and the Limits of Justice*, Cambridge: Cambridge University Press

Savage, M., Barlow, J., Dickens, P. and Fielding, T. (1992) *Property, Bureaucracy and Culture: Middle-Class Formation in Contemporary Britain*, London: Routledge

Slater, D. and Tonkiss, F. (2001) *Market Society*, Cambridge: Polity Press

van Zanten, A. and Veleda, C. (2001), 'Contextes locaux et stratégies scolaires: clivages et interactions entre classes et classes moyennes dans la périphérie urbaine', *Revue du Centre de Recherche en Education* 20: 57–87

White, P. (1994) 'Parental choice and education for citizenship', in Halstead, M. (ed.) *Parental Choice and Education: Principles, Policy and Practice*, London: Kogan Page

Williams, R. (1959) *Keywords*, London: Fontana

Chapter 3

Shifting class identities?

Social class and the transition to higher education

Diane Reay

Introduction

We are living in a period of rapid change and over the last twenty years radical changes have occurred in every sphere and level of society. A number of competing theories have emerged to explain these changes and their impact on identities. At one end of the theoretical spectrum, it has been argued that we have entered a new postmodern period, characterised by fragmentation of experience, the dissolution of structural forces such as social class and gender, a diversity of lifestyles and the loss of predictability (Aronowitz and Giroux 1991). At the other end of the theoretical spectrum, modernist theorists argue that, despite a fragmentation of structures, the weakening of traditional ties and the breakdown of 'ontological security' (Giddens 1991), these changes do not mean that the metanarratives of social class, race and gender have ceased to say anything useful about identities in the new millennium (Phillips 1999).

A particularly influential theory, which reflects on self-identity at the beginning of the twenty-first century, has been Beck's (1992) thesis of individualisation. According to Beck the certainties of the industrial era have been eroded and a new set of risks have emerged. These risks range from global risks stemming from the threat of environmental disasters and nuclear wars to risks which individuals need to negotiate routinely in their everyday lives. For Beck, while individuals' life chances remain highly structured, they are increasingly likely to seek solutions on an individual rather than a collective basis. Experiences are individualised in a process in which setbacks and crises are viewed as personal failure even when they are connected to processes beyond the individual's control (see also Bhatti, this volume).

Clearly, these theories have much to say about the development of class identities in the new millennium. Valerie Walkerdine, Helen Lucey and June Melody (2001), steering a theoretical path that draws on both modernist and postmodernist conceptions, argue that in order to understand social class injustices in contemporary society it is crucial to recognise class identity in two ways; both as a phantasmatic category that is discursively constructed but also as a category that still retains considerable power to explain social, cultural and material differences between individuals. In this chapter I want to keep both personal biography and the psyche in play with structural processes by working first with an analysis of social class as an identity designation lived out by individuals materially, socially and culturally. However, I also want to argue for the importance of understandings at the level of the individual psyche in which denial, dis-identification, defensiveness, pride and shame are familiar and often competing responses to living class on a day-to-day basis (Skeggs 1997; Savage *et al.* 2001). At the same time I draw on Beck's thesis of individualisation to illustrate how class-differentiated levels of risk generate widely differing attitudes and predispositions to the transition process and the field of higher education.

It is also important to recognise the ways in which identity is relational and marked out by differences and exclusions. As Stuart Hall (2000: 18) reminds us, 'identities function as points of identification and attachment only because of their capacity to exclude, to leave out, to render "outside" abjected'. We construct a sense of who we are through understandings of who we are not. Thus identity always invokes practices of inclusion and exclusion and these are becoming manifest in the field of higher education (Reay *et al.* 2001). We only need to look at the presentation, formation and re-formation of national and ethnic identities across Europe to see the power of such exclusionary and inclusionary processes. Class identity is more problematic at this specific historical juncture; a period in which class consciousness across English society is widely recognised as fragile and fragmentary and class identities are variously denied, disputed or devalued. However, at the same time as class as a concept is increasingly problematised (Pakulski and Waters 1996), individuals' propensity for generating classificatory systems to separate out 'us' from 'them' continues unabated. It is clear from existing research that these classificatory systems are rooted in class differences. For example, Ball *et al.*'s study into parental choice (1996) found that while middle-class parents were not directly employing the language of class, the myriad euphemisms they utilised to separate out 'the sorts of children' they wished their own offspring to go to school with from those they wished to avoid was powerfully grounded in class identifications. Universities have traditionally been considered the province of the privileged in society. Yet, in the new era of mass higher education, very similar processes to those operating within the field of schooling can now be identified within HE. One major consequence is that universities like London Metropolitan, Middlesex and South Bank are increasingly pathologised for having large working-class and ethnic intakes.

In this chapter I explore social class in the process of transition to higher education. I concentrate predominantly on the social group the New Labour government professes to be keen to attract into higher education despite taking away grants and introducing fees: young and mature students who as recently as ten years ago would have been very unlikely to be applying to university.[1] In particular, the focus is on how class and 'race' issues interrelate in students' anticipations and aspirations in relation to higher education. I explore the students' experiences of intended destinations at the point of transition, how they viewed various HE institutions and their perceptions of 'fit'. I also examine how a sense of self, and in particular 'a classed self', influenced the meanings they ascribed to higher education, and how they related to the field and the divisions within it. But I also focus on the consequences of change and transition for these students. We glimpse the inequities of the process in their words and particularly in the heightened sense of anxiety many of them communicated and I argue that there are powerful social justice implications, which sanitised versions of social mobility fail to convey. As a consequence of this failure to recognise the transition process as powerfully class differentiated, the movement of working-class students into the middle-class world of higher education is often viewed superficially as a straightforward process of class transition in which the working-class young person becomes a middle-class adult. I suggest the experience is much messier and more problematic than that: first, a lot of the working-class individuals moving into HE are already adults and second, there is no easy transition, no seamless process. The working-class applicant has to do a lot of psychic reparative work from dealing with fear and anxiety about the unknown to, in extreme cases, reconciling two different senses of self (Lather 1991). Here we catch glimpses of Bourdieu's 'duality of the self' (1999: 511) in which the working-class individual is caught between two irreconcilable worlds. In addition to the working-class accounts of transition to higher education, a number of quotations are also included from middle-class students in order to highlight the ways in which class differences added up to significant injustices.

'Square pegs in round holes': fear and fitting in

> I don't see the point in spending my time with people who are not going to be able to relate to me and I'm not going to be able to relate to them. We are from different worlds, so I think I've had enough of that in my life … I don't want to feel as if I have to pretend to be someone I'm not.
>
> (Janice, black, working-class lone parent)

Bourdieu writes of how objective limits become transformed into a practical anticipation of objective limits; a sense of one's place which leads one to exclude oneself from places from which one is excluded (Bourdieu 1984: 471). Many of the working-class students expressed high levels of ambivalence about the more elite universities. 'Fitting in' is a multi-faceted process in which there are those who have to fit in and others who have to be fitted in with. It was the minority of working-class students, who had the possibility of going to an elite university, who expressed the most anxiety about university choice. For them, the 'good' university is not the uniformly positive place it represents for white, middle-class students. In contrast to their middle-class counterparts, working-class students often allude to the problems inherent in going to places 'where there are few people like me'. Candice, a black, working-class student, hints at both a collective fate she is trying to escape and concerns around her difference when she discusses her desire to go to 'a good university':

It's been really scary thinking that you could have made the wrong decision, very anxiety inducing ... I think it's more difficult if no one in your family's been there. I think in a funny sort of way it's more difficult if you're black too... because you want to go to a good university but you don't want to stick out like a sore thumb. It's a bit sad isn't it. I've sort of avoided all the universities with lots of black students, because they're all the universities which aren't seen as so good. If you're black and not very middle class and want to do well then you end up choosing places where people like you don't go and I think that's difficult.

Embedded in Candice's text, as well as those of other high-achieving working-class students, are complicated issues around the crossing of psychological barriers which involves a recognition of 'difficulties' but still allows them to aim for a university place that outstrips the collective expectations of 'people like us'. At the same time Candice's dilemma illustrates the ways in which class and 'race' are interwoven in the higher education choice process, and how their effects can amplify and deepen anxiety, as well as, for some, offset one another. Candice's words suggest both a class and ethnic distance, at least in relation to more prestigious universities, that she clearly feels it will be difficult to bridge. Candice goes on to talk eloquently about a specific racialised and classed anxiety that accompanies what appears to her to be an almost overwhelming amount of choice:

Yes, it's been really, really difficult. It ended up being very stressful because I was doing it in such a void. I'd got no idea of how much was involved, that there was such an enormous number of universities to choose from and that you could end up making some really stupid mistakes. It's been really scary thinking that you could have made the wrong decision, very anxiety inducing. I know so little about it all and my family know nothing about it so it was a big thing finding out everything for yourself. So I did find it very stressful not knowing how to go about it, not really knowing what to look for. I mean school helped quite a lot but basically it's your life and that's quite scary thinking you could mess it up because you don't know enough.

(Candice, black British, working class, predicted 2As and a B)

The anxiety and sense of confusion is also evident in Sheila's account. Sheila mentions being confused ten times in her interview. She outlines a process fraught with difficulties and indecision:

It is hard, because you've got to make all these decisions, and half of us aren't even sure of what we want to do. It is quite strenuous and it is quite tiring and it's confusing, especially when you don't know what you want to be. And like, you are being forced to find out what you want to do, and you don't know, because I think we are so young. I'm only eighteen and I'm being asked all these questions – Sheila, what do you want to be? And Sheila doesn't know, Sheila is confused and I guess I'm still confused.

(Sheila, black British, working class)

Both Candice and Sheila express very similar feelings of 'being in the dark' to those Walkerdine *et al.* (2001) found among their successful working-class girls. But it is not just an issue of working-class femininities. Like Candice, Shaun has also found the whole process 'scary':

It is very, very worrying, because I haven't got any safety nets anymore. I really don't know what I'm going to do if the worst happens, if I don't get the grades for university, I am really, really scared. It really is scary.

(Shaun, white working class, predicted an A and 2Cs)

All the students were having to deal with the pressures of having to get good enough grades and, to different degrees, were attempting to grapple with 'risky opportunities' (Beck 1995); however, only the working-class students used such powerfully emotive language of fear and anxiety. The young people from established middle-class backgrounds where there is a history of university attendance far more often have a coherent story to tell about university choice; one with an easily discernible plot, and a clearly defined beginning and end, despite episodic uncertainty and stressful periods. There are extensive familial reserves of expertise. Unlike in Shaun's case, if 'the worst' happens there are 'safety nets'. No one talked of 'being scared' or 'in the dark':

There's a family tug company in South America, which is a sort of relation on my mother's side, which, they pay my school fees, so it might be tactful to go and do a bit of work with them, and I might find it very interesting, and they employ family, so it is always a fallback if I am desperately unemployed in three years' time.

(George, white middle class)

The 'void' Candice talks about is filled with cultural, academic and social capital. Nick is reading the same subject as his father did at university. His interest in music began in primary school and has been a constant throughout his education:

Well, just since I've been born, I suppose it's just been assumed I am going to university, because both my parents went to university, all their brothers and sisters went to university and my sister went to university and so I don't know if I've even stopped to think about it. I've always just thought I am going to go to university, and I don't know, I have kind of grown up with the idea that's what people do, most people do that. I mean, quitting school has never been an option for me. If I really wanted to I think my parents would probably support me, but I've just never even considered it as an option, I have always assumed I have been going to university and the choice has just been which university, rather than will I go at all, I suppose that's just the way my parents are, they just send us to university.

(Nick, white middle class)

The students from professional middle-class backgrounds, and particularly those at the two private schools, have stories to tell about the gradual, continual shaping of specific academic dispositions in which higher education choice is the logical end product of a host of earlier academic choices. In their texts choice is presented as rational, orderly, clear cut, almost beyond question, very unlike the chancy, uncertain process Candice, Sheila and Shaun are caught up in.

Working-class fears and anxieties about the move into higher education are interwoven with desires to 'fit in' and feel 'at home'. Here we see just how alien the elitist culture of the old universities can appear to both young and mature working-class students:

I was put off Goldsmiths, the interview there was really, really stressful. Oh, it was so stressful, it was two men and we'd done mock interviews here but it wasn't like that, this was kind of like what I'd imagined to be a conversation round a dinner table in a really upper-class, middle-class family and I was like 'Oh my God, I'm not ready for this. This is not for me'. It was awful. It was like they wanted me to have really strong views about things and I'm more maybe this maybe that. But they wanted someone who knew for certain what their feelings were but I kind of found myself thinking should I say this or should I say that? It was terrifying.

(Maggie, white working class)

Maggie went on to say that the experience made her feel that she was totally out of her league. In the new, highly class-differentiated field of higher education with its premier division, where less than 10% of the students are working-class, and its first and second divisions, where universities' position in the league table maps onto the proportion of working-class students recruited, 'out of my league' succinctly encapsulates the situation she found herself in. This sense of class-cultural alienation was there in other working-class students' accounts. Ong told me of his visit to a Cambridge college:

It was a complete shock, it was different from anywhere else I have ever been, it was too traditional, too old-fashioned, from another time altogether. I didn't like it at all. It was like going through a medieval castle when you were going down the corridors. The dining room was giant long tables, pictures, it was like a proper castle, and I was thinking – where's the moat, where's the armour? Save me from this. You know, you expect little pictures with eyes moving around, watching you all the time. And I just didn't like the atmosphere, not one bit.

(Ong, Chinese working class)

You get a sense in Ong's words that Cambridge is worlds away from his experience not only spatially but temporally as well. But more than that there is a sense of university as a dangerous place. I suggest that his description of being fixed by numerous watching eyes acts as a powerful metaphor for middle- and upper-class contempt for social 'inferiors' (Carey 1992). All too often a sense of working-class inferiority comes from having to see themselves through middle-class eyes. While that can be avoided in working-class contexts it is far more difficult to avoid in that archetypal middle-class institution – the elite university – hence Ong's overwhelming sense of being surveilled.

'Outcasts on the inside': exclusion and exclusivity in higher education

But we are not just talking about either the unfair levels of risks for working-class students which far exceed those of the middle-class students, or the cultural elitism many working-class students find off-putting. As I stated earlier, identity is about difference and differences generate exclusions. Exclusionary processes shape the field of higher education in a variety of ways but most obviously in the hierarchical ordering of the higher education field itself. Bourdieu argues that:

> By putting off, prolonging and consequently spreading out the process of elimination, the school system turns into a permanent home for potential outcasts, who bring to it the contradictions and conflicts associated with a type of education that is an end in itself.
>
> (Bourdieu 1999: 422)

Bourdieu's 'outcasts on the inside' are now clustered largely in 'ethnic' and 'working-class' universities, shunned by those fractions of the middle classes with high levels of either cultural or economic capital or both. The consequences are increasing class and racial segregation within HE in which university schemes for widening access and participation are having little impact on wider processes of polarisation and pathologisation. Although Beck (1992) argues that risks have become individualised across all sections of society it is still the working classes who are most at risk in education:

> It is clear that children of the most culturally and economically disadvantaged families cannot gain access to the different parts of the school system, and to the higher levels in particular, without profoundly modifying the economic and symbolic value of degrees (and without, at least apparently creating risks for the holders of such degrees). But it is just as clear that these students are directly responsible for the devaluation that results from the proliferation of degrees and degree-holders, meaning the new arrivals, who are its first victims. After an extended school career, which often entails

considerable sacrifice, the most culturally disadvantaged run the risk of ending up with a devalued degree.

(Bourdieu 1999: 423)

The extent of the devaluation in contemporary Britain is evident in recent statistics to emerge from the Higher Education Statistics Agency. In 1998–9 almost a third of all graduates, over 40,500, got clerical, secretarial or administrative jobs compared with 37,800 going into professional occupations (*Sunday Times*, 19.11.00, see also Bhatti, this volume). Awareness of the threat of devaluation was apparent in what many of both working- and middle-class students said: 'South Bank University has a reputation somehow of being an ethnic university and I think that's not good for getting jobs afterwards' (Annas, African middle class). 'Everyone says London Metropolitan is a working-class university so I don't think it's a very good place to go to' (Janice, black working class).

The advent of mass HE has created spaces within academia for working-class students but it has also lead to the creation of new stigmatised universities and new stigmatised identities. This elitist, hierarchical and highly class-differentiated field presents working-class students with a difficult conundrum. Entwined within desires for self-advancement for working-class students are difficult impulses which raise the spectre of both denial and pathology; a pathology that implicates both self and others like oneself. Such desires are far from straightforward and are often complicated by their potential for psychic damage as who one is and where one comes from are imputed with deficit:

> I would rather not do a degree than do my degree at the London Metropolitan University … It's a bit like, you know, that Groucho remark, I don't want to be a member of any club that will have me.
>
> (Lesley, white working class)

We can see the double bind confronting working-class students. The places they can feel comfortable and at home in within HE are seen to be deficient in some way. Throughout the working-class students' accounts we catch glimpses of the working classes as the 'other' of higher education. This positioning as 'other' causes tensions for the working-class students; tensions which raise powerful issues around authenticity, shame and belonging (Archer *et al.* 2001; Reay 2002). The dilemma they have to deal with is encapsulated in the comment of Julia, a mature working-class student, that 'I wouldn't go to any university that would have me'. Both Lesley and Julia's words convey 'a duality of the self' in which a tarnished past identity coexists uneasily alongside a desired new improved identity. Unsurprisingly, the generalised feelings that new universities are not good enough signify very differently for these working-class students than they do for middle-class students. The middle-class students are not implicating themselves when they talk about avoiding new universities, although such avoidance is racialised as well as classed (Ball *et al.* 2002). Entwined within desires for self-advancement for working-class students are difficult impulses which raise the spectre of both denial and pathology; a pathology that implicates both self and others like oneself. Such desires are far from straightforward and are often complicated by their potential for the sort of psychic damage that Skeggs (1997) describes in relation to her working-class, female students.

Shame and the fear of shame haunts working-class relationships to education (Reay 1997; Plummer 2000). The conundrum for many of the working-class students was that they were caught between two opposing shames. First there was the shame of overreaching and failing. This sense of failure was not simply academic, it implicated the individual far more holistically in that a number of them seemed to feel that they failed to be the 'right' person for traditional universities even when their level of achievement qualified them to apply. But if the first shame did not engulf, a second shame, that of ending up in 'a second-class university' (Lesley), threatens:

> At the end of the day you want to say you've been to university and be proud of it, when people put their little university in brackets it's like that's where I did it. Not do it in really messy joined up writing so they can't understand it because you're ashamed of where you went to.
>
> (Angela, Irish working class)

While they do not engage directly with issues of class, their narratives are steeped in class distinctions. Their rationale resonates with Beverley Skeggs' working-class women students' dis-identifications from their current class positioning (Skeggs, 1997). Working-class students like Angela, Julia and Lesley, whilst recognising 'their place', imbue this with connotations of deficit and were attempting to leave. For them the spaces which have opened up within higher education for minority and white working-class students were, by definition, degraded places they sought to avoid, aspiring instead to the places of more privileged others. All three were caught up in processes of dis-identification from their current social positioning. As Julia said, 'I didn't want to go somewhere that would accept me as I was, because I'd had GCSEs and two failed attempts at A levels'.

In Angela, Julia and Lesley's comments we can see how symbolic violence can be enacted at one's own expense (Bourdieu, 1990). There are powerful resonances with the attitudes of the working-class men in Sennett and Cobb's (1972) *The Hidden Injuries of Class* and at the same time a key difference. While the stigma associated with being working class kept Sennett and Cobb's manual workers where they were, it is propelling these three out of working-class places and into much more unfamiliar middle-class terrain. There is a complex psychological paradox here, because such acts of symbolic violence, the engagement in processes of dis-identification, are pivotal to Julia, Angela and Lesley thinking themselves into other, more privileged, spaces. Bourdieu's 'duality of the self' is evident in these working-class experiences of upward mobility, generating 'a habitus divided against itself, in constant negotiation with itself and with its ambivalences and therefore doomed to a kind of duplication, to a double perception of the self, to successive allegiances and multiple identities' (Bourdieu 1999: 511). And yet it is important to recognise the hopes and desires that also characterise the transition process. All the students in the sample, both working- and middle-class, wanted to go to university. The transition, for working-class students in particular, is difficult and sometimes painful, yet there are also gains. I have written about the optimism and self-transformation of working-class applicants to higher education elsewhere (Reay et al. 2002). Julia, Lesley and Angela, despite the contradictions and psychic costs, were also involved in self-transformation, responding creatively to difficulties and pressures, building their own identities.

Living with material constraints

Class differences, exclusions and inequalities do not only operate at the level of the psyche. We also need to examine how class differences are lived out materially. Far more working-class than middle-class students talked about undertaking paid employment in both term time and the vacations while studying for a degree. Only a handful of the privately educated boys contemplated undertaking paid work during term time when at university, while a majority of the state-educated students were. However the greatest constraint on university choice is predicted A-level grades and achievement at A level is highly predicated on the amount of time available to study. Across our questionnaire sample of 502, a third of the students from the established middle classes were currently in paid employment compared with two-thirds of students from 'unskilled' households. Only one private school student was working more than 15 hours while those working over 10 hours a week were heavily concentrated at the lower end of the socio-economic scale. Such practices make the possibility of attaining grades, which would make elite universities a realistic goal, easier for some and far more difficult for others. Rick, a white working-class student, while perhaps stating an extreme case, sums up a collective conundrum for working-class students currently contemplating higher education:

> Not much of a choice really, it's either poverty or failure, cos I think having to work three days a week won't leave enough time to do the right amount of studying, and anyway if I'm in it for the experience of learning new things I need time to be able to do that ... to get some enjoyment out of it, so I guess it's poverty.
>
> (Rick)

We can also see the continuing powerful influence of structural factors in the class-differentiated ways students spoke about the impact of geography on their choices. The transcripts of the working-class students were saturated with a localism that was absent from the narratives of more economically privileged students.

Material constraints of travel and finance often mean they are operating within very limited spaces of choice in which, for example, an extra few stops on the tube can place an institution beyond the boundaries of conceivable choice. Khalid is an extreme example of working-class localism, but most of the working-class students felt geographically constrained: 'You see City University is at walking distance from my home, Westminster is also walking distance, but it's not that short as it is to City University. So I'm sort of still thinking' (Khalid, working class, Bengali student).

A number of the FE students spoke about working out the relative costs of travelling to different London HE institutions and, while travel costs were not their sole criterion of choice, they clearly played a major role in delineating the possible from the impossible: 'Yes, I live near Putney Bridge, and Roehampton, for locality Roehampton appeals, because I can go home for tea. And I also thought about being a poor student and I thought well, it's about 90 pence on the bus' (Debbie, Scottish working-class FE student). Alomgir makes a direct link between his lack of choice and his social positioning:

> We need to study close to home because you've got to look at the economic situation. I mean we're not middle-class in the way that a lot of people can just go to any university they want, far from home … Myself, most of us, in fact all of us are part-time employed so we can support our studies. It's quite sad, it takes up time, consumes a lot of time because I do about twenty-four hours a week if not more than that.
>
> (Alomgir, Bengali working-class student in focus group discussion)

Unsurprisingly, most of the working-class students in our study ended up in the new 'working-class' universities; their trajectory into higher education shaped by a mix of material constraints, desires to fit in and fears about overreaching themselves.

Conclusion

Far from heralding a new era of equal opportunities within higher education, the advent of mass entry into higher education has instituted a process of unequal opportunities in which a majority of working-class students are segregated in low status universities at the bottom end of the universities' league table. Very different experiences of being a student and concomitantly, very different student identities are generated through these processes of exclusion and division. Whilst middle-class students often move away from home and are unlikely to be working long hours in the labour market, working-class students were constrained both geographically and financially. Most of the working-class students in our study were staying in the parental home and anticipated long hours in the labour market while studying. In this sense, the traditional idea of a student lifestyle, with its combination of independence, dependence, leisure and academic work was beyond the reach of many of the working-class students. Being a student for them meant something different from the conceptions and experiences of their middle-class counterparts. But as the chapter has illustrated there is a difference between those HE applicants who settle for 'working-class'[2] spaces within academia and those who aim for middle-class spaces. The small numbers of working-class students who attain a place in one of the elite universities confront not only academic work but often considerable identity work; the refashioning of the working-class self into a middle-class persona, a painful psychic process in which who one is and where one comes from are imputed with deficit and old devalued identities either have to be discarded or overlaid with respectability. A new research study also indicates that they benefit far less than their middle-class counterparts. Research by the Council of Industry and Higher Education shows a significant earnings divide between graduates from lower and those from higher social groups, irrespective of what institution they attend (Tysome 2002).

This chapter has only begun to touch on the fears and desires that accompany such a difficult transition out of one class and into another. Kelly (1984) points out the gap in theories of social and cultural reproduction; the inability to explain 'the ones who got away'. Educational theorists fail to even engage with the overt psychological processes entailed in upward social mobility, let alone look beneath at the more hidden layers of compromise and compromising; the psychic struggles and stresses. However, the upwardly mobile working classes, such as the students in our research study, are implicated in an unfamiliar anxiety-inducing process; one that involves shedding at least part, if not all, of their earlier class identity (Lynch and O'Neill 1994). They are utilising one system of meritocratic individualism, the school system, in order to attain a place within another, that of higher education. How then do they reconcile the sense of self they started out with? What sorts of hybrid identities are created in the process? And why, when they have worked so hard in order to make the transition, are the benefits far lower than for their middle-class counterparts?

During the King's College Widening Access and Participation Scheme we asked the minority ethnic, predominantly working-class, young people what they were looking for in a university. Their responses echo those of the working-class students on the ESRC higher education choice project: to fit in, feel comfortable, be somewhere where there is a mixture of students from a wide range of backgrounds. Yet, if these young people aim high and apply to institutions in the pre-1992 sector of HE they will have little chance of being at ease with themselves. They too will be caught up in a double bind where going to one of the more elite universities often means social marginalisation, various feelings of shame, denial and defensiveness about their social backgrounds, and the difficult task of constructing a middle-class self without middle-class resources. If social justice is an aspiration in the arena of higher education, then it is the elite universities, and middle-class attitudes more generally, not just working-class students, that will need to change.

Notes

1 These students were part of the sample for an ESRC project on choice of and access to higher education. The research team for the project comprised myself, Jacqueleine Davies, Stephen Ball and Miriam David. The data collected included both qualitative and quantitative material. After piloting, a questionnaire was administed to 502 school students across six institutions, using tutors to select representative tutor groups for us. The questionnaire deployed a variety of elicitation exercises. Individual interviews were then conducted with 120 students. These were all taped and transcribed in full. At first those who had volunteered through the questionnaire were interviewed, but then attempts were made to broaden the sample both to address imbalances, notably in relation to gender, and to include a range of interesting cases, for example, first-generation students (nearly all of the FE students (19 out of 23) were first-generation), and Oxbridge entrants in state schools. Tutors and other key personnel were interviewed in all six institutions (15 in total), as well as a sub-sample of 40 parents. Supplementing these three data sets were field notes from participant observation. I attended a range of events in all six institutions, including careers evenings, HE careers lessons, Oxbridge interview practice and tutor group sessions on the UCAS process. Grounded coding techniques were employed in the analysis of interview data. The transcripts were open coded initially but as analysis proceeded coding concentrated on the major emergent issues. Work on developing the characteristics and dimensions of the primary codes was extended by using axial coding and constant comparison procedures. All the qualitative data was entered into Nudist, a qualitative data analysis package, which allowed for the verification or disconfirmation of the relevance of issues emerging through manual coding. Nudist also allowed for a number of frequency counts in relation to the interview data and was used to search, sort and manage the database.

2 Even to speak of 'working-class' spaces within academia is to stretch a point. According to the *EducationGuardian University Guide* (2002) the new universities with the most working-class students are Bolton (41%), London Metropolitan (41%), Teeside (45%), and Wolverhampton (45%). Yet, as the percentages illustrate, these are still predominantly middle-class places.

References

Archer, Louise, Pratt, S. and Phillips, D. (2001) 'Working-class men's constructions of masculinity and negotiations of (non)participation in higher education', *Gender and Education* 13, 4: 431–450

Aronowitz, S. and Giroux, H. (1991) *Postmodern Education*, Minneapolis: University of Minnesota Press

Ball, S. J., Bowe, R. and Gewirtz, S. (1996) 'Circuits of schooling: a sociological exploration of parental choice of school in social class contexts', *Sociological Review* 43, 1: 52–78

Ball, S. J., Reay, D., and David, Miriam (forthcoming) '"Ethnic choosing": minority ethnic students, social class and higher education choice' to be published in *Race, Ethnicity and Education*

Beck, U. (1992) *The Risk Society*, London: Sage

Beck, U. (1995) *Ecological Enlightenment: Essays on the Politics of the Risk Society*, Atlantic Highlands, NJ: Humanities Press

Bourdieu, P. (1984) *Distinction*, London: Routledge and Kegan Paul

Bourdieu, P. (1990) *The Logic of Practice*, Cambridge: Polity Press

Bourdieu, P. (1999) in Bourdieu, Pierre and Accardo, Alain, Balazs, Gabrielle, Beaud, Stephane, Bonvin, François, Bourdieu, Emmanuel, Bourgois, Phillippe, Broccolichi, Sylvain, Champagne, Patrick, Christin, Rosine, Faguer, Jean-Pierre, Garcia, Sandrine, Lenoir, Remi, Oeuvrard, Françoise, Pialoux, Michel, Pinto, Louis, Podalydes, Denis, Sayad, Abdelmalek, Soulie Loic, Charles and Wacquant, J. D., *Weight of the World: Social Suffering in Contemporary Society*, Cambridge: Polity Press

Carey, J. (1992) *The Intellectuals and the Masses,* London: Faber and Faber

Giddens, A. (1991) *Modernity and Self-Identity*, Cambridge: Polity Press

Hall, S. (2000) 'Who needs identity?' in de Gay, P., Evans, J. and Redman, P. (eds) *Identity: A Reader*, London: Sage in association with the Open University

Kelly, J. (1984) *Women, History and Theory,* Chicago: University of Chicago Press

Lather, P. (1991) *Getting Smart: Feminist Research and Pedagogy with/in the Postmodern,* Routledge: New York

Lynch, K. and O'Neill, M. (1994) 'The colonisation of social class in education', *British Journal of Sociology of Education* 15, 2: 307–324

Pakulski, J. and Waters, M. (1996) 'The reshaping and dissolution of social class in advanced society', *Theory and Society* 25: 667–691

Phillips, A. (1999) *Which Equalities Matter?,* Cambridge: Polity Press

Plummer, Gillian (2000) *The Failing Working-class Girl,* Stoke-on-Trent: Trentham Books

Reay, D. (1997) 'The double-bind of the "working-class" feminist academic: the failure of success or the success of failure', in Zmroczek, C. and Mahony, P. (eds) *Class Matters: Working-Class Women's perspectives on Social Class*, London: Taylor and Francis, 18–29

Reay, D. (2002) 'Class, authenticity and the transition to higher education for mature students', *Sociological Review* 50, 3: 396–416

Reay, D., Ball, S. J., David, M. and Davies, Jacqueleine (2001) 'Choices of degree or degrees of choice? Social class, race and the higher education choice process', *Sociology* 35, 4 : 855–874

Savage, M., Bagnall, G. and Longhurst, B. (2001) 'Ordinary, ambivalent and defensive: class identities in the Northwest of England', *Sociology* 35, 4: 875–892

Sennett, R. and Cobb, W. (1972) *The Hidden Injuries of Class*, Cambridge: Cambridge University Press

Skeggs, B. (1997) *Formations of Class and Gender*, London: Sage

Sunday Times (2000) 'Downwardly mobile graduates', p. 7, 19 November

Tysome, T. (2002) 'Unwashed must brush up on their social skills', *Times Higher Education Supplement*, p. 3, 17 May

Walkerdine, V., Lucey, H. and Melody, J. (2001) *Growing Up Girl,* London: Palgrave

Chapter 4

Social justice and non-traditional participants in higher education

A tale of 'border crossing', instrumentalism and drift

Ghazala Bhatti

Introduction

This chapter is concerned with the experiences of non-traditional participants in higher education for whom, until recently, the very idea of obtaining a degree was an impossibility. The opportunity of entering institutions of HE has consistently eluded their school friends and family members. The circumstances leading to their entry into HE, the experience of HE itself and its aftermath left them facing a 'different', though not in every case a certain, future. 'Border crossing' (see Vincent, this volume) into the predominantly middle-class arena of the university threw into sharp focus the degree of instrumentalism and drift deployed by individuals, both in terms of decision making and as a coping strategy. It is suggested that in retrospect, those with *instrumental* tendencies are more likely to achieve desired outcomes, whereas others who study various subjects for the sake of self-improvement and knowledge acquisition *per se*, find themselves *drifting* into a disconnected, ambivalent world outside the university. The consequent disillusionment can be directly related to the type of degree obtained as well as the perceived status of the HE attended. The notion of 'success', which remains problematic for traditional non-participants in HE, is presented reflexively and as requiring careful consideration.

The Higher Education Funding Council of England (HEFCE) and target setting

The present government's aim is that by 2010, 50 per cent of young people should benefit from higher education by the time they are 30 years old. According to HEFCE figures only 28 per cent of entrants are currently from social class III, IV and V and only one in six of those groups enter HE, as compared to nearly half of those from social class I and II. Every HE institution is expected to have recently submitted a widening participation strategy and action plan to HEFCE. A consideration of widening participation is also required by the new Quality Assurance Authority (QAA) code of practice on recruitment and by the new audit-based quality assurance system proposed by HEFCE and QAA. Arguably there is still a

Table 4.1 HEFCE Performance Indicators

Participant group	All UK HEIs %
Young entrants	78
From state school	85
From social class III/IV/V	25
*From low participation areas	12
Mature entrants	22
*Mature/low participation areas	15

Source: Based on 1999–2000 Higher Education Statistics Agency (HESA) data.

long way to go before educational and social reforms can transform the life chances for many people. Lifelong learning (Smith and Bocock 1999, Marks, 2002), if properly resourced, may offer better hope for social inclusion. What measures can be taken to make the outcome of HE experience a fulfilling one for those whose 'familial habitus' did not equip them with strategies for surviving the unfamiliar social and academic demands of university life? Whether HEIs will ever arrive at government targets for mass higher education and better degree completion rates without additional provision and adequate resources remains to be seen. HEFCE Performance Indicators based on 1999–2000 Higher Education Statistics Agency (HESA) data reveal a disturbing trend. Taken at face value, they present a picture where the absence of equity is paramount.

This chapter focuses on the experiences of some of the individuals who fall in the two categories defined by * in Table 4.1. They are located in communities which have the lowest HE participation rates in the UK. To ignore the experiences of such graduates may render them invisible and lead to the continued exclusion of future HE participants from similar social and cultural backgrounds.

Some details about the sample

The data were collected mainly through long, detailed interviews between 2001 and 2002 from 16 graduates, representing various disciplines, who attended four universities (two new – post-1992 – and two old). They graduated in the period between 1998 and 2001. Additionally, the sample included six university lecturers, each with a minimum of seven years' teaching experience in HE. Two distinct self-selected samples of traditional 'non-participants' in HE were chosen to look at dissonance and continuity of experience during and after the degree. The common factor in every case was that these individuals were the first people to graduate in their immediate and extended families. One sample was drawn from a predominantly white group of mature (25- to 38-year-old) men enrolled on the three-year Community and Youth Studies (C&Y) BA Honours degree programme and the other was an opportunistic sample of six younger (22- to 28-year-old)

Asian – Bangladeshi and Pakistani – women graduates who successfully completed their first degrees. As this is a self-selected sample based in England, it cannot claim to be representative of the entire range and breadth of traditional non-participants in HE in Britain, but it does highlight some areas of concern which may benefit from future research. Further details about the sample are presented below.

Southern universities

The sample comprised ten men from manual occupational backgrounds with a history of unemployment and casual work in the family. These include six white, two African Caribbean, one Indian and one Pakistani man.

Northern universities

The sample comprised six women from homes with a history of manual/semi-skilled work and unemployment. These include three Bangladeshis and three Pakistanis.

Social justice issues?

Recent research which has engaged with issues concerning social justice in education has emphasised the contradictory ways in which seemingly good intentions may be reflected in practice. The implementation of many recent educational policies has been shown either overtly or covertly to damage young people's future (Gillborn and Youdell 1999; Parsons 1999). The challenges inherent in negotiating 'choices' post-16 and in higher education (Ball et al. 2000, 2002) have been well documented. Even though conceptually we might seek to avoid binaries, certain terms in educational discourse have now come to possess a phantom presence, where what is left unsaid is in a sense as potent as what is said. These terms which hint at omission have implications for social justice in terms of equality of condition and equality of outcome. Improvements in education, be it at school or university, also point to the subtext of 'exclusion', 'failure' and 'sink' institutions populated by association with students who have a 'low market value' (Tomlinson 1997). Where 'educational fatigue' (Schuller and Bamford 2000) exists for a few, impenetrable educational closure may remain entrenched for many. For university tutors, caught at the interface between policy and practice, the very act of empowering students whom society has previously 'failed' remains a profoundly difficult challenge.

The concept of justice, which can be usefully deployed for a discussion of higher education for those whose experiences inform this chapter, includes both redistributive justice and cultural justice which focus on equality of outcome rather than just equality of opportunity devoid of outcomes (Lynch 1995). It also has to engage simultaneously with the contested and shifting positions of identity and power (Hall 1992; Werbner 1996) because higher education, in seeking to extend aspirations, cannot act in isolation from the willing agency of the participants. A glimpse at the difficult journey into higher education, for those whose 'familial habitus' (Reay 1998) did not present education beyond schooling as a real possibility, makes it clear that any attempt to pathologise their communities would simply undermine and misrepresent such students' struggles and their lived experience.

Gewirtz's (1998) extension of the definition of social justice based on Young's (1990) and Fraser's (1997) propositions suggests a useful starting point (see also Gewirtz and Cribb, this volume). Many types of 'justice' are interlinked when the issue of entitlement in higher education is considered. The position taken up in the research reported here is that applicants from the poorest sections of working-class communities in Britain are entitled to higher education. Their degrees, gained after some sacrifice, similarly deserve respect and should ideally lead to better career opportunities. Yet, the connection between their pre-university and post-university experience is nebulous and far from straightforward. A degree does not automatically set them on an 'upward' path. Differences based on social class, intersected by gender, learning disability and ethnicity continue to exert powerful influences during HE and persist later in the job market. The issues explored below unmask, among other things, the extent of added responsibilities which currently fall on those university tutors and courses which accept 'risky' students. Higher education on demand when twinned with the dream of widening participation raises fundamental questions about social justice.

Community and Youth Studies students and the idea of university education

What is it that entices traditional non-participants into higher education? The data gathered here present a fluid, shifting reality which is complex and difficult to compartmentalise neatly. For C&Y students, previous school-based experience of educational closure is counterposed against the temptation of breaking new ground educationally. Their reflections on the challenging circumstances which propelled them into the university in the first place are embedded within particular social and cultural contexts.

> Me? At uni? It's only when I got to W— Borough Council that I realised how impossible life was suddenly. There were all them excluded kids in a sin bin. Just like me, only I used to be in remedial classes. I could actually *see* a younger me, messing around – and I thought to myself 'Oh my god things have not changed!' I had to get out, right out, get trained *do* something before all *my* kids ended up there forever.
>
> (Roger, 30, white, ex-car mechanic)

Roger's eleven-year-old son got excluded from school. A father of three, Roger is working at a pupil referral unit and as a part-time residential care worker in the south of England.

> I got thrown out at 13. Do you know I couldn't for the life of me tell you what it was for, flicking chalk around, or dancing in the corner of the class? It was not as though I was the only one, but *my day had come* as they say. What I remember best is the hiding I got from Dad. I left home (in Ireland) at 14 when mum died. So now twenty years later what do I do? I graduate! Wow!
>
> (Phil, 34, white, once a bricklayer, now a full-time paid worker with the homeless in London)

> I mean you get involved with the kids in the neighbourhood, don't you? I got involved and got into skiving school. Now I work with those who are 'at risk'. I know *exactly* where they are coming from. I am so happy I got a chance to get to university – late in life though it was!
>
> (Ashley, 38, African Caribbean)

Ashley was once a London bus driver, night security worker, then unemployed, disabled through hearing impairment, now working full time with a group of disaffected young people in a youth centre.

The above are fairly typical experiences of students who populate C&Y degrees in Britain. These are mostly individuals who struggle to obtain a full-time degree alongside part-time jobs and domestic responsibilities. With some (African Caribbean and Asian) exceptions, the majority of the students tend to be white. It takes a few years for these 'failures' of the schooling system to pick up courage and find out about HE courses which might accept them. They are absolutely 'terrified' of failing again, yet jubilant when they gain admission into the university. The admission interview at the university includes an invitation to explore in writing any issues of social concern they might wish to choose. The topics selected include refugees and asylum seekers, teenage pregnancies, truancy, drug-related petty crime, eating disorders, child abuse and self-harm. These topics are related to candidates' personal experiences, obtained first-hand or through working part time or volunteering in the deprived communities with which they are familiar. If an offer is not made, an access course is suggested with an invitation to re-apply on successful completion.[1] Some students leave the course after two years with a diploma. Others go on to write an original, empirical research-based dissertation in an area of interest. These students have to overcome many barriers – intellectually, materially and emotionally – in order to qualify successfully. This last point is equally true of the women I discuss later in this chapter.

Learning to think again – a process of transformation

It is a long journey from the first nervously handwritten diagnostic essay where all kinds of previously undetected needs surface, from dyslexia and dyspraxia, texts full of grammatical errors and polemical outpourings, deep subjectivities and self-doubt, to the point where three years later, students are able to write analytically, and defend their ideas confidently with reference to academic sources. In the course of the degree many find new identities, either in their local communities or in the job market or both, though this 'does not cut any ice' on campus. Their journeys are reminiscent of Lather's (1991) students who were on an often painful journey of self-discovery (see also Reay, this volume). Their reflections on their increasing knowledge and transformation capture their multi-dimensional, shifting positionality. They engage in what Bloomer (2001) has termed 'lateral connectivity'.[2]

> Let's put it like this, good work doesn't show. The riot doesn't happen, some street hooliganism doesn't happen, little old ladies don't get bags snatched in certain lanes. There is less bad behaviour on the buses. Soon youth and community workers will work themselves out of a job because they don't get noticed! And no one will even notice they are missing ... until the next riot ...
>
> (Murad, 31, Pakistani, youth worker)

> I work with people the teachers don't want to know, and many tutors in this university would *certainly* not want to know. Do I get teachers' respect? Of course not. No one wants the likes of me on school governing bodies or anything like that ... It's an image thing ... I have a funny blue strand in my hair and I wear an earring. I am the young people's advocate when they get into trouble with the police. It's a thankless job on a shoestring budget. So long as my group learn sailing, get some D of Es [Duke of Edinburgh awards], learn how not to be racist or homophobic, learn the meaning of ground rules for group work, learn to respect each other when no one in society has respected them. Then I reckon I have done a good day's job! I never got any of that when I was growing up. I need to make it different for other young people.
>
> (Alan, 34, African Caribbean, community worker)

> Before this course I didn't question things openly. Now I do. I read the broadsheets. Funny word that! I pick arguments with my mates at home (Manchester) when they call corner shops 'Paki shops'... small everyday things like that ... I have changed they tell me. I don't feel I've gone posh or anything like that ...
>
> (Jimmy, 28, white, community worker)

Most of the learning takes place through reading and discussions and several one-to-one tutorials where constructive criticism is provided. These tutorials are demanding for both tutors and students.

Full participation or studied avoidance?

All ten participants said that they did not socialise with either 'traditional' or mature students on other courses unless they happened to live in university accommodation. This suggests a profound sense of difference from other undergraduates. A vast majority of C&Y students live at home and commute to university. In this respect they are very much like the prospective working-class university students in Ball *et al.*'s (2002) study, who needed to save money on rent (for other examples, please see Reay, this volume). Living at home may also curtail the C&Y students' chances of interacting closely with other (middle-class?) undergraduates with whom they are unfamiliar. With a few exceptions, their social life on campus was limited to other students like themselves. There were no mechanisms for formal liaison between courses, although other students, trainee teachers for example, may well have learnt something useful from the experiences of these once-excluded pupils.

By their own account, learning which led to personal autonomy took place *after* degree completion when knowledge acquired at university was tested in the work place. They were, in the words of one graduate, 'wiser, sensible and with fewer real friends!' Interestingly, all the graduates felt their degrees had not made any difference to their perceptions of their own social class positions, though others around them, family and old friends, saw them differently. Guilt, insecurity and uncertainty of the kind found by Reay (1998, 2001 and this volume) in terms of border crossing into the predominantly middle-class domain of higher education was subsumed by a sense of betrayal verging on anger and outrage, on behalf of themselves and others. Friends and family, who deserved better educational opportunities too and had been denied them, were mentioned voluntarily. The issue of knowledge, including self-knowledge, is extremely complex. Gaining knowledge was a situated, non-linear, multi-focused process and its long-term impact was unpredictable.

Instrumental and altruistic motives

The degrees chosen by these students are guided by the prior knowledge they bring to the course, which suggests that they could not afford to contemplate 'just any old degree'. They also feel the need to work in communities within which they 'feel comfortable' and to whom they 'could pay something back'. They sought out this particular degree because within community education it held out the possibility of moving from part-time 'sessional' work to better-paid, full-time salaried posts. Although their choice is constricted by their family commitments and economic circumstances, it is also judicious and job-related. As far as opportunities for career development are concerned, their choice of a degree as mature students was always instrumental:

> I love music, but I wouldn't have done a degree in that. What job can I get with that, except dodgy DJ[disc jockey]-ing!
>
> (Alan)

I mean there is no point larking around [reference to students doing Fine Arts degrees] enjoying yourself all the time. That won't get you a job will it? There's kids to feed and council tax to pay at the end of the day.

(Phil)

There are constant references to the 'real life' outside the university and the need to be in control. The following is a typical sentiment expressed by nearly all C&Y graduates.

No point being dead clever with a degree and that, and be on the dole. No thanks! I know that now (after graduating) I can work in many areas and help people. First you have to stand on your own two feet. If I can't help myself how will I help others?

(Roger)

On an optimistic note, it is significant that all C&Y graduates who were interviewed had obtained full-time employment within one year of leaving the university. Their choice of university degree had paid off. It is also important to note that in this particular, relatively small, sample, ethnicity alone did not account for differences in outcome (see also Modood and Shiner 1994).

What the tutors said

Why do I teach them?... I find your typical students too tame and unchallenging. This lot tries my patience to breaking point ... once you've pitched your knowledge against *their* experiences, you realise how empty life is without the Jimmys and the Mandys of this world. You realise how our society *really* treats people ... other colleagues who don't teach students like these don't really respect my work ... All they talk about is the RAE! [Research Assessment Exercise which grades departments and awards funding on the perceived quality of research undertaken].

(John)

They are threatened by women tutors to begin with ... They have very high expectations, specially if they gave up a full-time job to study ... You need a strong, united, tutor team with a high commitment to teaching ... the same rules on standards, on deadlines, despite the sob stories they'll tell ... They have been let down so many times before, they will try *anything* to do less work. It's their frantic lives ... They'll tell tales about other tutors ... 'so and so said you only need two references (in essays) for a good mark', when they know very well the baseline is critical analysis of 8 to 10 texts. *You* let them get away with it, and you've lost their respect forever. It's a risky business, your integrity is on trial.

(Hilary)

The amount and quality of tutor time and effort which goes into facilitating probably the most disempowered students in the British university system into more confident, articulate graduates is difficult to sum up concisely. It is interesting to note that the tutors feel their work is not acknowledged by their peers. It seems that in the 'hierarchy of knowledge' (Brown and Scase 1994) or in the 'market value of undergraduates', non-traditional students of the kind described above were *not* a good investment for universities, at least as far as the RAE was concerned.[3]

Will such degrees which seek to offer students coping strategies by creatively building on their pre-university experiential knowledge manage to survive the 'status market' within HE? One tutor expressed his doubts:

> C&Y students bring in the money, but they don't do the image of the department any good... do they? They work with people no one else wants to work with. They pierce their bodies *and* their nails, they colour their hair all shades of purple. They look like they have just walked in from Greenham Common or the Mardi Gras. They talk loudly and are not always respectful to all lecturers unless they receive respect first. They wouldn't care whether it was a government minister or the vice chancellor! Heaven knows we have tried to teach them good manners along the way. They will tell you to your face that they will respect you *only* because you helped them truly learn and you didn't patronise them. It doesn't do the image of the department any good to have *these kinds of students* sitting outside on benches, drinking coke and water in class, laughing loudly, actually *challenging* their teachers. They are not 'obedient' like the nursing students, nor full of red tape like the social work students. I think sooner or later the university will close down this course. Never mind if some of our C&Y students are going on to do master's degrees in other universities, never mind if one even gets an ESRC studentship for a PhD now and then! In today's educational climate it does not do to empower poor people. You may help them to read Freire and Giddens but that doesn't lead to good RAE results! They leave me no time for research! Then we will be asked about 'widening participation'... [original emphasis]
>
> (Tony, who has worked with 'these types of students' for over a decade)

It was suggested that by their very association with 'risky' mature students from working-class backgrounds, the tutors' future within the institution is also placed at 'risk'. The oppositional pull exerted by the demands of RAE on the one hand and tutors' obligation to these 'time-consuming students' on the other, is often expressed in tutors' conversations. Although at the time of this research the tutors' commitment to their C&Y students was their primary concern, it is difficult to predict how much support will continue to be provided for such students and their tutors in the old universities in future.

From 'the slum' to the campus and back again

The second sample of 'non-traditional' graduates was composed of Bangladeshi and Pakistani women who had different experiences within HE. For them, predictably, it was not only social class, but also gender and ethnicity which came into play, shaping their experiences. Researchers studying the effects of educational markets on ethnic minorities have documented how certain educational markets are targeting ethnic minority students (see Macrae *et al.* 1997). Such students might be 'guided' towards less prestigious urban colleges (Tomlinson 1997). Those interviewed had under-achieved at school and had re-taken GCSEs and A levels before embarking on university degrees. Their initial experiences after leaving school resembled those described by Eggleston *et al.* (1986) more than 15 years ago. Unlike the 'young entrants' in the HEFCE table above, these women typically started their first degrees at the age of about 20. This was what happened to a Pakistani and two Bangladeshi graduates:

> I went from school, to sixth form college, to another college and then to a (new) University. If my teachers had bothered to explain to me at school what a rubbish place the local college (of further education) was, I would never, *never* have gone in there! My stupid degree in media studies is worth nothing ... here I am, two years down the line and nothing! I feel sick, my parents even borrowed money for me. I have fought with them not to send my younger brother and sister to that place! It's better they stay at home ... and there was so much racism there too!
> (Zenab, British-born and educated Pakistani, 24-year-old unemployed in 2002)

> But my degree is in the bag and ... I am dependent on my family. I hate that! None of my white friends are still job hunting. Me? Well, of course my family is dead proud of me but what good is it if I can't get a job? My mum thinks I will be happier when I get married and have a family ... That is the life I was trying to avoid till I was 26 ... all through school, A levels, all through my degree. I wanted to be somebody who could help others in the family ... get my aunts to educate my cousins ... things like that.
> (Sadia, 24, Bangladeshi, born and educated in Britain, BA in
> Humanities from a new university, unemployed in 2002)

> Life is harder if you are a graduate and unemployed and if you wanted to work, have a career, because all your cousins and school friends make fun of you!
> (Jamila, 25, Bangladeshi, born and educated in Britain, BA Business Studies
> from a new university, worked for one year then made redundant in 2001)

These women wanted to obtain jobs after qualification. Not succeeding caused a sense of double failure, once because of a troubled path through compulsory schooling and then again when in their opinion all their hard work during their degree 'came to nothing' in the job market. They were seeking equality of outcome. Anything short of that was 'failure despite success'. They suffered loss of face (real or imagined) in their families, for whom, ironically they wanted to be role models and whom they wanted to help. The other relevant detail which tarnished the initial joy of academic 'success' was that, in their families, the boys were not doing as well academically as the girls. The myths which began to circulate, born out of incomprehension, a sense of betrayal, despair and anger, were articulated:

> Now my brother makes fun of me too. He thinks the system doesn't want Muslims to succeed even if they get educated. May be he is right? It is not fair is it? It is impossible to win …
>
> (Sadia)

The implications of drifting and making 'wrong degree decisions' for individuals in such families do not remain confined to that person alone. According to these women, the close-knit nature of families ensures that the 'news travels everywhere from Manchester to Bradford to Leeds to everyone who is remotely connected to you' and with that many myths travel too. They were only too aware of the 'race-related' gendered positions they occupied. This affected them as individuals, as members of their particular families, as well as their wider communities. Social class was not consciously acknowledged as a barrier because before their graduation they believed that education would compensate for earlier educational losses. Although their achievements were seen as 'successes' by their institutions of higher education, these women felt that their university tutors did not really care enough about their future beyond university education, exactly in the same way as career teachers in their schools had not really cared.[4] 'They were older and more experienced' and they 'should have steered me off the stupid course!' They also blamed themselves for not being better informed, very much like the younger sample in Ball *et al.*'s (2000) study. Now, looking at her education reflexively, Zenab realised that her education had been 'rationed' (Gillborn and Youdell 1999) and she put it down to prejudice against her religion, gender and culture.

The painful detail in which disillusionment and lost opportunities were defined were interwoven with a lack of self-confidence and growing self-doubt.

> When the girls [neighbours] ask me about universities and things, I feel uncomfortable … not easy is it?… There are good universities and bad universities. I picked a bad one. Until two years ago I used to tell them to go to X University. Now I don't know any more.
>
> (Aliya, 24-year-old Pakistani, Business Studies graduate)

> I just tell my close friends I messed up my life. I had all the chance in the world and I messed up …
>
> (Zenab)

Maybe I should have let someone else in the family do a degree. They may have done better than me! I don't trust myself any more.

(Jamila)

It seems that these women did not get appropriate career advice, either at school or at the new university they attended. They had imagined that a degree would automatically lead to a job and financial security but that was not to be. A lack of *instrumental* motives, and lack of information combined with a shifting meaning of 'success' led them into the current position. They had not met anyone who had done the same degree before them, which might have prompted them to reconsider their choice. They had just drifted from one educational establishment into another in the hope that things would work out in the end.

At the beginning, in the first two years I was happy. I was at the university! Now? Now I think I was in a dream world then. Life has changed for everyone else and I am back where I was before.

(Sadia)

These women's families lacked the social and material capital which might have given them another chance. The courses they had attended were intended for personal fulfilment as well as better employment opportunities in fields where they could 'help others', where 'others' include family members in the first instance and then the general public. This desire echoes Osler's (1999) findings indicating that young people wanted to obtain entry into a course which would enable them to be self-sufficient and autonomous within the job market and while simultaneously enabling them to help their own communities.

For the first cohort of working-class Pakistani and Bangladeshi women, navigating their way through the undulating terrain of HE, it seems there are structural obstacles due to the intersection of gender and ethnicity aligned to the social class position they occupy. The high level of moral support and encouragement from their families was in the end not enough. Ill-informed decisions concerning choices of degree and (mostly new) universities in their cases proved unforgiving for five out of six women in the employment market. Two women said they could obtain jobs at the local supermarket but they chose not to. Others working there were peers from school days 'who did not have to do A levels and a degree to get the same job'. The women all have in common close ties to their families and a strong sense of their religious identity which seemed to have offered them hope when other practical support mechanisms failed. In contrast, Reay's account (this volume) of minority ethnic and white working-class students poised to enter elite universities reveals individuals going through a process of *dis*-identification with their existing selves.

The tutors' views

The tutors said they worked hard with all their students irrespective of who they were. In reply to specific questions about Bangladeshi and Pakistani women students, except for one instance, mostly generalisations were offered, generalisations which revealed their lack of knowledge of the students' hopes and later experiences.

> It would be good if they could be more assertive. I thought on the whole Sadia was hard working and interested. She always handed in her work on time. No problem really. Not academically, any way though I do remember we referred her for extra help to the study skills tutor in the second year and we discovered that she was mildly dyslexic. No major problems there …
>
> (Trevor)

> The bright sparks get into Y University (old university in the same city). Those who tend to come to us are students who missed UCAS the first time round, or they were on a gap year for two years! Can you imagine missing UCAS deadlines and the clearance too! Can you believe it? We do our best once we get them here. Some do really *really* well and get into jobs straight-away. Others? Well, it's like anywhere else. Everyone cannot possibly find a job of their first choice, can they?
>
> (William)

> We do offer vocational courses as you know, but our Asian students are not always in them, not the girls any way. Can't understand this really. Some drop off within the first year but most stay on I would say. They seem happy enough.
>
> (Hugh)

Tutors were unaware of the level of disillusion which affected 'successful' Asian women graduates. As far as they were concerned, they had helped their students to obtain good degrees. They tried to give good references for jobs if anyone applied for one. What happened in the job market was not, and could not be expected to be, their main concern. The tutors did not know and were not interested in finding out which Asian-origin students were Bangladeshi and which Pakistani. The question about ethnicity was perceived as irrelevant.

What the tutors were concerned and more curious about was the way in which any additional money paid to universities for increasing access would actually be used directly for student bursaries. According to these tutors, institutions of HE are interested in acquiring resources to do with widening participation, but not always in translating those acquisitions into appointments of more tutors who can best support further work with non-traditional participants. It seems that a host of increasingly complex factors are at work at institutional and structural levels when it comes to 'widening participation'. On the basis of the present data it is difficult to say whether the situation and concern among tutors in old universities is different as compared to that in the new universites.

A single-minded pursuit of success

In the sample of six women, one woman had a different focus. There was in her account a strong and defiant reaction to past poverty and a lonely struggle to 'get a decent education'. This was expressed by Amna, a 'successful' GP. She had attended an old university. Amna had become focused on a utilitarian version of 'education' early on in her school career. In her opinion, anyone who had the academic ability and yet managed to do a degree which did not lead to gainful well-paid employment was just foolish.

> You would be an utter stupid fool, if you have the brains and the grades, *not* to do medicine or a medicine-related course if you are a Pakistani Muslim woman in Britain. Medicine ... or dentistry, or if you are really desperate, then even a degree in psychology is a safer bet. Teaching is a naff idea ... unless you particularly enjoy verbal abuse from white kids. It was bad enough when we were at school! God knows what it's like now ... Besides, you only get one chance for a career [paid career, motherhood implied as a second career]. I hated it when my parents pushed me into medicine. Now I am *so* grateful to them! I mean I have been able to pay back a little bit, help my [unemployed] brother. I am pushing all my [extended] family to avoid dead subjects at university. In fact, I think Pakistanis should boycott courses which turn them into *khotas* [donkeys] ... You might think that is a very cruel thing to say, but it is a question of survival ... There is no getting away from it, there are real tough times ahead if you do a dead degree specially if your parents are not loaded with money and you don't happen to be white!
>
> (Amna: British-born and educated Pakistani, 28-year-old medical doctor)

It is only possible to make sense of such stark and instrumental motives towards HE if the pressures on women like Amna are understood within a wider framework of 'justice'. Asian doctors' post-qualification career paths in some inner cities can continue to be full of struggle (Hattersley 2002), so in a sense Amna's scepticism may not be altogether misplaced. Such was the hold of past experiences, including poverty, that Amna did not desire an identity which would take away the support structure embedded within her family. She was brought up with strong moral values within a tightly knit family unit. She did not want to walk away from her responsibilities to her family, even though she said she would be better off economically if she were to move away from her city of birth. Her siblings were dependent on her for advice and financial support from time to time. She had elderly parents who were ill and she wanted to be around for them. Her sense of herself, her career, and of her place in her community were intertwined.

Amna had re-taken her A levels to improve her grades, but once she got to university she began to really enjoy the challenge presented by her courses. She was full of praise for her lecturers and felt that Britain held out hope for women from her background, 'provided they get straight As in A levels'.

> Let's face it, you have to be better than your white peers to be selected in the first place. Disability is a no no in medical degrees and then your colour can be the biggest handicap when it comes to good courses at good universities. Where medicine is concerned it's a ruthless game. It is quite simple really.

Amna's story shows the dangers in an over-simplistic use of descriptors such as 'social class' and 'success'. Her objective social class position might have changed over time, but unlike other recently qualified doctors in her year, Amna told me she was supporting at least eight people in her family. Where Asian women are concerned, might the real losers in the long term with the possible exception of people like Amna (currently needed in the National Health Service) be precisely the sorts of students whose voices are represented here? It is clear that, for these graduates, it is justice in terms of equality of outcome which matters.

Similarities and differences

The instrumental way in which Amna saw medicine was somewhat similar to the way in which C&Y graduates regarded their degrees. Graduates from working-class backgrounds, who did *not* share at the very outset some sort of instrumentalism found themselves adrift. They found the disillusionment of 'educated unemployment', which led to a heightened sense of despair, unbearable. Interestingly, the need to be accountable to those more needy than themselves is what working-class men had in common with working-class women. This characteristic – the need to care – runs across the whole sample of graduates irrespective of gender, age or ethnicity.

When it came to aspirations, it seems C&Y graduates were more judicious and realistic in their self-appraisal and in finding their way into a course whose post-qualifying employment opportunities are almost 90 per cent (career information in the two universities). The predominant feeling in both groups of graduates, men and women, was that if a degree does not lead to a 'safe bet' in terms of paid employment, it is not worth considering. Some realised this at the outset, others retrospectively. All those interviewed said they would not have gone to university if they had to get student loans. This does not augur well for the future education of such social groups (also see Ainley 1994). These students were living in communities with very high levels of material deprivation and actual or threatened unemployment. Those graduates who did not 'succeed' for whatever reason had to pay dearly for 'wrong' choices.

Concluding remarks

This chapter looked at the experiences of 16 graduates from working-class families who entered and then survived HE in England, and at the views of some of their tutors. For these first-ever graduates in their families, the rapidly changing aspect of post-16 education and post-university labour markets has left structural inequalities largely intact. The social and material difficulties experienced during, and sometimes even after, a challenging passage through (re-)education are sometimes re-drawn instead of being demolished. For different reasons, then, all these graduates returned to work within their own communities, be they C&Y graduates or Amna, who is a medical doctor. Yet, in their own terms, for those who had instrumental motives it can be said that higher education *did* lead to positive outcomes for individuals.

Added resources are needed for state-funded schools which educate future undergraduates, particularly those students currently facing material and educational disadvantages in their communities. If universities are to address past schooling-related disadvantages and actively build on what schools tried, but were not always enabled to achieve, then better resourced and more nuanced policies are urgently needed in the HE sector. A mentoring scheme of positive role models, matched for similar socio-economic and ethnic backgrounds in different professions may prove to be helpful. A culturally sensitive and well-informed career advisory service may also help. (No one mentioned the career service in the universities. This could either be because they did not use the service or because they did not find it helpful.) Wishful thinking of 'improvement' in the context of 'lifelong learning', 'widening participation' and 'higher education on demand' will, devoid of targeted resources and careful monitoring, relegate poorer sections of certain communities to a quiet exclusion and educational closure. For those graduates who took part in this research it is clear that equality of outcome is the *only* form of 'social justice' which they recognise.

Notes

1   For a discussion of widening participation through access courses see Thomas (2001). For non-completion of access courses see Reay *et al.* (2002).
2   'Changes in young people's educational careers and attitudes to learning were frequently linked to their lives outside formal learning institutions, and particularly to their personal and social lives. Changes in their educational values and attitudes were part of wider patterns of transformation – of person and identity – underlining the importance of lateral connectivity' (Bloomer 2001: 433).
3   For a comment on the effects of RAE on an institution of higher education see Bassey (2002).
4   There is research evidence of teachers' low expectations of Asian girls at school. See Bhatti (1999). Is it possible that this may also be happening at university level?

References

Ainley, P. (1994) *Degrees of Difference: Higher Education in the 1990s*, London: Lawrence and Wishart

Ball, S. J., Maguire, M. and Macrae, S. (2000), *Pathways and Transition Post-16: New Youth, New Economies in the Global City*, London: Routledge

Ball, S. J., Davies, J., David, M. and Reay, D. (2002) '"Classification" and "Judgement": social class and the "cognitive structures" of choice of Higher Education', *British Journal of Sociology of Education*, 23: 51–72

Bassey, M. (2002) 'Take Care!', *Research Intelligence* 80: 1

Bhatti, G. (1999) *Asian Children at Home and at School*, London: Routledge

Bloomer, M. (2001) 'Young lives, learning and transformations: some theoretical considerations', *Oxford Review of Education*, 27, 3: 430–449

Brown, P. and Scase, R. (1994) *Higher Education and Corporate Realities: Class, Culture and the Decline of Graduate Careers*, London: UCL Press

Eggleston, J., Dunn, D., Anjali, M. and Wright, C. (1986) *Education for Some: The Educational and Vocational Experiences of 15–18 Year Old Members of Minority Ethnic Groups*, Stoke-on-Trent: Trentham

Fraser, N. (1997) *Justice Interruptus*, London: Routledge

Gewirtz, S. (1998) 'Conceptualizing social justice in education: mapping the territory', *Journal of Education Policy*, 13, 4: 469–484

Gillborn, D. and Youdell, D. (1999) *Rationing Education: Policy, Practice, Reform and Equity*, Buckingham: Open University Press

Hall, S. (1992) 'New Ethnicities' in Donald, J. and Ali, R. (eds) *'Race', Culture and Difference*, London: Sage

Hattersley, R. (2002) 'Obscure charm of the inner city', *Guardian*, p. 10, 20 August

Lather, P. (1991) *Getting Smart: Feminist Research and Pedagogy with/in the Postmodern*, London: Routledge

Lynch, K. (1995) 'The limits of liberalism in promotion of equality in education', Association for Teacher Education in Europe Annual Conference, Oslo, 3–8 September

Macrae, S., Maguire, M. and Ball, S. J. (1997) 'Competition, choice and hierarchy in post-16 education and training market' in Tomlinson, S. (ed.) *Perspectives on Education, 14–29*, London: Athlone

Marks, A. (2002) 'A "grown up" university? Towards a manifesto for life-long learning', *Journal of Education Policy* 17, 1:1–11

Modood, T. and Shiner, M. (1994) *Ethnic Minorities and Higher Education*, London: Policy Institute/UCAS

Osler, A. (1999) 'The educational experiences and career aspirations of black and ethnic minority undergraduates', *Race, Ethnicity and Education* 2, 1: 39–58

Parsons, C. (1999) *Education, Exclusion and Citizenship*, London: Routledge

Reay, D. (1998) '"Always knowing" and "never being sure": familial and institutional habituses and higher education choice', *Journal of Education Policy*, 13, 4: 519–529

Reay, D. (2001) 'Finding or losing yourself? Working class relationships to education', *Journal of Education Policy*, 16, 4: 333–346

Reay, D., Ball, S. and David, M. (2002) '"It's taking me a long time but I'll get there in the end" Mature students on access courses and higher education choice', *British Educational Research Journal*, 28, 1: 5–20

Schuller, T. and Bamford, C. (2000) 'A social capital approach to the analysis of continuing education: evidence from the UK Learning Society research programme', *Oxford Review of Education,* 26, 1: 5–19

Smith, D. and Bocock, J. (1999) 'Participation and progression in mass higher education: policy and the FHE interface', *Journal of Education Policy*, 14, 3: 83–299

Thomas, L. (2001) *Widening Participation in Lifelong Learning*, London: Continuum

Tomlinson, S. (1997) 'Diversity, choice and ethnicity: the effects of educational markets on ethnic minorities', *Oxford Review of Education*, 23, 1: 63–76

Werbner, P. (1996) 'Essentialising the other: a critical response' in Ranger, T., Samad, Y. and Stuart, O. (eds) *Culture Identity and Politics: Ethnic Minorities in Britain*, Aldershot: Avebury

Young, I. M. (1990) *Justice and the Politics of Difference*, Princeton, NJ: Princeton University Press

Chapter 5

Education and community health

Identity, social justice and lifestyle issues in communities

Lyn Tett

Social exclusion and social justice

'Social exclusion' has come into common parlance recently, particularly through its use in a number of EU, UK and Scottish policy documents (CEC, 2000; DfEE, 1998; Scottish Executive, 1998).

> [However,] the excluded do not constitute a defined group in the population: there is no single clear-cut definition of 'social exclusion'. Categories such as the 'unskilled', 'ethnic minorities', 'the unemployed' cover a range of circumstances.... So 'exclusion' does not bring a precise target into view but a range of associated issues.
>
> (OECD, 1999: 15–16)

Generally the term has been associated with the long-established and deep-rooted problems of poverty and unemployment that have been exacerbated by growing social and economic inequalities. In response to these problems the stated aim of the social inclusion policies of governments that are designed to bring about social justice is to ensure that all citizens, whatever their social or economic background, have opportunities to participate fully in society and enjoy a high quality of life. These rather bland and meaningless phrases have been used to argue that education and lifelong learning have a central role to play in this process. This is because it is suggested that lifelong learning programmes have the potential to 'change people's lives, even transform them' (Fryer 1997: 24) and give excluded people an economic and political voice through participation in the labour market and enhanced citizenship.

The part that the state is to play in combating social exclusion and promoting lifelong learning is, however, more ambiguous. The impact of globalising tendencies in the economy and culture and the associated trends towards individualism and declining support for welfarism have led governments to seek the promotion of more active and engaged citizens. The goal of policy is now to change behaviour in civil society (individuals and organisations) rather than simply provide a service. As Rhodes (1996: 655) has argued, the management of contemporary states involves '"less government" (or less rowing) but "more governance" (or more steering)'. Similarly, John Field has argued that the use of the term 'social exclusion' throughout Western Europe reflects a policy change. He suggests that 'rather than struggling against the social causes of inequality, the new language of exclusion implies that government's task is to promote "inclusion" into the existing social order' (Field 2000: 108).

In this new context issues of socio-economic inequality and the concern for wealth redistribution as part of a programme of social justice have been seen as less important and ideas about how inequalities are viewed have changed. As Ann Phillips argues:

> An earlier discourse of economic egalitarianism has given way to a new emphasis on individual responsibility. Extremes of income and wealth are no longer presented as undesirable in themselves. The only undesirable element is that they may lock certain members of society into an inability to take care of themselves. The state then has a responsibility to ensure that opportunities for self-advancement are made equally available to every citizen, an obvious responsibility in relation to education and training.
>
> (1999: 13)

The retreat from economic egalitarianism has also had an effect on how notions of social justice have been considered. For example, there has been a waning sense of the social obligation of the 'haves' to the 'have nots', which means that the old appeals to duty and the responsibility of society to its less fortunate members have fallen on rather deaf ears. One example is the British Social Attitudes Survey, reported on in December 2001, which found that attitudes to the poor had hardened.

> In 1994, 15 per cent attributed the plight of the poor to "laziness or lack of will power"; in 2000, this had risen to 23 per cent. Conversely, in 1994, 30 per cent blamed poverty on "injustice in our society"; in 2000, this had dropped to 21 per cent.
>
> (*New Statesman* 2001: 6)

This shift in attitudes, at its most extreme, can become a fear of the excluded themselves. This group have been described by some commentators such as Charles Murray (1994) and others from the radical right as becoming an 'underclass' who have effectively dropped out of society and live from a mixture of crime and welfare benefits. Others, such as MacDonald (1997) have identified the structural issues such as unemployment and poverty that lead to social exclusion but the popular media has not taken up these, more thoughtful, arguments. This means that appeals for greater spending to alleviate poverty and promote social justice are often couched in terms of an investment, assuaging middle-class fears of the poor. A corollary of these approaches is that rather than government doing things directly, it is required to persuade citizens to change their ways. Thus in the field of health, government has encouraged a widespread search for 'active measures' that place responsibilities on citizens to improve themselves, for example, by eating healthy foods and taking exercise.

What is clearly missing from this discourse, however, is the recognition that low wages, insecure employment, and dependence on means-tested benefits all contribute to social exclusion and poor health. Income inequality matters in any consideration of social exclusion because 'income is both the basis of social participation through consumption and a reflection of the power of people in their economic roles' (Byrne 1999: 79). From this viewpoint social exclusion is an active process that is about exclusion from power as well as material assets. As Madanipour and colleagues (1998: 22) point out:

> Social exclusion is … a multi-dimensional process, in which various forms of exclusion are combined: participation in decision making and political processes, access to employment and material resources, and integration into common cultural processes. When combined they create acute forms of exclusion that find a spatial manifestation in particular neighbourhoods.

This means that social exclusion can only be understood as a relational term that is really about the social processes that reproduce inequalities of power and resources, reinforce low self-esteem, undermine status and lower expectations. Combating social exclusion and increasing social justice thus requires re-distributive measures as well as enabling the needs and interests of marginalised communities to be articulated and acted on.

How the problem of social exclusion is conceived leads to different solutions. If the problem is seen in terms of a discourse of individual responsibility and pathology then the solution lies in changing the lifestyles of these individuals. If, on the other hand, it is recognised that social exclusion is a structural issue that arises from the fundamentally unequal nature of society then the solution is conceived differently. Moving towards a more socially just society requires the recognition that the people living in excluded communities are not the problem, rather they are the solution. People have varying degrees of agency but their actions can often make a significant difference to their conditions.

There are opportunities to use the spaces created by these policy ambiguities to work for more inclusive strategies for social justice. This is helped in Scotland by the recognition of the Social Justice Department of the Scottish Executive that social exclusion is a relational term that derives from inequality.

> Some communities and groups face concentrations of deprivation and exclusion, sometimes as a result of structural inequalities and labour market effects, and sometimes due to discrimination and inequality. Building strong, thriving communities is central to our … strategy. We need to work together to plan for greater inclusion and to support communities to … take ownership of their own futures.
>
> (Scottish Executive 2000: 4)

How these spaces might be widened in relation to health and social justice is discussed in the next section.

Education, health and social justice

Health is an important social justice issue since poor health and premature death in the UK is strongly linked to inequality, poverty and social class. A great deal of research has shown the impact of these factors on health, both in terms of the diseases people die from and the illness they suffer (Acheson 1998; Annandale and Hunt 2000; Benzeval *et al*. 1995; Scottish Executive Health Department 2001; Wilkinson 1996). For example, a baby whose father is an unskilled manual worker is one and a half times more likely to die before the age of one than the baby of a manager or professional employee. In addition, the poorest children are twice as likely to die from a respiratory illness and more than four times as likely to be killed in a road traffic accident as those from social class I (Leon *et al*. 1992). As Graham (2000a: 90) puts it 'social class is written on the body: it is inscribed in our experiences of health and our chances of premature death'. Similarly people's experience of the place where they live is also fundamental to the quality and meaning of their day-to-day life and health. These include social relations with people, the physical fabrics of the locality and the local geographies of services and facilities. Research is beginning to demonstrate that, in combination, features of place can be either sustaining or undermining of psychosocial well-being and health (Gattrell *et al*. 2000: 166).

This chapter puts this large-scale research into a local context by examining the ways that a group of people experiencing poverty, poor housing, and stress have assessed the impact of these factors on their health through participating in education through a course called 'Health Issues in the Community'. This course has involved people from a range of socio-economically excluded areas and groups throughout Scotland in identifying and investigating local concerns about the health issues that affect them. People involved in existing groups, such as mental health users' groups or minority ethnic women or people who use the local community centre, have been recruited by local tutors to participate in the course. Tutors are drawn from both the health and education professions, have a course pack that provides a variety of teaching and learning materials about health inequalities and a guide to student-centred learning approaches. They all undertake induction training and have support from a national co-ordinator as well as access to a wide range of supplementary learning and teaching materials. Because it is delivered locally the course has provided opportunities for people to express their own views, and to question official assumptions, explanations and definitions of health and illness, particularly where they differ from their own experience. Materials are generic so tutors are able to draw on people's lived experience of individual and community health problems to build a curriculum based on the issues that the participants believe are important to them and their communities.

The assumption underpinning the course is that social action in the health field is about educating ourselves to see that the control of our health is fundamental to the control of our lives. While individually focused medicine does not consider the social origins of many illnesses, the community health movement has attempted to do so. Rather than blame ourselves for our ill health, the focus is on the damaging social experiences that produce ill health and, furthermore, there is an understanding that remedial action needs to be social. This view of health focuses on the socio-economic risk conditions such as poverty, unemployment, pollution, poor housing and power imbalances that cause ill health. It also emphasises that 'people's experiences of health are more about the quality of their emotional and social situation than about their experience of disease or disability' (Labonte 1997: 9). The perspective taken by the course is that an important way that inequalities in health can be tackled is to find ways of strengthening individuals and communities so that they can join together for mutual support. As Whitehead points out, 'research shows that by people joining together you can strengthen the whole community's defence against health hazards' (Whitehead 1995: 25).

At the end of each course, which is accredited by the University of Edinburgh, participants investigate and write about a health issue in their community as part of their assessment. To date nearly a hundred people have completed these essays and a selection of their writings has been published in three books edited by Jane Jones (Jones 1999a, 1999b, 2001). I will be drawing on these published writings to illustrate this chapter by using the words of the participants to demonstrate the impact that these health issues had on their lived experience and the action they took to bring about change. I will do this by focusing on two aspects of the impact of poverty on the health of the participants in the courses: first, in relation to women and families and then in relation to housing factors. The names of the students are pseudonyms.

Women, identity and family

A gendered division of labour in which women take primary responsibility for childcare and domestic labour sustains family life in Britain. These combined responsibilities make for long working days that are structured by other people's needs (Graham 1994: 116). Students on the course were all too aware of this. As one pointed out:

> A woman is the prime carer; money manager and financial wizard; purchaser of all food, clothes and household necessities. Try to imagine how difficult and impossible it is for her to manage [on a low income]. This is not a short-term problem but is the reality day after day. Coping with this daily is extremely detrimental to a woman's mental health.
>
> (Anne, in Jones 1999b: 18)

Another suggested:

> Poverty breeds ill health. Whether food is nutritious is not the main issue, just being able to buy food of any description is the first priority. Poverty is powerlessness. There is no choice as to where you live. Poverty is not being able to keep a warm comfortable home, thereby being unable to combat dampness and condensation. Poverty is defeat. The feelings of hopelessness and worthlessness can lead to the downward spiral of drug taking and alcoholism, which are ways of escaping from miserable surroundings and the awful day-to-day living and isolation.
>
> (Fiona, in Jones 2001: 29)

This raises an important issue about the development of social agency. The first step in developing a more active approach is that people recognise that they are strategic actors who make choices in response to their oppressive social situations. Graham (1994), in her study of women and smoking, showed how mothers created a space – symbolic if not real – between them and their children and filled this space with self-directed activity. Smoking a cigarette provides such an activity that can be accessed instantly when mothers feel their breaking point has been reached. The women reported how they tried to weave other, more self-directed, routines into their schedules of childcare and housework. She pointed out that:

> Parents bringing up children on low incomes spend more of the little they have on collective necessities, like food and fuel, than do better-off households. It is a strategy for survival that leaves a mother constantly aware of her family's poverty: of what they have not got and what they cannot do. It is a lifestyle of enforced exclusion from the communities to which they belong.
>
> (1994: 119)

Students on the course illustrated this:

> Stress is an inevitable part of life for those living on the breadline. The constant worry about making ends meet, about looking after your family and their needs. For people in poverty, the stress of being unable to cope can be a killer.
>
> (Sandra, in Jones 1999b: 7)

> When you live in poverty you are forced to make choices between items which others take for granted, such as heating, lighting or a nutritionally balanced meal. Managing on a low income is a constant worry because you cannot afford to take part in anything social like Gala days, school fetes, day trips to the beach or even school uniforms for the children.
>
> (Emma, in Jones 2001: 24)

Women take responsibility for their family's health and this inevitably leads to stress, especially for those living in poverty. As one minority ethnic student commented:

> In my community it is a responsibility of the family to look after the elders. Husbands have long hours of work from 7am to 9pm, and they can't share household responsibilities. Women do not have time for themselves, looking after young children, providing help to the elderly, looking after husbands coming in late at night. The one woman in the house performs all these jobs.
>
> (Aisha, in Jones 2001: 19)

Another student who lived in a socio-economically excluded community suggested:

> To wander round a glossy supermarket with very little money in your purse – it's little wonder this leads to depression, a sense of never coping and always having to make a choice between heating your home or buying a wholesome varied diet for your family.
>
> (Maggie, in Jones 1999b: 25)

The way that women do put their own health last, giving their main priority to looking after their children or family, became more and more apparent as the course tutors worked with different groups of women. An example of this was one student's definition of what she meant by health.

> If you're healthy enough to get up in the morning to do what you've got to do without having to worry about being exhausted or breaking down by dinner time. That's my idea of health. I've got to be healthy for my family.
>
> (Beth, in Jones 1999a: 16)

Here women reflect societal assumptions about their identities being drawn mainly from their roles as carers for their children and others where their core work is focused around maintaining family life. For women to prioritise their own needs is to challenge both the cultural assumptions about women's place in society and the patriarchal division of labour (see Van Every 1996).

Housing and health

Statistically owner-occupiers have lower risks of death and better health than people who rent their homes (Macintyre *et al.* 2000). Research suggests that socio-economic status, the physical and social features of the home and the area and psychological characteristics such as self-esteem interact to produce these outcomes (ibid. 138). Poor housing is one of the major health issues identified by many socio-economically excluded communities. As one student put it:

In my community due to poor housing design and inadequate heating systems families are forced to live with dampness. If they did heat their houses
properly they probably would not be able to afford to eat, and are therefore
forced to live with dampness in their homes.

(Frank, in Jones 1999b: 8)

High-rise flats that are a common feature of socially excluded communities and
the isolation this type of housing causes is another factor that leads to stress and
depression. 'Isolation is a major problem in the flats as you can go for days without seeing anybody' (Cathy, in Jones 1999b: 9). Animosity between neighbours is
also a problem when people are living, quite literally, on top of each other. This is
often combined with overcrowding, especially for those with large or extended
families.

Participants in the course demonstrated that one way of ending the spiral of
despair regarding poor housing and ill health is through community development.
This means that rather than seeing dampness and the noise pollution caused by
poor housing as an individual trouble that must be solved by an individual taking
action on his or her own, the reasons behind the problem are examined. This
requires the rejection of the view that it is a particular lifestyle that causes problems and the adoption of a sceptical view about why these problems are described
in this way. One example, reported on by Neil (in Jones 1999b), was 'I know of a
person who when complaining of dampness to his landlord was told that he
breathed too much because the landlord didn't want to do anything about it!'
Another student suggested:

The way forward is through the community development process where individuals come together and tackle the problem as a public issue rather than a
private one. Their strategy then becomes forcing the housing department to
address the problem of poor housing and developing effective procedures in
dealing with noisy neighbours.

(Alan, in Jones 1999b: 35)

Through the process of developing strategies for tackling their identified problems and taking their issues to the wider community, a group can grow in
confidence and eventually will be able to take well-thought-out solutions to policy makers. One group involved in the course eventually gained better insulation,
soundproofing and heating through a long campaign of local and wider action. As
one member of the group put it: 'This had an instant effect on improving people's
health both directly and indirectly by reducing people's stress and anxiety levels.
Your home should be a place where you can relax, unwind and escape from the
outside world' (Jimmy, in Jones 1999b: 35).

Contesting health as a lifestyle issue

It appears that the medical dominance over the definition and analysis of health and illness is still disproportionately influential in health policy and practice (see Carlisle 2001; Graham 2000b; Purdy and Banks 1999). It is still a struggle for policy makers to give priority to the political and social determinants of health and to make the connections between the psychosocial effects of lack of control over the social and material conditions of people's lives, and poor health. Moreover, there is a pervasive assumption that it is people's individual lifestyles that need to be changed in order to improve health rather than their social and material conditions. Contesting these official definitions of health was therefore a key issue in working with communities on their own health issues. This had a number of implications that are explored below.

Just as the assumption that pervades education is that it is not the fault of the schools if they fail to educate disadvantaged children but largely the fault of their mothers (see Luttrell 1997) so this same assumption pervades views about where responsibility lies for maintaining children's health. An important aspect of the course, therefore, was to help women to prioritise their own health needs and to analyse the structural issues that led to their ill health and that of their families. In one area a survey was undertaken by a group of women of the health provision that was needed in their community. The information from the study led the project to create some protected time for women, with childcare, so that they might have the space to think about their own health. A number of groups were set up that created an opportunity for women to reappraise their role and begin to find time for themselves and be able to take action to change their lives (see Jones 1999a: 17).

One aspect of women's tendency to see themselves as individually responsible is that they can easily become isolated, especially when they are on their own with the children. One student remembered how she felt when she first found herself with total responsibility for her children with no friends or family nearby to help. 'I felt alone, isolated and scared. The fear was the worst, especially at night, after the children had gone to bed, as I sat alone in the quiet darkness worrying about all the things that could go wrong' (Diane, in Jones 2001: 36).

Another woman described her feelings of inadequacy when she was a young mother trying to raise three children on a very low income. She also showed how getting together with others had helped her. She said:

> It was a struggle to pay the rent, feed them and try to clothe them. It would have been all too easy to say 'to hell with it' and to escape into oblivion with drink or drugs. I knew the feelings of helplessness, but also of guilt. I thought it was all my fault. At the time I didn't realise how ill I was although I would never have gone to a doctor anyway, as I felt so ashamed and thought that I would be blamed and lectured to. (Then I got to meet some other people

through the toddlers group and I realised I wasn't alone.) Coming together made me feel part of a whole. It helped end my isolation and hopelessness.

(Elsie, in Jones, 2001: 30)

Once people feel that they are able to take action then much can change. For example, one student was exasperated with the media blaming people for their own poverty and, with others, enlisted community education staff who helped them work out their agenda and what action to take. She explained:

Healthy diet was a big issue and it was the priority. The shopping centre was the only place in our town that you could get fresh fruit and vegetables but the prices were way above most people's budgets. We decided to take action first of all about telling people what were healthy foods. Then we went to our local farmer to buy our fruit and vegetables so that we could sell them cheaper, only adding on the cost of petrol. The group sent out leaflets giving information on where to go to buy cheaper fruit and vegetables, the response was staggering. Everyone knows what a healthy diet is but they just can't afford it.

(Hetty, in Jones 2001: 33)

A challenge for people is to see the potential that effective social action has in de-privatising their pain. By making public poor people's experience of the burdens they carry, in both public and private settings, it becomes possible to see their problems as the direct result of the countless contradictions inherent in their social position. One aspect of this is challenging the stigma associated with mental health and the medical solutions that are offered. Participants in the course described their worries about going to the doctor with their symptoms and their fears about the impact this will have on their children. For example, one student said: 'It is really frightening to say what you feel. You think, if I tell them that, the bairns [children] will get taken away. You're frightened of being labelled a bad mother' (Joan, in Jones 1999a: 91).

Another participant who lived in an overcrowded flat in a tenement building with anti-social neighbours described how these pressures led to stress and then to depression. She said:

It got to the stage that I decided to go to the doctor. I explained my problem to him, then the pen comes out and the miracle cure in the doctor's eyes is to prescribe anti-depressants, that's what I was sent away with. I got outside the surgery and thought to myself no way am I going to rely on pills to help me with my problem. I thought I'd like to tackle this on my own, so I would get up early in the morning and walk practically everywhere all day long.

(Kate, in Jones 1999b: 9)

Moving from an individual solution, however, to one that comes from collective action is the next step but this usually needs the intervention of 'skilled helpers' (see Brookfield 2000). One way in which the Health Issues in the Community course provides such help is to show how apparently private troubles are actually public issues (Mills 1959). Two students commented on the ways in which their understanding of mental health had changed:

> I had been on tranquillisers but I felt so ashamed about it that I hid it from everyone. Then this young woman spoke up about her experience in the discussion group and I realised that lots of women had had the same feelings. You have to learn that it isn't your fault but you need people to talk to about it first.
>
> (Laura, in Jones 1999a: 130)

> I'm involved with the Stress Centre now that got set up really because a group of us started to think about what would have helped us more than just getting a prescription. We decided that it was somewhere to go to get a bit of support and someone to talk to, so we talked to a lot of different people and eventually the Centre was set up. Working there has done a lot for my self-confidence and I know that we can help people. It takes time but it can be done.
>
> (Norah, in Jones 1999a: 133)

Working with a community to increase self-determination and take control over its collective resources is an important task for educators. Building organisations, taking action to redistribute resources, ensuring that community voices are heard, all have direct health benefits. This is because lack of control over one's own destiny promotes a susceptibility to ill health for people who live in difficult situations where they do not have adequate resources or supports in their day-to-day lives (see Annandale and Hunt, 2000). Clearly many of the people who participated in this course have involved themselves in action that has enabled them to move from a position of relative powerlessness to one of greater empowerment in relation to the issues about health that are important to them.

Conclusion

A wide range of research that has examined the areas of socio-economic status, occupational health and stress has shown consistently that powerlessness, or lack of control over destiny, is a high risk factor for disease. It demonstrates that being poor, low in the hierarchy, without control and living in chronic hardship increases susceptibility to higher morbidity and mortality rates (Wallerstein 1992: 199). Learning that contributes to empowerment can, on the other hand, reduce these risk factors by enabling participants to be decision makers, 'developing mutual identification and transforming perceptions of self-blame through an analysis of the social context of problems' (ibid. 204).

The personal and social damage inflicted by inequality, social exclusion and restricted opportunity is now officially recognised by governments in the UK. An important component of social inclusion is learning which should represent a resource for people to help them identify inequalities, probe their origins and begin to challenge them, using skills, information and knowledge in order to achieve and stimulate change. Through learning, competing values can be reviewed, their relevance for society can be assessed, and, slowly, newly emerging values can be transmitted (see Fryer 1997).

Clearly, whilst learning alone cannot abolish inequality and bring about social justice it can make a real contribution to tackling social exclusion through education in relation to the health issues identified for action. If people can be helped to challenge deficit views of the health of their homes and communities then a small step has been taken in enabling their voices to be heard. Enabling communities to name and frame their health problems for themselves and build their own 'really useful knowledge' (see Johnson 1988) thus becomes an important benefit of learning. Shifting the emphasis away from disease and ill health and individuals' lifestyles and towards the ways in which well-being can flourish in communities, has been an important outcome of this course. A community development approach to health enables community groups to establish for themselves what their health issues are and provides a means through which they can explore the root causes of their problems. The impact of such work can be seen in three broad areas. First, an increase in agency and thus better health through increased self-esteem, confidence and empowerment; second, more local control over decision making thus improving the delivery of health services to meet locally identified needs. Finally, a holistic approach to health can contribute towards the creation of an alternative framework through which to understand health issues from a broad-based, sustainable perspective.

The importance currently attached to personal responsibility allows structural inequalities to be minimised and instead treated as 'choices' and 'lifestyle issues'. This is reinforced by a prevailing climate that shrugs off social injustice since, when we no longer feel able to change our circumstances, we would rather believe them to be equitable and just. The course, Health Issues in the Community, has provided a small counterweight to this climate by providing opportunities for people to express their own views, and to question those official assumptions, explanations and definitions of the causes of ill health that focus on lifestyle issues. In a field where official definitions can exert a powerful influence over the content of communication the project has sought to help local people focus on health information that is meaningful to them because it comes from their own experience. By taking action, for example over housing or high food costs or the stigmatisation involved in mental health issues, local people assume a degree of control and create, rather than receive, meaningful knowledge. Learning together collectively and then taking action based on what has been learnt is an empowering process as people start to take back some control over their own destiny and directly improve their own health and that of their communities. As Margaret Davies argued in 1913:

Even a little knowledge is a dangerous thing. It causes a smouldering dis-content, which may flame into active rebellion against a low level of life, and produces a demand, however stammering, for more interests and chances. Where we see ferment, there has been some of the yeast of education.

(Quoted in Scott 1998: 56)

It is important, however, to remember that education cannot compensate for soci-ety since as long as people are struggling under adverse socio-economic conditions then we cannot forget the force of structural inequalities on their lives. Social justice requires not only the recognition of people as active agents working for change in their own communities but also the redistribution of power and material assets to those that have been excluded if real change is to be achieved.

References

Acheson, D. (1998) *Independent Inquiry into Inequalities in Health*, London: The Stationery Office

Annandale, E. and Hunt, K. (2000) (eds) *Gender Inequalities in Health*, Buckingham: Open University Press

Benzeval, M., Judge, K. and Whitehead, M. (1995) *Tackling Inequalities in Health*, London: King's Fund

Brookfield, S. (2000) 'Adult cognition as a dimension of lifelong learning' in Field, J. and Leicester, M. (eds) *Lifelong Learning: Education Across the Lifespan*, London: Routledge

Byrne, D. (1999) *Social Exclusion*, Buckingham: Open University Press

Carlisle, S. (2001) 'Inequalities in health: contested explanations, shifting discourses and ambiguous policies', *Critical Public Health*, 11, 3

Commission of the European Communities (2000) *A Memorandum on Lifelong Learning*, Brussels: Directorate General for Education, Training and Youth

Department for Education and Employment (1998) *The Learning Age – a Renaissance for a New Britain*, London: The Stationery Office

Field, J. (2000) *Lifelong Learning and the New Educational Order*, Stoke-on-Trent: Trentham Books

Fryer, R. (1997) *Learning for the Twenty-First Century*, London: DfEE

Gattrell, A., Thomas, C., Bennett, S., Bostock, L., Popay, J., Williams, G. and Shahtahmasebi, S. (2000) 'Understanding health inequalities: locating people in geo-graphical and social spaces', in Graham, H. (ed.) *Understanding Health Inequalities*, Buckingham: Open University Press

Graham, H. (1994) 'Surviving by smoking' in Wilkinson, S. and Kitzinger, C. (eds) *Women and Health: Feminist Perspectives*, London: Taylor and Francis

Graham, H. (2000a) 'Socio-economic change and inequalities in men and women's health in the UK' in Annandale, E. and Hunt, K. (eds) *Gender Inequalities in Health*, Buckingham: Open University Press

Graham, H. (2000b) (ed.) *Understanding Health Inequalities*, Buckingham: Open University Press

Johnson, R. (1988) 'Really useful knowledge, 1790–1850' in Lovett, T. (ed.) *Radical Approaches to Adult Education: a Reader*, London: Routledge

Jones, J. (1999a) *Private Troubles and Public Issues, a Community Development Approach to Health*, Edinburgh: Community Learning Scotland

Jones, J. (1999b) *Writing about Health Issues: Voices from Communities*, Edinburgh: Moray House Institute of Education

Jones, J. (2001) *Writing about Health Issues: Voices from Communities Volume 2*, Edinburgh: Moray House Institute of Education

Labonte, R. (1997) 'Community, community development and the forming of authentic partnerships' in Minkler, M. (ed.) *Community Organising and Community Building for Health*, New Brunswick: Rutgers University Press

Leon, D. Vagero, D. and Otterbiad, P. (1992) 'Social Class differences in infant mortality in Sweden: comparisons with England and Wales', *British Medical Journal*, Vol. 305

Luttrell, W. (1997) *School-smart and Mother-wise*, London: Routledge

MacDonald, R. (1997) *Youth, the 'Underclass' and Social Exclusion*, London: Routledge

Macintyre, S., Hiscock, R., Kearns, A. and Ellaway, A. (2000) 'Housing tenure and health inequalities: a three-dimensional perspective on people, homes and neighbourhoods' in Graham, H. (ed.) *Understanding Health Inequalities*, Buckingham: Open University Press

Madanipour, A., Cars, G. and Allen, J. (eds) (1998) *Social Exclusion in European Cities*, London: Jessica Kingsley

Mills, C. W. (1959) *The Sociological Imagination*, Oxford: Oxford University Press

Murray, C. (1994) *Underclass: the Crisis Deepens*, London: Institute of Economic Affairs

New Statesman (2001) 'Editorial', 3.12.01

OECD (1999), *Overcoming Social Exclusion Through Adult Learning*, Paris: OECD

Phillips, A. (1999) *Which Equalities Matter?*, Cambridge: Polity Press

Purdy, M. and Banks, M. (1999) *Health and Exclusion: Policy and Practice in Health Provision*, London: Routledge

Rhodes, R. A. W. (1996) 'The new governance: governing without government', *Political Studies*, 44, 4: 652–667

Scott, G. (1998) *Feminism and the Politics of Working Women*, London: UCL Press

Scottish Executive (1998) *Social Inclusion Strategy for Scotland*, Edinburgh: Stationery Office

Scottish Executive (2000) *Social Justice Annual Report*, Edinburgh: Stationery Office

Scottish Executive Health Department (2001) *Health in Scotland, Report of the Chief Medical Officer*, www.scotland.gov.uk

Van Every, J. (1996) *Heterosexual Women Challenging the Family: Refusing to be a Wife*, London: Taylor and Francis

Wallerstein, N. (1992) 'Powerlessness, empowerment and health: implications for health promotion programs', *American Journal of Health Promotion*, 6, 3: 197–205

Whitehead, M. (1995) 'Tackling inequalities: a review of policy initiatives' in Benzeval, M., Judge, K. and Whitehead, M. (eds) *Tackling Inequalities in Health: an Agenda for Action*, London: King's Fund

Wilkinson, R. G. (1996) *Unhealthy Societies: the Afflictions of Inequality*, London: Routledge

Chapter 6

Male working-class identities and social justice

A reconsideration of Paul Willis's *Learning to Labour* in light of contemporary research

Madeleine Arnot

Introduction

The publication of Paul Willis's *Learning to Labour* in 1977 represented a landmark in the study of social identities and social justice in education. Willis's seminal thesis about why working-class boys get working-class jobs, when first published, was described on its back cover as 'an uncompromising book which is certain to provoke considerable controversy'. Twenty-five years later, the book is still one of the most cited texts in the sociology of education. In an extraordinary way, Willis's text links the 'problem' of working-class education which has framed social democratic policy discourses since 1944 with contemporary concerns about identities, culture and social change. Re-reading Willis, I want to argue, has significance beyond the immediate concerns of the book. The various re-readings of the book, only some of which I refer to in this chapter, exemplify some of the complex theoretical and methodological shifts in the study of identities and social justice. I shall argue that, despite the numerous rigorous criticisms of Willis's theory of working-class culture and the social-cultural reproduction of working-class inequalities, the themes of his study still represent an important symbolic marker in the study of gender and social class identities and in the development of critical research methodologies associated with transformative politics. Arguably, the book also represents a more grounded and situated analysis of identity than is currently on offer. Re-reading the text therefore proffers the chance to reflect critically upon our current theoretical project on social identities, social justice and schooling. I begin that discussion by illustrating three rather different readings of the book, before exploring how male class identities are now being researched and related to issues of social justice.

Connecting identity, agency and structure

Willis's research was conducted with a group of 12 working-class boys attending Hammerton school in the huge industrial conurbation in the Midlands. The town was then working class with only eight per cent classified as professional middle class. The population was around 60,000 with one of the highest activity rates in the country. Women were especially active in the labour force (some 79 per cent), most of whom were involved in manufacturing in metal and metal goods, and the rest worked in food, drinks and tobacco industries, mechanical engineering, vehicles, bricks, pottery and glass, and distribution. Unemployment in the early 1970s in this area was only one per cent under the national average. As Willis noted Hammerton was 'something of an archetypal industrial town. It has all the classic industrial hallmarks as well as those of modern monopoly capitalism in conjunction with a proletariat which is just about the oldest in the world' (6).

The Hammerton 'lads' studied by Willis had developed their own strong 'anti-school' culture – a culture which they had developed creatively out of the materials, resources and insights available to them. Their praxis – the creative development, transformation and reproduction of aspects of the larger culture – paradoxically and critically led them to certain kinds of work. The effect was 'the manual giving of their labour power' to the structures of Western capitalism. This giving, 'a compact with the future' as Willis described it, took working-class destiny and reformed it into new purposes. Part of that process involved what he called the 'partial penetration' of the 'really determining conditions of existence of the working class' (3) which belied official versions given to them by the school and society.

> The tragedy and the contradiction is that these forms of 'penetration' are limited, distorted and turned back on themselves, often unintentionally, by complex processes ranging from both general ideological processes and those within the school and guidance agencies to the widespread influence of a form of patriarchal male domination and sexism within working-class culture itself.
>
> (Willis 1977: 3)

Using his data, Willis offered an explanation about the failure of the educational system to improve the chances of these 'lads'. Central to his analysis was the role of labour power and in Part 2 of the book, Willis explored the relationship of patriarchy (and to a lesser extent racialism) to capitalism. The meaning of labouring and labour power to these 'young non-academic and disaffected males' was understood in the context of these other social divisions. Thus Willis demonstrated empirically how the cultural pattern of the educational failure of manual working-class children was different from other middle-class and working-class patterns found in schools – it had its own logic, experiences, relationships, choices and decisions. In this analysis, the extraordinary conjunction of structural and subjective possibilities were brought together in the description of the experiences and identifications of one particular group of youth.

Learning to Labour therefore spoke to the concerns of social justice which at the time were focused upon male working-class educational experiences and offered an analysis of class identities which resonated with current sociological discourses.[1] From a social justice perspective, the analysis went to the heart of the liberal democratic meritocratic ideals of schooling which in the post-war settlement offered schools a contradictory dual repertoire (CCCS 1981) – the pursuit of economic growth coupled with the desire to encourage greater social equality and cohesion. This dual repertoire at the centre of Labour's reform efforts brought together vocational and liberal discourses within the school. Economic rationalism coupled the promotion of individual skills and competencies with the tapping of working-class pools of talent and the promotion of a more educated society. In contrast, Willis's research exposed the injustice and forms of 'institutional repression' (Willis 2000: 38) associated with such a repertoire for manual working-class boys. Credentialism, the boys understood, could no more lead to the 'dismantling of the whole class society' (ibid. 38) as it could improve the chances of the manual working class. According to Willis:

> Prevented from pursuing alternative flowerings of their capacities or subversive courses of growth, credentialism enslaves ['the lads"] powers and seeks to trap them in the foothills of human development … From the collective point of view, lived out in the culture of 'the lads', the proliferation of qualifications is simply a worthless inflation of the currency of credentialism, and advance through it, a fraudulent offer to the majority of what can really mean something only to the few.
>
> (ibid. 38–39)

However, the consequences of revealing such 'institutional repression' were not necessarily negative. Curiously, Willis's account of the transitions of young working-class males into manual labour confirmed to teachers that not only could they not be held directly responsible for working-class failure but that by hearing the collective voices of 'the lads', teachers could begin to address the realities of the boys' lives and intervene on their behalf in transformative ways. Distancing himself from the more deterministic functionalism of social/cultural reproduction theory, Willis positioned himself within what he saw as the radical educational practice which was being nurtured by the Centre for Contemporary Cultural Studies at Birmingham University at that time. Reflecting on his work, he wrote:

> If we have nothing to say about what to do on Monday morning, everything is yielded to a purist structuralist immobilising reductionist tautology: nothing can be done until the basic structures of society are changed but the structures prevent us making any changes. … To contract out of the messy business of day-to-day problems is to deny the active, contested nature of social and culture reproduction: to condemn real people to the status of passive zombies, and actually cancel the future by default … It is a theoretical as well as a political failure.
>
> (Willis 1997: 186 quoted in Skeggs 1992: 182)

Willis firmly believed that by using ethnographic methods to explore in depth the forms of human creativity or 'art' and their social consequences, the possibility existed of radicalising teachers' practice and addressing the injustices associated with capitalism as an economic and social form. In his more recent book *The Ethnographic Imagination* (Willis 2000) he describes how the study of social 'penetrations', such as those of the 'lads', is a means of widening and deepening the 'always contingent and reflexive body of knowledge about humankind' about 'how humans use resources for meaning-making in context'. 'Cultural practices of meaning-making are intrinsically self-motivated as aspects of identity-making and self-construction: in making our cultural worlds we make ourselves' (Willis 2000: xiv). In *Learning to Labour*,

> the ethnographic study of culture therefore had a general role to play in point-ing to injustice and in contributing to, maintaining and extending norms of social justice and human decency. There are specifically internal connections here for a perspective attuned to the lived penetrations of social agents, i.e. understanding what *in situ* practices themselves 'say' about social justice.
>
> (Willis 2000: 120)

Collecting the voices of those who might otherwise be silent must be done, according to Willis, in the spirit of 'respecting, recording, illuminating and learn-ing from forms of sensuous subordinate meaning-making and self-making, even as they may be distorted and constrained by their unpropitious conditions' (ibid. 120). The ethnographer, in Willis's eyes, may give those studied potential power through the politics of 'naming', they might 'open up the invisibility of symbolic work, and thereby offer opportunities for the redirection or limitation of the repro-ductive consequences of lived penetrations'[2] (ibid. 121). Other namings could thus be put into circulation in official discourses thus 'interrupting or denying the smooth functioning of expert government regulation and the legitimisation of inequality' (ibid. 121). Referring to contemporary worlds, such ethnographic studies can develop greater theoretical understandings of the impact of the 'struc-tures, social relationships and "behind back" social change' which generate new kinds of desires and new kinds of survival and thus new kinds of identity expressed in new kinds of collectivity and new kinds of politics (ibid. 121).

Such ideals, however, were never likely to be achieved easily nor in a linear fashion. Indeed through describing in such vivid detail the ways working-class 'lads' worked on and with material circumstances and their 'objective possibili-ties', *Learning to Labour* suggested that the egalitarian efforts of school could be diverted and even negated by the self-reproduction of working-class subordina-tion. The pleasure which the lads took in having 'the laff', fun and the pisstake (Willis 2000: 38), 'their tumble out (rather than transition from) school' (ibid. 41), their random selection of jobs and their 'resistant dignity' (ibid. 39) were shown to prepare them for the logic of labour under capitalism – 'an intended and con-servative reproduction' of the social structure. Critical modernist and later postmodernist educators in the UK and abroad not surprisingly received the book with a certain amount of political ambivalence.

Nevertheless, the power of Willis's text lay in the richness of his account of the survival of the 'lads' and in the potency of his analysis of social inequality. Its sociological legacy in the fields of education and youth cultural studies can be found in the continuing focus on the extraordinary creativity of various groups of youth in responding to their positionality. Indeed the analysis of creativity in identity construction, identifications and alliances arguably has now become the major focus of sociological studies of social justice. At the same time, the relevance of *Learning to Labour* has been greatly affected by post-structuralist readings of such a 'modernist' and politically committed agenda (Skeggs 1992).

Methodological agendas for social justice

In retrospect, it is easy to see why *Learning to Labour* was seen as a methodological and theoretical turning point, paving the way not just for critical ethnographies but also for later post-structuralist readings of identity. It was described as a key marker in the development of social scientific epistemology, integrating an analysis of structure and agency that was unprecedented. The critical ethnographic methods employed by Willis were interpreted, therefore, as a significant epistemological break with the structures of positivism and rational theory (although arguably these had already been challenged by Hargreaves' (1967) and by Lacey's (1970) studies of school life). As Wexler (2000) recently commented, Willis's analysis of the reproduction of inequality moved away from more 'neutral', 'atheoretical' studies of boys, 'adding empirical quality to a more general theoretical introduction of critical theory to education' (98).

Willis's political agenda however was to be challenged by a number of methodological critiques. Beverley Skeggs' review of *Learning to Labour* commented upon the extent to which Willis's political project in the name of social justice had committed the reader to a highly romanticised celebratory view of the working-class 'lads'. She points to the 'seductive' nature of the text – noticing its deployment of rhetorical devices such as the use of 'we', its encouragement to evolve a personal response to the subjects before discussing the sociological theory about their situation (the division between the first and second parts of the book), the use of dramatic incidents which would 'do a soap opera proud', the vicarious access to an unfamiliar world, the appeal of Willis's political commitment with its celebration of agency over structure and domination, his optimism and the sympathy he generates for 'the lads'. However, the consequences led to 'a reconfirmation' for middle-class socialists 'of the revolutionary potential of the working class – if only they weren't so sexist and racist' (1992: 188).

Post-structuralist and postmodernist re-readings of the study went further and questioned the extent to which the book marked not just a political but also a methodological turning point. Post-structuralist and postmodern feminists, in particular, pointed to the various ways in which Willis's project had left unresolved central questions about, for example, the role of theory, especially in relation to issues of agency, identity and praxis. In this reading, Willis was trapped within the narratives of 1970s critical theory. Using a postmodern yardstick, Patti Lather (1991) for example, criticised Willis for his *a priori* use of neo-Marxist theory. She argued that there was no sense of the ways in which Willis's perspective as researcher might have been altered by the data. The role of theory was therefore presented as 'non-dialectical, unidirectional, an imposition that disallows counter-patterns and alternative explanations' (67). The methodological stance of such critical Marxist theory was that it essentially privileged externality, created a unitary analysis of 'the lads' and left the researcher paradoxically in a politically neutral position, distanced from his subject.

Ironically, Willis was taken to task for his failure to develop any further dialogue or praxis with the boys in his study. Gore argues that, although Willis pointed to 'the productive aspects of power', he had concluded with 'elucidation of the oppressive structures which kept the lads in their class position' (Gore 1993: 96). His concept of 'partial penetration' – the ability of people to pierce through cultural contradictions in incomplete ways that did not lead to ideology critique – was itself incomplete since it did not offer insights into the possibilities for intervention. Thus although the 'language of possibility' had its beginnings in such a text, the move from an awareness of structural constraints to transformative work had not been made. Strong tensions still existed between the 'discursive foci on critique and possibility' (Gore 1993: 96).

Thus, although Willis had identified the area of resistance to authority as an important corrective to the overly deterministic correspondence, he was seen as maintaining a quasi-positivist or scientific realist approach to research. Without problematising the research process itself, the dangers of objectification and the distanced relationship between subject and object (Lather 1991), Willis had apparently reproduced 'covert forms of positivism' or a 'scientific realist approach to research' that had led in the final instance to the sustaining of an 'essential male gaze of social subordination and domination as knowledge practice' (Wexler 2000: 98).

The consequences of such readings of *Learning to Labour* were substantial. On the one hand, Willis's theory of class resistance through youth cultural forms took hold of the sociological and political imagination (Brown 1988) – its emphasis on identity construction became the dominant sociological research paradigm. On the other hand, as a result of such criticisms, Willis's book was understood to represent a modernist text *par excellence* by a new generation of social scientists trained in post-Enlightenment thinking. The consequence arguably, as Beverley Skeggs notes, was that the political and theoretical integrity of Willis's analysis 'has been lost in much of the game-playing of postmodern discourse' (1992: 193).

Masculinity as class opposition

A different, more positive, reading of *Learning to Labour* has been proffered by those concerned with the processes of gender identity formation. In the context particularly of the development of a sociology of masculinity, Willis's book represents a major break with past theories of gender socialisation. Willis had, in effect, shown how identity construction – the production and construction of gender identities – could be researched. Since the publication of *Learning to Labour*, as Connell (1995) argues, few have doubted that the social construction of masculinities is a systematic socially negotiated process. Nor have they been able to avoid the complex interface between the social structure and culture. Paradoxically, in this context, *Learning to Labour* did not pave the way just for critical ethnographies but also for post-structural readings of gender identity and gender identity work.

As Connell (1995) noted, Willis's contribution was to place the study of gender well within the analysis of working-class cultures in education, at the interface between schooling and the economy and shop floor culture, and within the study of anti-school cultures. Significantly, the book focused not just upon class specificity but also upon 'a study of masculinity in practice'. For Connell, Willis's study along with Tolson's (1977) seminal text *The Limits of Masculinity* were the first of their kind. Both suggested that school was the site in which multiple masculinities were generated, often in opposition to school authority and curriculum structures. Since then, many studies have explored the range of subject positions inhabited by boys inside and outside schools (for example, Brown 1988; Mac an Ghaill 1994; Sewell 1997/8). Thus, even though the formal dichotomy of 'lads' and 'ear'oles' was soon challenged by Brown's (1987) ethnography of 'ordinary' working-class boys – those who wanted to 'get on' and 'get out' of their destinies – his study along with the many others which followed focus on the *relational* world of boys. Boys were shown to be actively shaping gender relations as much as social class relations and to be constructing their masculinity within the fluid relations of gender, ethnicity, class, age and sexuality. Rather uniquely, as early as the 1970s Willis had brought together the study of class, gender and race relations in a complex and sophisticated way.

Willis had also shown the ways in which different masculinities and indeed particular forms of (heterosexual/white) hegemonic masculinity were created, regulated and reproduced within the same school. According to Connell, Willis had effectively demonstrated

> the *relations* between the different kinds of masculinity: relations of alliance, dominance and subordination. These relationships are constructed through practices that exclude and include, that intimidate, exploit and so on. There is a gender politics within masculinity.
>
> (Connell, 1995: 37)

After Willis, school studies focused on patterns of hegemonic masculinities rather than socialisation. Cultural differentiations rather than just economic differentiation, as Connell notes, became central to the study of working-class identity formation.

Ahead of its time, *Learning to Labour* explored the contradictory and negative consequences of gender, and to a lesser extent, race on white working-class boys' identities. Willis offered pivotal insights into how masculinity/sexuality could become the key to social class resistance to unjust systems. Willis described his work as 'creative explorations and re-articulation of received dominant social codes and reproduction: working class/middle class, black/white, male/female. Binaries can be played off against each other and miscegenated or ironically positioned to reveal third terms' (Willis 2000: 37). The dualism of masculine and feminine which contemporary post-structuralist writers such as Bronwyn Davies (1989) see as central to the discursive framing of identities in modern society were explored through Willis's analysis. In *Learning to Labour*, he considered how such dualisms work for working-class lads trapped within the objective structures of capitalism. His analysis of the 'lads" culture demonstrated that forms of social class (anti-school) resistance are based on the celebration of traditional sexual identities which ultimately confirm the cycle of social class reproduction (MacDonald 1981: 153). It is this insight that arguably still has not been challenged. His research showed that boys were adopting, adapting, and reworking gender dualism rather than being socialised into one or other category. 'The lads' "identity work" involved them critically in the inversion of mental/manual divide associated with capitalist economies, and the matching of hard physical labour with what we would now call the 'narrative superiority of masculinity'.

The way in which such dualism worked in the school setting was configured by the realities of schooling for working-class male youth. Willis saw that 'the lads' understood what the price of conformism to the state educational agenda was for the manual working classes. Conformism would entail collusion by the working classes in their own educational suppression. As Willis argued, the working-class 'lad' 'must overcome his inbuilt disadvantage of possessing the wrong class culture and the wrong educational decoders to start with' (Willis 1977: 128). To succeed, however, would have meant the emasculation of the working-class youth. These English 'lads' celebrated their masculinity against school norms of docile, conforming and diligent pupils. By labelling such pupils as effeminate and 'cissies', the 'ear'oles', the 'lads' affirm their pugnacious and physical masculinity in an anti-school culture. They thus confirm their respect for their masculine identity, derived from their families and peer group and see its fulfilment in hard physical manual jobs. A critical aspect of *Learning to Labour* therefore is the discussion of what Willis called 'cross-valorisation' of, on the one hand, manual labour with the 'social superiority of masculinity' (148). In an account that has many resonances with contemporary post-structuralist discussions of identifications, dis-identifications and subject positionings (e.g. Skeggs 1997), Willis describes the identity work of "the lads". He comments that not all divisions are viewed as oppressive. 'For "the lads", a division in which they take themselves to be favoured (the sexual) overlies, becomes part of, and finally, partially changes the valency of a division in which they are disadvantaged (mental/manual power)' (148).

According to Willis, 'the lads' invert the mental–manual hierarchy by transposing it onto the gender dualism and male–female hierarchy. In effect, the mode of production and class oppression are reproduced in part through the equivalence established between the mental/manual division of labour and between masculinity and femininity. This also paves the way for the reproduction of male manual labour power on the factory floor:

> The important inversion however is not achieved within the proper logic of capitalist production. Nor is it produced in the concrete articulation of the site of social classes of two structures which in capitalism can only be separated in abstraction and whose forms have now become part of it. These are patriarchy and the distinction between mental and manual labour. *The form of the articulation is of the cross-valorisation and association of the two key terms in the two sets of structures*. The polarisation of the two structures becomes crossed. Manual labour is associated with the social superiority of masculinity and mental labour with the social inferiority of femininity. In particular manual labour is imbued with a masculine tone and nature which rends it positively expressive of more than its intrinsic focus in work.
>
> (148)

Willis's analysis of the struggle of the working-class male in the context of a dominant class resonated well with that of Bourdieu (1977) who argued at that time that working-class men have much to lose through educational success in such a culture.[3] Protecting themselves from social mobility and indeed from emasculation, working-class men find ways of expressing their sexuality. Bourdieu argued that biological (male/female) and gender (masculine/feminine) determinations 'exert their influence on linguistic (or sexual) practices and imagery through the structure of homologous oppositions which organise the images of the sexes and classes' (Bourdieu 1977: 51 quoted in MacDonald, 1981; Arnot, 2002). In acquiring dominant linguistic and cultural forms, what is at stake is not just the accusation of class disloyalty, but also the negation or repudiation of masculine sexuality defined in terms of virility, pugnacity and self-assertion. Taking on bourgeois culture (a way of speaking, self-presentation through gesture, dress and so forth) also implies a particular relation to one's body – hence, the different names for parts of the body (the femininity and daintiness of *la bouche* against the roughness and violence of *la gueule*) in bourgeois and working-class speech. By inverting the classification between class cultures, Bourdieu argued, working-class men celebrate their masculine sexuality and their physical (manual) culture by punctuating their language with 'coarse' and 'crude' words and 'broad and spicy stories' – a theme which also emerges strongly in *Learning to Labour* and, interestingly, in contemporary poststructuralist research on boys' laddish behaviour in today's schools.

In ways that resonate well with contemporary concerns about localised social identities, Willis argues that the interconnections he uncovered between gender and class were specific to particular positionings of youth. In an interview, he demonstrates his awareness of the formation of multiple identities and multiple articulations of binary categorisations. He comments thus:

> I wasn't arguing that a certain working-class male masculinity was forever linking manualism and masculinity, but that these were different binary systems with their own histories, and that in other situations, you might have different articulations of gender, patriarchal and capitalist categories. There is a real instability in the way that gender systems and capital systems or capital relations are articulated with each other.
>
> (Willis quoted in Mills and Gibb 2001: 400)

Gender relations, identities and family life

Whilst Willis's classic had exposed the 'brutality of capitalist productive relations' (McRobbie 1980: 41), its social justice agenda arguably had failed to address the brutality of male power over women and indeed white oppression of black groups within the working class. Thus whilst setting a new agenda around concepts of masculinity, Willis had neglected to explore more fully those empirical data which demonstrated precisely the complex interaction between masculinity and femininity and its harsh consequences for working-class women. Angela McRobbie, for example, paid homage to the extraordinary creativity of Willis's and Hebdige's (1979) studies of male adolescents since both showed how these young men took

> ... already coded materials from their everyday landscapes (and though this is not spelt out, from their fantasies) and mould them into desirable shapes into social practices and stylish postures. Both accounts drew on the notion that control and creativity are exercised from within subordinate class positions and that, as a result of this subordination, cultural gestures often appear in partial, contradictory and even amputated forms.
>
> (McRobbie 1980: 40)

But at the same time, she also saw that, through the language of adolescent male sexuality, Willis had illustrated but had not sufficiently analysed the ways in which class and patriarchal relations work together, 'sometimes with an astonishing brutality and at other times in the teeth-gritting harmony of romance, love and marriage' (38). McRobbie argued, like other cultural theorists of the time, that Willis failed to get to grips with this powerful role of sexuality in working-class male cultures. She commented that :

> ... 'the lads' may get by with – and get off on – each other alone on the streets but they did not eat, sleep or make love there. Their peer group consciousness and pleasure frequently seem to hinge on a collective disregard for women and the sexual exploitation of girls.
>
> (McRobbie 1980: 40)

As one of 'the lads' says of his girlfriend:

> She loves doing fucking housework. Trousers I brought up yesterday, I took 'em up last night and her turned 'em up for me. She's as good as gold and I wanna get married as soon as I can.
>
> (ibid. 38)

What McRobbie found striking was how 'unambiguously degrading to women is the language of aggressive masculinity through which "the lads" kick against the oppressive structures they inhabit' (38). Willis was taken to task for his failure to comment critically on, for example, the way a female teacher's authority was undermined by being labelled a 'cunt', the way 'the lads' mime masturbating of a giant penis for amusement; their litany of sexual obscenities and the way they publicly expressed their disgust for menstruation (jam rags) at every opportunity. The violence of the imagery, the cruelty of 'the lads" sexual double standard, the images of sexual power and domination become the 'lads" last defensive resort. By dignifying these racist, sexist and homophobic 'lads' McRobbie and later Skeggs (1992) argued that Willis's project failed to understand the articulation of male power and domination.

Feminist critics also pointed to the impression gained in *Learning to Labour* that male manual work depended solely on the cultural reproduction of machismo from father to son,[4] the male pride in physical labour and contempt for pen-pushing. Willis had thus failed to integrate these aspects of working-class culture into an analysis of the working-class family. Like most cultural theorists of the time, the family was outside the sphere of analysis. It was represented in some ways as a 'softer sphere in which fathers, sons and boyfriends expect to be, and are, emotionally serviced' (McRobbie 1980: 41). The private experiences (relations with parents, siblings and girlfriends) behind 'the lads" hard outer image, and their immersion in working-class culture outside the public sphere, were largely ignored. As McRobbie noted, working-class culture 'happens as much around the breakfast table and in the bedroom as in the school and in the workplace' (44).

This debate still resonates with current writing on masculinity. Recently, Willis (quoted in Mills and Gibb 2001) recognised the strength of this feminist critique about the reduction of patriarchal relations to class, the underestimating of the importance of the home and domestic relations, and the uncritical reproduction or celebration of 'sexist conventions, forms and prejudices'. Yet, twenty-five years after this analysis of *Learning to Labour*, the internal dynamics of family life are still not seen by social and cultural theorists as being as significant as economic change in framing youth identities, although there is more recognition that families should be central to social justice concerns. The more family takes centre stage, the more likely it is that gender identities are not just located within the division of labour, but are also located within two other axes of gender power identified by Connell (1987) – that of *power relations* and what he called *cathexis* (emotional/sexual selves and attachments). As we shall see, these latter two axes are beginning to emerge in accounts of gender identities (in particular studies of masculinity), although the connection to social justice is often not made explicit.

A more fully *sexed* notion of working-class culture that Angela McRobbie so powerfully called for, is only now the subject of most contemporary social justice research on identities and education. Christine Heward (1996), for example, challenges contemporary scholarly work on masculinity which still tends to relate masculinity to particular 'normative understandings of family relations'. These normative models tend to take up the theme of father–son relations as critical to the development of male gender identity and mother–daughter relations as critical to female gender identity. Freudian psychoanalysis and Parsonian sex-role theory, she argues, have legitimated this view of the sexual division of labour in the family. As a result, there is still little analysis of how masculinities are negotiated, experienced and worked on in relation to more holistic notions of the psychosocial gendered power dynamics of family life.

As Heward pointed out, a boy's identification with his father (even if the father was absent most of the time) was seen as central to the construction of masculinity which was understood in the context of 'the world of work and power'. Willis, like Tolson (1977), had built his theory of the 'lads' using the father's position in the labour market and class culture as 'an important differentiator in the construction of masculinities' (Heward 1996: 36). Using seven male biographies, Heward demonstrates how 'the ambivalence and alienation which characterise father–son relations' are rooted in the 'vast range of complexities of power, emotion and sexuality nexus *within* families'. Each biographical example illustrates how the dynamics between mothers and fathers and the son's negotiations of those dynamics are problematic, contested and unpredictable. Thus young men's experiences of family life are deeply shaped by both parents. Heward argues: 'The importance of mothers in the process of identity formation should be acknowledged rather than dismissed as anti-models who have performed their initial nurturing function' (Heward 1996: 48).

The relations of self to structure in this analysis become far more complex than just the gender and generational transmission of working-class work cultures. Gender regimes and power relations, particularly in the family and work places are being transformed not least by women 'turning away from exploitative male heterosexuals'. Intimate relations are transformed, childcare regimes have changed and female and male patterns of employment and work cultures have shifted. As Heward argues, 'women and relations between men and women are a potent source of change in intimate relations' (1996:48) – thus it would seem essential today that in order to understand today's 'lads' we must look to the third of Connell's elements – that of emotional life, and to explore 'intra- and inter-family gender relations within structural contexts'. 'This would permit a wide variety of outcomes to be envisaged and make mothers integral rather than peripheral to the process of constructing masculinities' (Heward 1996: 48).

Other recent research of working-class boys in English secondary schools has highlighted the centring of mothers in boys' lives. For example, in their analysis of the contemporary practice of masculinity in schools, Nayak and Kehily (2000) highlight the contradictory role of mothers in working-class boys' humour. Like Willis's findings, 'having a laff' for these boys represents one of the means by which different positions of domination and subordination amongst boys are established and regulated, allowing some boys to exert power over others. Humour used as an 'unofficial resource' in the culture of manhood. In Willis's terms such humour had significance as preparation for the styles and rituals of the male shop floor culture, or a form of class cultural resistance. However, today such humour has become the means by which white working-class heterosexuality is affirmed. 'Wind-ups, joke telling, funny stories, spontaneous gags, mimicry', Nayak and Kehily found, become the 'unseen forms of communication, validating or rejecting male forms of behaviour' (111).

In a working-class West Midland community (not dissimilar to that researched by Willis) which is now experiencing deindustrialisation and the dismantling of car and metal industries, Nayak and Kehily found that such dominant forms of heterosexuality have become a way of coping with both local and global processes of change to their community. Young men were 'hardly learning to labour'. Having a laugh today is 'every bit as dedicated to a counter-culture of humour as "the lads" in Willis's study, but it is less about gaining power and more about feeling entitled to it'.

> We contend that heavy industrial humour may become a means of recuperating masculinity in a post-industrial economy. The values embedded in schoolboy pranks, jokes and funny stories then act as symbolic codes which young men may learn to 'be masculine' *in the absence of secure manual work*. [Author's emphasis added.]
>
> (Nayak and Kehily 2000: 112)

Where Willis's study observed the class significance of such humour, Nayak and Kehily's see cussing, blowing matches, ritualised insults and funny/spicy stories as the undercurrents at work behind English heterosexual masculinity. Significantly such behaviour reinforced hyper-masculine egos by exploring the deepest sexual taboos about sons' relationship with their mothers. The ritualised insults played with the idea of their mothers as slags, sluts and whores. For example: 'Your mother's been raped so many times she puts a padlock on her fanny'; 'Your mom's got so many holes in her knickers you can play Connect Four' (quoted in Nayak and Kehily 2000: 114). These highly personal comments were a source of great distress for some boys, some of whom were reduced to tears in public. However, by mobilising sexist discourses of power such as mother cussing, boys achieved superior positions in the group. They could even collude with male teachers' jokes about their mothers being 'slags'.

Whilst it is widely recognised that shifts in the economy and in educational funding have led to increased economic dependency of young people on their families, the significance of the household domain and the internal relations between parents and their children are still largely being ignored in critical sociologial studies of the transition to work and adulthood (Brannen *et al.* 1994). Ball, Maguire and Macrae's (2000) recent study of post-16 male and female youth in new urban economies, however, is notable for its findings from their individual case studies which reveal just how important was the influence of families in offering and generating resources for identity formation. Even if there was conflict, the '[f]amily remains ... a key source of belonging for all except a small minority of young people' (144). Parents interpret the world and instil attitudes and dispositions which are assessments of 'possibilities and impossibilities' within objectively inscribed conditions. Ball, Maguire and Macrae argue that such attitudes form part of what Bourdieu (1990: 57 quoted in Ball *et al.* 2000: 144) called a 'matrix of perceptions'. 'Most young people were found to be operating within a "framed field of reference" (Foskett and Hesketh 1996), 'loose or tight, established by their parents' (Ball *et al.* 2000: 144).

Although working-class families today might appear to concede decision making to their children (e.g. school choice, occupation and training opportunities especially in globalised economies), they nevertheless feel concern. And, according to Ball, Maguire and Macrae, 'mothers are at the forefront of all this'. Admittedly class and economic factors might affect mothers' ability to 'divert their emotional involvement into generating academic profits for their children'. As the authors point out, the

> choreography of decision making within families is complicated. Different parents defined their participation and the autonomy of their children in different ways. As a minimal position, most parents had a clear view of unacceptable decisions and what was 'best' for their children.
>
> (Ball *et al.* 2000: 144)

These biographical case studies of working-class male youth suggest considerable dependence on their mothers. One must not forget that, particularly in the absence of fathers, mothers can be the only source of stability and control. In *Goliath: Britain's Dangerous Places* Campbell (1993) vividly documented how, during the violent explosions in British cities in the late summer of 1991, working-class mothers sustained the viability of the home over and above male unrest, severe policing and violence. Mothers were the resource which the working-class communities relied upon to sustain the semblance of order within collapsing economic and material conditions. In these conditions, social justice research can no longer fail to take such gender realities into account.

Arguably, contemporary sociological research has taken Willis's acknowledgement of working-class family culture further and has queried the powerful association between fathers and sons as the only influence on the construction of working-class male identity. Clearly fathers play a major role in representations of working-class masculinity, but the construction of male heterosexuality is also played out within the emotional relationships of parents and other family members. Recent post-structuralist research on masculinity has therefore developed even further the insights Willis introduced into the study of gender identities, although not necessarily within the same discourse of social justice.

Contemporary 'lads' in a performance discourse

Willis's ethnographic study of the response of working-class youth to their schooling and their social and economic positioning exposed the social contradictions of post-war illusions of meritocracy. From a policy perspective, *Learning to Labour* offers a unique platform from which to consider the nature and extent of contemporary socio-cultural and economic inequalities. Following Willis, we can now ask: does the school with all its performance and standardising cultures now include rather than exclude such working-class youth? Has the individualising of educational achievement led to the transformation of such young men who had previously prepared themselves, in resistance, for their destinies as unskilled manual labour?

The book, it seems, has greater, not less, relevance in the current school climate in the UK when the processes of social exclusion have become even more acute than in the more lenient times of full employment and social democratic philosophies. Today, young men in the manual working classes (those who are variously called 'status zero' or the 'underwolves' (Wilkinson and Mulgan, 1995)) have even less investment in the economic future, even less prospect of making the transition into continuous work of the sort described by Willis in the late 1970s. Paradoxically with the heightened pressure on young people today through a competitive, tightly regulated and divisive performance-driven school system, research in the UK suggests that today's 'lads' appear to be pushed to even more extreme alternative cultures, and there appears to be a spread of a laddish behaviour (although not working-class culture) amongst other groups of boys.

Willis's theory of class reproduction was challenged, as he himself recognised (Willis 1979; Willis *et al.* 1988),[5] by the loss of male labour in manufacturing industry in the UK. By 1989, the industrial sector made up only 25 per cent of jobs in the country while the service sector accounted for almost 70 per cent of employment. Such economic restructuring and the contraction of manufacturing industry in the UK had the greatest impact on those boys whose fathers worked in factory or other industrial jobs. The loss of their fathers' jobs was to reduce young men's expectations of finding 'real work' (Haywood and Mac an Ghaill 1996, 2001). The collapse of the youth labour market, the replacement of factory work with new technologies and the expansion of the service industries all fundamentally affected the opportunities for these young men's employment after school. Willis's 'lads' could no longer expect the conventional transitions from school to work through traditional apprenticeships and familial contacts.

Evidence from more recent studies of working-class masculinities (Mac an Ghaill 1994; Sewell 1997, 1998) suggests that the reforms of schooling from the late 1980s to the mid-1990s exacerbated rather than reduced school resistance. By increasing emphasis upon performance and on competition within and between schools, and by raising the stakes in terms of compliance to a school culture that was class-oriented, schools were more rather than less likely to be viewed as hostile institutions, especially since the sorting and selecting functions of schools were made more visible. The new school ethos bore little relationship to the realities of economic dysfunction and community breakdown. As Haywood and Mac an Ghaill (1996, 2001) argue, in areas in which working-class youth are already marginalised, surveilled and excluded from the productive life of society, the reconstruction of schooling according to market principles was most likely to force confrontations between young black and white working-class boys and their teachers. It was these confrontations that created and sustained counter-hegemonic masculinities among such youth that were both anti-academic and anti-school.

Mac an Ghaill's (1994) ethnographic research in Parnell comprehensive school in a predominantly working-class inner-city industrial area also in the Midlands confirmed the presence of a group of what he called 'Macho Lads' who celebrated a powerful version of heterosexual machismo not dissimilar to that of 'the lads' in Willis's study. As Haywood and Mac an Ghaill argued, de-industrialisation had created 'a crisis in white working-class forms of masculinity'. The responses of the 'Macho Lads' to the new ethos of schooling involved celebrating alternative sources of gender power. Gender power based on what Mac an Ghaill called a *hyper-masculinity* was not so much the mechanism through which they could celebrate manual labour, it appears to be the main source of their identity (Mac an Ghaill 1994: 71). Still inverting the values of the school system, still retaining highly traditional gender values, today's 'lads' now choose to celebrate the 3 Fs – *fighting, football and fucking*. (See also Connell's (1989) account of unemployed white working-class men in Australia and Canaan's (1996) study of predominantly white working-class youth in the Midlands.) In short, these 'lads' coped with the multiple uncertainties of their position by promoting an exaggerated concept of heterosexual masculinity. By 'behaving badly', they regained control of their lives.

Contemporary white and black 'lads' thus appear to find ways of celebrating manhood without relying on a work identity. The generational connections between hard male physical labour and working-class masculinity described by Willis are not always possible, although as Mac an Ghaill argued, white working-class lads in Parnell School still held on to outdated modes of masculinity that centred around traditional manual waged labour. In contrast, the African/Caribbean and Asian 'Macho Lads' in Parnell School appeared to have less commitment to work in the locality, were more used to unemployment and economic insecurity. In Mac an Ghaill's analysis the major difference between 'the lads' of the 1970s and 'the lads' of the 1990s appeared to be in terms of the purposes/significance of their counter-school culture.

According to Sewell (1997, 1998) male heterosexuality was also found to have played a major role in the responses of a group of African/Caribbean boys in schools. In order to succeed, aspiring black youth had to assume a form of 'race-lessness' and lose their community and ethnic identity to avoid the wrath of their teachers. The reaction to this racelessness was the counter-promotion of a new black identity which took the form of what bell hooks (1993) called 'phallocentric masculinity' amongst those who found comfort from exclusion in hedonism and an anti-school black machismo. Yet these African/Caribbean 'lads' who were in 'retreatism or rebellion' were not necessarily less positive about learning than girls. However, teachers in this case study were obsessed with the dangers of black male sexuality.

What has therefore become a major issue in current research on social justice issues is *the norm of male heterosexuality*. Today, a much preferred theoretical position for most masculinity researchers is that of post-structuralism which offers insights into 'a certain game of truth' (Martino 1999: 240). From such a Foucauldian perspective, researchers can think about the various ways boys are inserted into the 'game of truth' in which they learn about what it is to be 'man' (ibid. 240). In this context, masculinity becomes a range of practices, a form of performativity which can shift in different locales, occasions, moments, and sites. There is no *a priori* theory of the subject. Instead the focus is in how boys consti-tute themselves as male subjects. The emphasis is upon the cultural techniques of boys, the 'polymorphous techniques of power' (Foucault 1978 quoted in Martino 1999: 240) which they experience and sometimes own. From a Foucauldian per-spective, the analysis has shifted away from the class significances of working-class masculinity to the various statuses given to masculinity in a partic-ular school culture, an analysis of how the desires of adolescent boys are channelled and relayed, and how the hierarchy of valorised and subordinated mas-culinities come into being (Martino 1999: 242).

Increasing interest in this aspect of male power has led to a multitude of pro-jects on white and black male heterosexuality amongst working-class youth in school. The argument now put forward is that this dominant hegemonic form of masculinity has been encouraged by schools, promoted extensively by the media (*Men Behaving Badly*, *Loaded*) and taken up now by a variety of different boys. Displaying styles of behaviour and modes of identification that ape 'the lads' cul-ture of the 1970s, all sorts of other boys are exploiting similarly aggressive forms of heterosexual and racist masculinity. Politicians since the 1990s have publicly declared *laddism* to be the cause of male working-class educational failure and the reason for all boys' alleged underachievement (Reed 1999; Francis 1999). What was understood in Willis's analysis to be a class cultural response to the conditions of material existence of the working classes and of the nature of schooling within capitalism is now being represented as a characteristic of mas-culinity itself irrespective of social class.

Evidence from recent research by O' Donnell and Sharpe (2002) and Frosh, Phoenix and Pattman (2001) suggest that laddishness has become the hegemonic form of masculinity which affects a range of boys who are positioned differently in the school system. For some, the explanation for this extension from the working classes to other social groups including even middle-class children is found (paradoxically) in the *remasculinisation* of schooling, with its new cultures of competition, standards, performance and exclusions (Mac an Ghaill, 1999). Jackson (2002), for example, argues the adoption of laddish behaviour is much stronger because of the changes in the educational system which are generating increased insecurity and pressure. Whilst boys appear to be using sexist and heterosexist discourses to frame their masculinity *vis-à-vis* femininity, she argues that from a social-psychological perspective, laddishness is also about coping with the fear of academic failure in a dominant culture of performativity. Middle-class boys might appropriate the culture of Willis's 'lads' because of the advantages of adopting the styles of disengagement and indifference of white working-class boys in such a heightened competitive environment. Some of the strategies which Becky Francis (1999) found boys now associate with 'laddishness' involve: procrastination; intentional withdrawal of effort and rejection of academic work; the appearance of effortless achievement; and disruptive behaviour. The presence of this competitive performance-oriented culture generates anxiety especially amongst boys whose gender identity is based upon achieving power, status and superiority.

Haywood and Mac an Ghaill (2001) argue that the shift from 'soft welfare' to harder market economies has lead to the restructuring of teaching which, in turn, has emphasised hierarchies of domination and subordination. They suggest that the restructured authority system, intensified surveillance, disciplinary codes, curriculum and testing, stratification technologies and the allocation and knowledge selection processes have resulted in a range of new hierarchically ordered masculinities. New discourses of entrepreneurialism and new masculine authoritarianism are being replaced by modern forms of 'technical bureaucratic knowledge'. In this context, there is less socialiability between teacher and taught and children 'are now conceptualised as value added knowledge containers'. The play of masculinities in school in this contemporary context therefore represents a complex dynamic which appears to have less oppositional, and thus has less transformative, political potential. Although as Reay (2002) recently argued, there is little evidence to suggest that traditional working-class masculinities and performance cultures in schools can be reconciled politically. For that to happen, those promoting working-class male educational success would need to address the centrality of masculinity as an identity forged out of deep traditional patterns of socialisation.

Conclusions

The debate about family life, cathexis and also 'laddishness' in schools, to some extent, has shifted away from Willis's account of working-class boys preparing to go into working-class jobs in their locality. The concept of 'the lads' has been extended in the media, in politics and even in boys' popular worlds to represent 'all boys'. As a result it is difficult to retrieve the touchstone of critical engagement signified by the class cultural studies of the 1970s. The transformative project developed in the critique of social democracy is not clearly reflected within the critical analyses of the globalised economy and performance-based choice cultures of schooling in the current decade. The relationship of young people's meaning-making and official discourses of education, between critique and possibility is not as clearly expressed: it is often implicit.

Paradoxically, although Willis's seminal text became a symbolic marker of modernist methodologies and narratives, at the same time it triggered, through the wealth of its description and theoretical insight, the development of post-structuralist tradition of studies of masculinities. As I have shown, many of the themes of contemporary post-structuralist work on masculinities were originally represented in *Learning to Labour* – most notably the working through of social classifications and dualism, the nature of meaning-making and identity construction, the situated relational worlds of identity formation, the complex cross-articulations of class, race, sexuality and gender. The epistemological break therefore was not necessarily as strong as it has been represented. At the same time, I want to argue that some of the strengths of Willis's analysis are precisely the weaknesses of contemporary accounts of gender.

Contemporary research on masculinities might suggest that Willis's analysis is less relevant in today's more fluid society. The argument would be that mono-causal analysis of power such as the social reproduction model with its concerns about rational subjects and predictable power relations and the 'romance' of working-class male creativity in the face of degradation could not adequately cope with the complexity of experience amongst contemporary boys. Can such a theory really account for the responses of boys to the restructured globalising economy? Post-structural research on school-based masculinities, on public discourses around masculinity and on male narratives and biographies suggests that we need a more dense, complex and social psychological analysis of power plays in schools, families and communities. As we have seen, since the publication of *Learning to Labour*, there has been what has been called a 'biographical turn' (Coffey 2001) amongst those interested in social identities. There is now a greater interest in how an individual's 'self-identity is constructed and negotiated through complex social processes' (53). More attention is being paid to the creation of 'choice' biographies, away from normative biographies. As Stanley and Morgan argued, biographical data (rather than ethnographic data) now challenges

> conventional sharp distinctions between structure and action, and, relatedly, individual and collective, as presenting an over-dichotomised view of social life. It means rejecting any notion that 'a life' can be understood as a representation of a single life in isolation from networks of interwoven biographies. In spite of the widespead assumption that autobiography is concerned with a single life, in practice, it is a very rare autobiography that is not replete with the potted biographies of significant others in a subject's life.
>
> (Stanley and Morgan 1993: 2 quoted in Coffey 2000: 54)

This new phase which Stanley and Morgan (1993) call the 'biographising of social structure and the structuralising of biography' can however also lead to romanticising the individual, the personal and their stories. Although schools are now seen as key sites for the 'active construction, production and reproduction of biographies and identities', only some studies are good at ensuring that 'personal narratives, individual lives and experiences are located within the situated, political and local contexts of education and schools' (ibid. 57). Indeed as leading masculinity scholars such as Mac an Ghaill (1999) admit, the post-structuralist approach whilst immensely valuable cannot easily read the significance of the collective forms that masculinity takes within new economies.

Willis's insights should be at the centre of our thinking about a society in which qualifications matter even more than before and the social exclusion of the manual working classes is even harsher. Willis's critical ethnography was never just an ethnography, nor just an example of social-cultural reproduction theory. His work causes us to reflect on how far society has changed since the 1970s, how much we as social scientists have developed our analysis of the meaning of education for different groups of youth, and how much we have gained and lost methodologically. But also contained within *Learning to Labour* was what Bernstein (1996) called 'a generative theory' about the relationship between schooling and the economy – the research questions it raised could be addressed and re-addressed time and again. I would like to conclude by quoting from *Learning to Labour*. In today's context, the following three observations about the relationship between identities and the social justice 'impulse' are especially meaningful.

> Masculinity must not ... be too simply posed. It has many dimensions and edges. In one way it is a half-blind, regressive machismo which brings self-destructive violence, aggression and division to relationships within the working class. In another way imparting something of what lies behind it, masculinity expresses impulses which can be progressive.

> Behind the expression of masculinity lies an affirmation of manual labour power and behind that (though mediated and distorted) a sense of the uniqueness of the commodity of labour power and of the way in which the general abstract labour unites and connects all kinds of concrete labour.

> The masculine disdain for qualification, for all its prejudice, carries still a kind of 'insight' into the divisive nature of certification, and into the way in which mental work and technicism are mobilised ideologically primarily to maintain class relations rather than to select the most efficient or to increase productive efficiency.

> (Willis 1977: 152)

Acknowledgements

The first draft of this chapter was presented at the American Educational Research Association, New Orleans 1–6 April 2002 at the session celebrating 25 years since the publication of *Learning to Labour*. I would like to thank Nadine Dolby and Greg Dimitriades for their invitation to participate in this symposium. I am also very grateful to Paul Willis for his comments on the first draft and for sending me the interview with Mills and Gibb and *The Ethnographic Imagination*, and to Carol Vincent for editorial comments on this version of the paper.

Notes

1 Willis himself described how the book 'hit a certain time in academic history, a certain time in Marxism, in cultural studies, educational sociology, a certain time in educational politics around an emerging disillusionment and disenchantment with the promises of comprehensive schooling' (Willis quoted in Mills and Gibbs 2001: 401).
2 More than consciousness raising which Willis considered to be potentially vacuous.
3 Willis argues in an interview with Mills and Gibb (2001) that he was much influenced by Bourdieu although interestingly he was not familiar with this particular article by Bourdieu which coincidentally explored the same ground (Personal communication).
4 It is relevant to note that Willis's childhood was shaped by the father–son relationship. He was brought up by his father alone after his mother's death when he was nine. Willis describes his father as having played a vital role in transforming a working-class culture into a process of social and intellectual growth (Willis quoted in interview with Mills and Gibb, 2001).
5 See Willis's own studies of male unemployment (Willis *et al.* 1988).

References

Arnot, M. (2002) *Reproducing Gender? Essays on Educational Theory and Feminist Politics*, London: RoutledgeFalmer
Ball, S., Maguire, M. and Macrae, S. (2000) *Choice, Pathways and Transitions Post-16: New Youth, New Economies in the Global City*, London: RoutledgeFalmer
Bernstein, B. (1996) *Pedagogy, Symbolic Control and Identity: Theory, Research, Critique*, London: Taylor and Francis
Bourdieu, P. (1977) 'The economics of linguistic exchange' *Social Science Information* 16, 6: 661
Bourdieu, P. (1990) *The Logic of Practice*, Cambridge: Polity Press
Brannen, J., Dodd, J., Oakley, A. and Storey, L. (1994) *Young People, Health and Family Life*, Buckingham: Open University Press
Brown, P. (1987) *Schooling Ordinary Kids: Inequality, Unemployment and the New Vocationalism*, London: Tavistock
Brown, P. (1988) 'Education and the working class: a cause for concern' in Lauder, H. and Brown, P. (eds) *Education in Search of a Future*, Barcombe, Lewes: The Falmer Press
Canaan, J. E. (1996) '"One thing leads to another": drinking, fighting and working-class masculinities' in Mac an Ghaill, M. (ed.) *Understanding Masculinities*, Buckingham: Open University Press
Campbell, B. (1993) *Goliath: Britain's Dangerous Places*, London: Methuen

Centre for Contemporary Cultural Studies (CCCS) (1981) *Unpopular Education: Schooling for Social Democracy in England since 1944*, London: Hutchinson

Coffey, A. (2001) *Education and Social Change*, Buckingham: Open University Press

Connell, R. W. (1987) *Gender and Power*, Cambridge: Polity Press

Connell, R. W. (1995) *Masculinities*, Cambridge: Polity Press

Connell, R. W. (1989) 'Cool guys, swots and wimps: the interplay of masculinity and education', *Oxford Review of Education*, 15, 3: 291–303

Davies, B. (1989) 'The discursive production of male/female dualism', *Oxford Review of Education*, 15, 3: 229–41

Foskett, N. and Hesketh, A. (1996) 'Student decision making and the post 16 market place' in N. Foskett (ed) *Markets in Education: Policy, Process and Practice (Vol. 2)*, Southampton: Doubleday

Foucault, E. (1978) in Hurley, R. (trans.) *The History of Sexuality*, Vol. 1, New York: Vintage

Francis, B. (1999) 'Lads, lasses and (New) Labour: 14–16-year-old students' responses to the "laddish behaviour" and boys' underachievement debate' *British Journal of Sociology of Education*, 20, 3: 355–371

Frosh, S., Pheonix, A. and Pattman, R. (2002) *Young Masculinities*, London: Palgrave

Gore, F. (1993) *The Struggle for Pedagogies*, New York: Routledge

Hargreaves, D. (1967) *Social Relations in a Secondary School*, London: Routledge and Kegan Paul

Haywood, C. and Mac an Ghaill, M. (1996) 'What about the boys? Regendered local labour markets and the recomposition of working-class masculinities', *British Journal of Education and Work*, 9/1, 19–30

Haywood, C. and Mac an Ghaill, M. (2001) 'The significance of teaching English boys: exploring social change, modern schooling and the making of masculinities' in Martino, W. and Meyenn B., (eds) *What about the Boys?*, Buckingham: Open University Press

Hebdige, D. (1979) *Subculture: The Meaning of Style*, London: Methuen

Heward, C. (1996) 'Masculinities and families' in Mac an Ghaill, M. (ed.) *Understanding Masculinities*, Buckingham: Open University Press

hooks, b. (1993) 'Hard core rap lyrics stir backlash', *New York Times*, 15 August

Jackson, C. (2002) '"Laddishness" as a self-worth protection strategy', *Gender and Education*, 14, 1: 37–51

Lacey, C. (1970) *Hightown Grammar: The School as a Social System*, Manchester: Manchester University Press

Lather, P. (1991) *Getting Smart: Feminist Psychology and Pedagogy within the Postmodern*, London: Routledge

Mac an Ghaill, M. (1994) *The Making of Men: Masculinities, Sexualities and Schooling*, Buckingham: Open University Press

Mac an Ghaill, M. (1999) 'New cultures of training: emerging male (hetero)sexual identities', *British Education Research Journal*, 25, 4: 427–443

MacDonald, M. (1981) 'Schooling and the reproduction of class and gender relations' in Arnot, M. (2002) *Reproducing Gender? Essays on Educational Theory and Feminist Politics*, London: RoutledgeFalmer

Martino, W. (1999) '"Cool boys", "Party Animals", "Squids" and "Poofters": interrogating the dynamics and politics of adolescent masculinities in school', *British Journal of Sociology of Education* 20, 2: 239–263

McRobbie, A. (1980) 'Settling accounts with sub-culture', *Screen Education,* 34: 37–50

Mills, D. and Gibb, R. (2001) '"Centre" and periphery – an interview with Paul Willis's, *Cultural Anthropology,* 16, 3: 388–414

Nayak, A. and Kehily, M. J. (2000) '"Learning to laugh": a study of schoolboy humour in the English secondary school', in Mac an Ghaill, M. (ed.) *Understanding Masculinities*, Buckingham: Open University Press

O'Donnell, M. and Sharpe, S. (2000) *Uncertain Masculinities*, London: Routledge

Reay, D. (2002) 'Shaun's story: troubling discourses of white working-class masculinities', *Gender and Education* 14, 3: 221–234

Reed, L. Raphael (1999) 'Troubling boys and disturbing discourses on masculinity and schooling: a feminist exploration of current debates and interventions concerning boys in school', *Gender and Education,* 11, 1: 93–110

Sewell, T. (1997) *Black Masculinities and Schooling: How Black Boys Survive Modern Schooling*, London: Trentham Books

Sewell, T. (1998) 'Loose canons: exploding the myth of the "black macho" lad' in Epstein, D., Elwood, J., Hey, V. and Maw, J. (eds) *Failing Boys?: Issues in Gender and Achievement*, Buckingham: Open University Press

Skeggs, B. (1992) 'Paul Willis, Learning to Labour' in Barker, M. and Beezer, A. (eds) *Reading into Cultural Studies*, London: Routledge

Skeggs, B. (1997) *Formations of Class and Gender*, London: Sage

Stanley, L. and Morgan, D. (1993) 'Editorial', *Sociology*, 27, 1: 1–4

Tolson, A. (1977) *The Limits of Masculinity*, London: Tavistock

Wexler, P. (2000) *Mystical Society: an Emerging Social Vision*, Boulder CO/Oxford: Westview Press

Wilkinson, H. and Mulgan, G. (1995) *Freedom's Children: Work, Relationships and Politics for 18–34 Year Olds in Britain Today*, London: Demos

Willis, P. (1977) *Learning to Labour: How Working Class Kids get Working-Class Jobs*, Farnborough, Hants: Saxon House, Teakfield Ltd

Willis, P. (1979) 'Shop floor culture, masculinity and the wage form' in Clarke, J., Critcher, C. and Johnson, R. (eds) *Working-Class Culture*, London: Hutchinson

Willis, P. (2000) *The Ethnographic Imagination*, Cambridge: Polity Press

Willis, P., Bekenn, A., Ellis, T. and Whitt, D. (1988) *The Youth Review: Social Conditions of Young People in Wolverhampton*, Aldershot: Avebury

Chapter 7

Avoiding the issue

Homophobia, school policies and identities in secondary schools

Debbie Epstein, Roger Hewitt, Diana Leonard, Melanie Mauthner and Chris Watkins

MM: Does the school have any particular focus on racist, sexist or homophobic bullying?

Teacher: Yeah, not homophobic. I would say that the policies on homophobia, that is an issue as well, homophobia as a cause of violence. I mean, quite often violence may start because of homophobic insults between boys. The school's policy on acceptance of people's sexuality, not discriminating against people, understanding. Quite honestly, I mean, that's not an issue that you make a lot of noise about in schools ever since the Tories. You know, you would be criticised, possibly. Maybe even the head teacher as well would be uncomfortable with pushing an issue like homosexuality or sexuality in a school like this.

Introduction

The quote above, from an interview with the head of history in a large comprehensive school in London, is drawn from our ESRC-funded project entitled 'The "Violence-Resilient" School: A Comparative Study of Schools and their Environments'.[1] In this project we sought to understand how different approaches to the management of schools could have the effect of reducing or producing violence in broadly similar neighbourhood contexts. What we were interested in, then, was not so much the amount of violence in any particular school, but how that compared with levels of violence in schools in similar areas with similar levels of reported neighbourhood violence. We were particularly concerned to trace the impact on those forms of violence related to 'differences that make a difference' (racist, sexist and homophobic violence and bullying, for example) of different regimes, cultures and approaches by the senior management teams of the schools we looked at. One of the key findings from our study was that, amongst these different forms of violence, harassment and bullying, schools found it most difficult to handle homophobic abuse and were most likely to ignore it. In this chapter, we explore the evidence of this, and consider some of the implications for schools, social justice and identity formation.

Social identities, as Stuart Hall (1996) argues, have as much to do with 'becoming' as with 'being'. He uses the term 'identification', rather than 'identity' to indicate the dynamic processes involved, suggesting that who you identify with, who you want to be and who you want to be with are key factors in thinking about 'identities'. But identity is not only about identification, and who you wish to be, but very much about who you wish to differentiate yourself from, to 'dis-identify' with, to use Beverley Skeggs' term (1997). She points out that 'to dis-identify we need to know from what the dis-identifications are being made. Recognitions have to be made, resisted, challenged for (dis-)identification to occur' (Skeggs 1997: 123).

In school contexts, identifications and dis-identifications are frequently made along lines of social difference and, perhaps more frequently than we would like to believe, are enacted through practices of exclusion, derision and bullying of various kinds. Carrie Paechter suggests (this volume) that masculinities and femininities can be understood as localised communities of practice. It follows from her argument that school policies may have a significant impact on formations of identity, since communities of practice develop in particular conditions and particular contexts. People may 'make themselves' through the constant reiteration of particular performative acts (Butler 1990), but they do so (to misquote Marx 1963) in conditions not of their own choosing. These conditions are, in part, produced by public policies and the policies of schools. In this context, we are interested in the conditions produced by the (lack of) policy in schools around one particular form of (dis-)identification – homophobia.

The chapter begins with a brief description of how we did the research. This is followed by a section on 'Visible homophobia'. Here we draw on our interview data to show how prevalent homophobic attitudes, teasing, harassment and bullying can be in schools, arguing that the forms it takes are gendered, racialised and classed. In this context, we would agree with Anoop Nayak (1997; 1999), who suggests that people often 'do' race through class, gender or sexuality, and so on. The next section, '(In)visible homophobia', explores some of the ways in which homophobia may be ignored in schools, becoming invisible, at least to the teachers. In this context, we draw attention to the ways in which the emphatic masculinities which often dominate in schools draw on homophobia as a resource for identity formation and protection. We then turn to the absence of school policies and, finally, the changing face of national policies in this area. Overall, our argument is that policies on homophobic harassment and bullying are unlikely to be well developed in schools and that this has significant consequences for social justice and identity in schools.

Methods

Our study of 'violence-resilience' included six schools located in different parts of London.[2] Access to schools was not easy to come by, since head teachers were justifiably concerned about the possible impact on their schools should research on violence within them become public knowledge and we will not, therefore, be describing them or their locations in great detail. Suffice it to say that we sought out schools within broadly similar neighbourhoods. Four of the schools were co-educational. Two were single-sex schools – one for boys, the other for girls. The project began with the collection of exclusion data from school records covering a two-year period from September 1996 to July 1998. Once we had completed this, we interviewed staff at different levels of seniority and groups of students from each school. Data on violent crime in the neighbourhoods of each school were collected, largely with the help of local authority community safety teams. Additional material was also provided by the Metropolitan Police Performance Information Bureau. While this provided us with some very useful profiles of the neighbourhoods of our schools, the police data was difficult to come by and often difficult to compare, since statistics were collected and analysed differently by different police teams.

Of course, definitions of violence are contested and difficult to arrive at. For the purposes of this project, we decided to differentiate between physical violence and what we called 'violence-related' incidents. Among the latter, we included various kinds of abuse, harassment and bullying. Interviews with staff, which were semi-structured, included a question about the prevalence of racist, sexist and homophobic violence and policies to deal with them. Interviews with students took place in groups and were more free-ranging, for the most part following their interests, although we did provide ourselves with a series of prompts we could use to ensure that we stayed on-task and covered the necessary bases with them. In the rest of this paper, we will be drawing on the interview material in order to explore both the prevalence of homophobia in the form of bullying, verbal harassment and casual talk and schools' approaches to dealing with it. We contrast what our respondents said about homophobia with their approaches to sexism and racism. In this context, we also draw attention to issues of class as they are expressed in the interviews. We also place our research within the wider context relating to sexual politics within which it was carried out. Finally, we come back to issues of identity and how policies (or lack of them) can feed into the resources which students and teachers draw on in their self-production.

Visible homophobia

We are not the first authors to draw attention to the prevalence of homophobia within schools[3] in Anglophone countries. For the most part, this literature has addressed directly the experiences of lesbian, gay and bisexual students or constructions of heterosexual masculinity via homophobia. Such qualitative work has made a valuable contribution to understanding constructions of social and cultural identity from a psycho-social perspective. More quantitative studies have contributed to our knowledge of the prevalence of homophobia in schools. For example, Douglas et al. (1997) found that 82 per cent of teachers surveyed in over 600 schools in the UK knew that homophobic verbal bullying took place in their schools and 26 per cent were aware of homophobic physically violent incidents. However, only 6 per cent of schools had policies directly dealing with homophobic bullying and violence. They comment that their work is likely to underestimate both the prevalence and degree of homophobic bullying taking place in the schools, given that this represents only those incidents reported to teachers. GALOP (1998) found, in their survey of over 200 lesbians, gay and bisexual young (that is, under eighteen) people in the UK, that 41 per cent said they had experienced physical violence and 90 per cent of these incidents had been at the hands of fellow students. Ian Rivers (1995) found 72 per cent of the 190 young lesbians and gay men who responded to his survey had either played truant or pretended to be ill in order to avoid homophobic abuse at schools.

Our findings, from a more qualitative research project, would bear out and illustrate the figures supplied in these quantitative studies. In all the schools we studied, we found examples of homophobia and heterosexism which were visible to staff and students alike. For example, both students and staff in all the schools talked about the use of homophobic language and the incidence of homophobic abuse. Many of the students interviewed commented on the regular, even mundane, use of homophobic terms (for example, 'pooftah' and 'batty boy') and, in some cases, on the punishments meted out to anyone (but especially boys) who appeared 'gay'. Indeed, the terms 'gay' and 'lesbian' were themselves in currency as terms of abuse. As one group of boys from Ferndale, our single-sex boys' school, explained:

MM: But do you think some of these incidents [violent incidents of various kinds] are to do with people being different because of their race, or they might be gay, or things like that?

Student 2: *No one* would be gay (laughs) in our school, because if they were ever found out then [they'd be dead].

Student 1: People are sensitive to not being gay in our class because they are always going on about it. You could say one thing, that may be a bit stupid or something and everyone would call you gay, and you would get punches sometimes.

MM: So that's just a complete, like the worst thing?…

Student 1: Yeah.

MM: So it's OK to make jokes … but not about being gay?

Student 2: No. In a boys' school, stuff like that. It's just stupid things like we were in PE the other day, and I was pushing my friend in the shower by accident and people were going 'Oh you're gay' and stuff like that.

Student 1: Sometimes, things like you look at a boy and smile, and it's just straightaway 'Oh you're gay'.

Student 2: Yeah. They're homophobic.

Student 1: Why are you looking at him and smiling?

Student 2:   I know there are certain boys in our class who are black will punch you for it. Not actually serious, just like a punch.

Student 3:   If you turn around and your hand hits a boy's leg or something, they'll say 'Oh you're gay'. Then they'll tell people outside the class sometimes and it gets …
(Ferndale School. Interview by Melanie Mauthner, 1 July 1999. Mixed group of 13- and 14-year-old boys in Years 8 and 9. Original emphasis)

The boys, here, report a rather extreme reaction to the fear of homophobia. '*No one*', they say, would ever be gay in their school. The fear of what would happen to someone identified as gay is such that one would never take the risk of coming out. At the same time, the level of petty, mundane interaction that they describe is probably what makes the most impact on the day-to-day lives and possibilities of students perceived as, or identifying as, gay. The boys detail the many, many ways in which a boy can become the target of a homophobic cuss. It seems that, for them, anything from smiling at someone, to touching someone accidentally, or saying one stupid thing can result in being called 'gay', which is, as they agree with the interviewer, 'the worst thing' that could happen. The prevalence of this type of insult in the school was illustrated by another group of three boys (all Year 10, about 14 years old) who commented that the epithet 'gay' was 'always involved in cussing', one that was heard every day ('Like you never go a day without …').

In some of the other schools we heard reports of students who did come out as gay or lesbian. For example, in an interview with two 14-year-old girls (interviewed by Melanie Mauthner, 8 July 1999) at Bellfield, a single-sex girls' school, the students talked about 'that girl in Year 7 [that is, aged about twelve] who was a bisexual'. In this discussion, these students talked of this girl as 'sweet' and 'proper brave', and said that, although other people 'would have like cussed her', they were friendly with her. However, this quickly moved to the following interchange:

Student 1:   And they were lesbians.
Student 2:   I don't like …
Student 1:   They're disgusting.
Student 2:   Walking round really proud of themselves and that.

Thus the move from reporting on a bisexual girl, showing how unprejudiced they could be, to expressions of disgust with lesbian behaviour, took place in an instant. Interestingly, particularly given that this was a girls' school, the shift seemed to be partly about anger at perceived unfairness:

Student 2:   What I hate is, they can kiss in the corridors, right, proper kiss. When I say kiss, it's nasty. They don't get told off, but if we were to bring boys in here and kiss them in the corridor, we'd be shouted at.

Student 1:   We're not even allowed to kiss our boyfriends on the front drive.

Student 2:   You're not even allowed to hold their hands.
Student 1:   Without a teacher watching you or the camera coming out.

What is at issue, here, is not whether girls are allowed to kiss – and women are generally allowed more leeway for touching and affectionate behaviour in public than men – but how the other students interpret this. Anger at the way they are treated by teachers (who, the students said, did not listen to them, likening the school to a 'prison' and a 'juvenile detention centre') has become redirected at lesbians, girls seen as having more freedom than the strictly controlled heterosexuality of the majority. This move can be seen as part of the work of identity. In order to know who you are, you need to know who the Other is, and the two girls, here, know that lesbians are that Other, excluded category against which Us can be defined (see, also, Epstein and Johnson 1998, particularly page 26). What we can see, here, is an inversion of power, common when people in majority or dominant groups feel threatened. Thus, for example, David Blunkett, in an echo of Margaret Thatcher on immigrants, sees asylum seekers as destabilising, potentially 'swamping' British society (*Observer*, 2.7.02). Similarly the jury in the Rodney King case in Los Angeles was able to view explicit video footage of a man, on the ground, being severely beaten by police with batons, and still find those visibly beating him not guilty of assault (see Gooding-Williams 1993, particularly the chapter by Judith Butler).

The anti-lesbian feeling expressed by these two girls should not be seen as belonging to them alone, but rather as one of the currencies available to girls within what Valerie Hey has termed the 'heterosexual economy' of the school (Hey 1997). That it had a negative impact on those girls at whom it was directed is evidenced in the story told by one of the women heads of year whom we interviewed:

> But I know a couple of girls in my year, for various reasons, are taunted. I mean, 'lesbian' is the sort of thing that's thrown at them like a, the worst sort of cuss that anyone could imagine. And one girl actually is refusing to come to school on and off and her mother is saying it's because of that kind of taunting.
>
> (Interview with Melanie Mauthner, 8 March 1999)

In an interesting analysis of their school, two Year-10 boys (aged about 15) at Appletown School commented to Roger Hewitt (16 May 1999) on the paradox of the 'huge amounts of homophobia' at the school. The boys identified four groups within the school: the Trendies (which included themselves); the Townies (who, they claimed, were most likely to be violent); the Lads (the majority in the school); and the Rude Boys (a black group, similar to the Townies). Interestingly, their categorisations referred only to the boys in this co-educational school. In line with Ian Rivers' finding, cited above, they commented that:

Apparently one out of every twelve kids, we have been told in our very PC PHSE (Personal, Health and Social Education) ... which means that effectively one out of every twelve is gay also, and as there is so much homophobia it kind of adds a weird paradoxical thing to it. A friend of ours who, I think more for attention-seeking purposes, whether it is actually true, I don't really know much about him, said that he was gay at a party and he was being hunted and had to skip [school], in order to get home, out of the way of these people.

These two students told a tale, which seemed to be intended to illustrate both their own anti-homophobic stance and their perception of the school's lack of support for middle-class students there:

Student 1:   There was a thing a little while ago where me and a friend wrote an article about a Townie – [X] is the biggest homophobe in the world and we wrote an article
RH: A person? ...
Student 1:   We are just talking about the ... magazine and a while ago in this magazine we wrote this article about this incredibly homophobic Townie in which we suggested he might be gay. He wasn't too happy, as you might imagine, and we did it to send up his homophobia because we were fed up with it. The school said that they had to come down hard on it. We got suspended for a couple of days and almost got detention over exams. They said that they had to come down hard on it so it seemed like they were being fair to middle-class and working-class kids.

There are several interesting points to be made about this extract. First, in a move which distances middle-class boys from homophobia, the boys associate it with the group they have previously identified as working-class and violent, the Townies. This is a middle-class strategy, identified by several writers in relation to racism (see, for example, Cohen 1988), which projects the unacceptable prejudice on to working-class others. Second and simultaneously, the boys fail to see that the effectiveness of their article, if any, depended upon the very homophobia they have previously identified in others. Thus, the politeness of middle-class (Trendy) homophobia is deployed in an attempt to combat the ugliness of working-class (Townie) homophobia. Third and perhaps as a consequence, the boys perceive the action of the school authorities as being a response to their middle classness, rather than to their actions in causing discomfort/embarrassment to another student. Finally, the extract draws attention to the failure of the school authorities to deal with the widespread and, it seems, virulent homophobia prevalent, with the result that, however misguidedly, these young men decided they needed to take matters into their own hands and combat homophobia themselves.

(In)visible homophobia

As mentioned above, we asked the teachers we interviewed a specific question about racist, sexist and homophobic violence. Several of the teachers responded on all three, saying that homophobia was a particular problem for them in their schools. Others, however, ignored this aspect of the question completely, almost as if it had not been asked. Thus teachers from the same school were able to throw very different lights on this problem. At City Heights, one of our co-educational schools, for example, one of the teachers commented that, 'there are homophobic, terrible homophobic attitudes' (Interview with Melanie Mauthner, 24 February 1999). However, another teacher at the school said:

> In my four years here I've yet to receive, erm, when you say 'homophobic'. I mean kids are going to call each other gay as a cuss, but it's, erm, I've not dealt with a case where I've dealt with a gay student yet, so I can't really speak for that. I have not dealt with that situation yet, so it's not a problem for me or anything like that, but I've just not dealt with one yet. So, but, er, kids always, you know, cuss each other, that kind of thing, you know, mother cussing is always rife.
>
> (Interview with Melanie Mauthner, 24 February 1999)

The underlying assumption of this latter attitude – that if one is not aware of lesbian, gay or bisexual pupils in the school, then homophobia is not a problem – is reminiscent of assumptions about racism in predominantly white schools that were pervasive in the 1980s and, to some extent, continue into the twenty-first century. Evidence from studies of racism and anti-racism in such schools shows that while racist language, and harassment of the small number of black pupils, was common, teachers often did not see/hear it. Commonly, successful in-service work with teachers led to them reporting many more incidents than they had previously seen or acknowledged (see, for example, Carrington and Short 1989; Epstein 1993; Epstein and Sealey 1990; Gaine 1987, 1996).

The homophobic incidents reported by both teachers and students were, almost invariably, to do with name-calling, verbal harassment and bullying, but rarely involved physical violence. This may contribute to teachers' tendency to either ignore or not take seriously such events:

RH:　　Right. What about homophobic language? Do you hear much of that?
Teacher:　Yes. Lots of that. I mean that's another thing that we didn't used to have. And so I don't think it's something to do with the school. I think it's a wider issue at the moment. Which has come back in calling, you know, boys, gay or poofs but not actually in reference to being gay at all. In fact that probably, that's not even going through their minds, you know, 'You are a homosexual', it's just a cuss which they use as an insult like 'your mum' or whatever.

(Head of Geography, Appletown, interviewed by Roger Hewitt, 8 March 1999)

It is interesting to note, in this quote that the teacher refers specifically to the naming of boys as 'gay or poofs'. This is in line with much contemporary work on masculinities and schooling, which links homophobia to the construction of male identities,[4] although, as we have noted above, anti-lesbianism has its own gendered dynamic too. It seems inescapable that part of the route taken by many young men towards establishing themselves within school hierarchies is in the form of macho 'laddishness'. Such performative masculinity is, it seems, one way for boys to establish themselves as definitely heterosexual; 'lads', after all, often (even usually) use homophobia and misogyny, themselves closely related processes, as resources for the construction of masculinities.[5] Others, writing about school-based masculinities, have called this version of masculinity 'hegemonic' (for example, Martino 1999). We prefer the term 'emphatic masculinities', given that the positions adopted by such young men, while they may be dominant in schools, serve them badly in their studies and in the world of work (Willis 1977; Willis and Kenway 2000). What we have noted in our research is that homophobia is related to the emphatic masculinities prevalent in school situations. These forms of masculinity often seem almost inescapable to young men in school contexts, even though there is evidence to suggest that they do not necessarily live them out very comfortably (see, for example, Frosh *et al.* 2002). Peter Redman and Maírtín Mac an Ghaill (1997) have written persuasively about the possibilities for different forms of masculinity which open up to young men as they enter post-compulsory education. They suggest that one of the reasons for this change is that at this stage young men need to identify with future work and university opportunities and build on those resources that will enable them to engage in the demands of these locations. Equally, the fact that post-16 education is no longer compulsory may mean that the kinds of 'laddishness' required of younger boys in schools become less salient.

One teacher was passionately concerned about the amount of homophobia to be found in schools, partly because his son, a pupil at another school, found himself the butt of much homophobic abuse:

> Without a shadow of a doubt. I, absolutely without a shadow of a doubt. My boy – it's homophobic stuff – he's thirteen. To my knowledge, he's a young boy who hasn't yet discovered his sexual identity and however, whatever he decides to do, he decides to become, for want of a better word, that's good enough for me. Me and his mother love him just the same. I am very very strict on homophobic behaviour, very very strict, but I am also strict on all forms of bullying and no doubt it's, a lot of it, is because of my son.
>
> I've got another son, the middle one he's probably the opposite, he's not a bully but he's the opposite. But I am strict and the problem his school's having … through this bullying and they're in a hard area but they've got a lot of middle-class kids as well and they failed OFSTED.

And I would actually, I don't, but I think it's probably unprofessional but I would like to go up the school, and say, you cannot miss it as much as what you are. There must be teachers in this school that are not seeing any ships [*sic*].

(Appletown, interview by Roger Hewitt, 17 March 1999)

The link made by this teacher between the problems experienced by his son's school, not only in behaviour but also in learning outcomes and inspection by OFSTED, is clearly important. In understanding schools' abilities to become 'violence-resilient', this is a link that assumes particular importance.

(Absence of) school policies

The schools we researched all had clear policies and practices to respond to racism. While these may not always have been successful, school management teams felt that they knew what they were doing and there was a consensus amongst staff and students that racism was not acceptable or defensible. As one of the teachers we spoke to explained:

Teacher: And this is how it was explained to me by the deputy head of [another school] and I actually stand by it. With racism most kids know the boundaries, it's political, they know the boundaries, you ring up the parents there is some form of support. In this school there would be lots of support from certain areas. I know I keep talking in middle class and working class. I don't mean to say that, but it's a way of differentiating the groups, you know.

RH: Yeah.

Teacher: You'll get a response, sexism you'll get a response but maybe not as much as the racism. Homophobic, in that particular school, and I think it's the same in this school, is most of the parents are just as homophobic, they won't admit it openly but they are just as homophobic and it gets said in the house and it's the norm.

(Appletown. Interview with Roger Hewitt, 17 March 1999)

Parental and local cultures of homophobia may, indeed, be a problem for schools trying to combat homophobic bullying and harassment. Certainly, issues like this were raised by a number of teachers in the different schools. There was a strong feeling that they would run into problems in making homophobia an issue for effective policy and practice. Teachers who considered it an important issue, were, nevertheless, quick to point out potential difficulties, and why it lagged behind racism and sexism in terms of school policies and practices:

Teacher: With homophobia it's quite difficult because you've got kids here that are fundamentalist Christians, kids who are Methodists, kids who are born-again Christians away, and those kids don't respond. As far as they are concerned it's against God, so therefore … And it's trying to educate them to accept that they may have these religious views, however, they are not acceptable within the school framework. And that's quite hard. I think that is difficult and I think it's hard for all schools really, because of the age that the kids are and the fact that it's not as clear cut as the black and white thing. It's you know 'It says in the Bible'.

RH: Do you think it's therefore in conflict with some sort of multicultural ideas?

Teacher: I think so. I think it is if I am perfectly honest. Because I think it's very very easy for a group of kids to unite because someone is picked on because they are black. I think the majority of kids I teach now, I hope, would be able to unite on the same basis on the fact that some person is being picked on because of their sexuality, but I know that there will be two or three in that group that would either overtly, or inside, be thinking 'Yes, but they are a homosexual. Why should they be given the same rights' and I think it's an ongoing issue. They reflect society. It's an ongoing debate in our society, and that's why in that sense we cannot fit an ivory tower in here. Their parents say these things. People in the chapter say these things, and so in a certain sense we reflect, but then we try and educate and move them on.

(Daleford teacher, interviewed by Roger Hewitt, 3 March 1999)

This teacher, from Daleford School, attributed the difficulty in dealing with homophobia to the presence of religious fundamentalists within the school. His head teacher's explanation was more along class lines:

Head: No, I'm just trying to think. Racist is, racist is most comprehensively [addressed] I suppose in terms of equal ops. policies. And in fact we're quite successful with that. Not that many, I can't think of that many exclusions that have a racist sort of basis. And kids, I think, are pretty much aware that you don't say those things. It's only very rarely it happens with particular kids possibly or a very odd situation. So while kids fight they, by and large, don't appear to fight from a racist cause. Sexist is more, the kids are more likely to say sexist [things], the company of sort of 'slags' and that sort of thing comes and they don't have the same taboo and would use that. But whether that actually leads to violence, I can't think, I would never really of looked sufficiently to see if it does.

I think it does quite often, I mean there are fights and arguments between boys and girls but I'm not sort of … And homophobic, I don't think we've addressed that, it's much more difficult to address and it doesn't come up so obviously amongst kids in school. Particularly in working-class areas I suspect. And so we often talk about the fact that we should do more about … But it's the racist one probably that the school has worked at hardest and is possibly the one that would have been most combustible if we hadn't.

(Interview with Roger Hewitt, 22 February 1999)

The difficulties expressed by these two teachers are compounded by the political context described at the beginning of this chapter. There is also a risk of resorting to explanations of behaviour that devolve responsibility away from the school in a manner which assumes there is nothing which can be done to solve the problems experienced. The placing of responsibility, here, on to working-class children and parents is reminiscent of the two Trendy boys discussed above.

The teachers quoted so far in this section of the chapter have all explained that policies to deal with homophobia lag a long way behind those to combat racism and sexism (which, itself, is less well dealt with than racism). However, they were able to point to attempts being made to take up this issue. What is, perhaps, a matter of more concern is the number of teachers for whom the response to our question about 'racism, sexism and homophobia' completely ignored the last. The female Deputy Head of City Heights responded to this question with a long discourse on everything other than homophobia:

MM: What about – is there any focus specifically on different types of violence – racist, sexist, homophobic?

Deputy: Yes, the actual logging system we operate has a box where you tick bullying, racist, sexist, other violent incidents, there are different categories, but because it's only used for the very serious incidents we have to do those surveys to back that up, because in the anti-bullying survey there are issues of race and gender come up, and we know that's an issue, prejudice is an issue with bullying, and people bully because it highlights a difference in one way or another. I think also it's worth mentioning that because we have a resource base we have disabled students, it has a beneficial influence on the students, they have to care for the safety of those students, and they can see quite graphically that these students cannot operate in an unsafe environment, and you can illustrate that, for example when you say 'Don't run!' you have a very good example because you might harm somebody in a wheelchair and you've got to see the world through other people's eyes, I think it makes them more aware. I wouldn't say – I haven't encountered – I suppose this would qualify as a tough school – I have very rarely encountered kids who are malicious and do things with intent. I think a lot of it is they are vulnerable, they can't help themselves and I think the staff know that, they haven't got the social skills and the interpersonal skills to manage themselves, or they're very traumatised or they're very stressed, but I would say that very very few of our students, maybe one or two of those hardcore offenders are really intending to hurt.

(Interview with Melanie Mauthner, 23 February 1999)

Public policy and homophobic bullying

The teachers who talked about how hard it was to develop effective policies against homophobia were not simply making excuses. This is clearly a difficult issue, compounded by the political context of the time when our research took place. Our fieldwork took place shortly before the Blair Government attempted, twice in one year (2000), unsuccessfully, to repeal Section 28 of the Local Government Act 1988.[6] Section 28 has never been used against any local authority or school and is so poorly drafted that it would almost certainly be impossible to use.[7] Although the Section had the support of the government of the time, the Department of the Environment (DoE 1988), in guidance issued within weeks of the passage of the Local Government Act 1988, stated categorically that it did not apply to schools. However, it has had enormous symbolic significance, and many teachers believe that they cannot address homophobia because of it, as illustrated by the quote which begins this chapter. The Deputy Head of Ferndale was quite explicit about this, saying: 'I think schools have been intimidated out of making that [homophobia] part of equal opportunities as visible as the other two [racism and sexism] by the Tory government and clause [that is, Section] 28' (Interview with Melanie Mauthner, 11 March 1999).

Since 1999 the policy landscape has altered somewhat, despite the fact that Section 28 has not, as yet, been repealed. At the time of the attempted repeal of the Section, those supporting this move appealed strongly to concerns about the effects of homophobic bullying in schools.[8] In an attempt to mediate between the lobby in favour of repeal and the conservative (and Conservative) campaign against it, the government sought a compromise position in its *Sex and Relationship Education Guidance* (DfEE 2000). While this document stresses the importance of 'marriage and stable family relationships', it also places on schools a duty to combat prejudice and homophobic bullying. In 2002 OFSTED recommended that: 'Schools should make sure that values relevant to education about sex and relationships are consistently adhered to within the school so that, for example, homophobic attitudes do not go unchallenged' (OFSTED 2002: 34). It remains to be seen whether schools do avail themselves of the opportunities provided by these changes to develop and implement their own policies or whether policy on homophobic harassment and bullying remains the 'Cinderella' amongst equal opportunities policies, as we found it to be in our research.

Conclusion

We have argued, in the chapter, that schools tend not to have (effective) policies to combat homophobic violence in the form of bullying and harassment. As we have shown, this is in spite of pervasive homophobia reported by students and some teachers. Some teachers and schools, while aware of homophobia as a problem that can lead to violence, shrink from developing policies to challenge homophobia because of fear of parents and/or negative publicity for their schools. Others ignore the issue, either not noticing or ignoring the existence of any problem.

What does this mean for the identity formations within schools? The absence of consistent policy on this aspect of social difference may legitimate homophobic bullying and harassment. If, as all the schools claimed, there is a consensus that racist and sexist harassment are not acceptable and would lead to sanctions, then the absence of such a consensus on homophobic bullying makes it an easy resource for teasing, insults and so on. In this way, the conditions not of their own choosing in which pupils (and teachers) make themselves are conducive to homophobia in ways that impact on those identifying as lesbian, gay or bisexual *and* those identifying as heterosexual. This dynamic appeared, in our research, to be at its most stark in the single-sex boys' school. However, it was present in the co-educational schools too and, in a somewhat different form, in the single-sex girls' school.

Schools have a responsibility to develop better policies and practices to challenge homophobia, not just to protect those young people who identify as lesbian, gay or bisexual, but in the interests of reducing the levels of violent and violence-related incidents that take place at and around the school. In this context, relationships within schools, the degree to which staff identify with school policies and communicate with each other and with pupils will also have a significant impact. Furthermore, the problems which teachers identify with their local communities and the attitudes of parents will not disappear if they are left unchallenged. The intertwining of policy at national and school level with formations of identity through the creation of the homosexual Other can be clearly seen through the data presented in this chapter. The challenge is for the Other to be included fully in school communities in ways which open up possibilities for more varied forms of identity than are currently possible.

Notes

1 'The "Violence-Resilient" School: A Comparative Study of Schools and their Environments' was funded by the Economic and Social Research Council (Award No L133251041) as part of its Violence Research Programme.

2 All names in this paper have been changed to preserve anonymity of participating schools. We would like to thank the heads of the six London secondary schools who allowed us access to research their 'violence-resilience', particularly those with problems of violence. Given the potential for damage to schools should they be subjected to publicity on these grounds, we are particularly cognisant of their courage.

3 This work includes: Mac an Ghaill (1994a; 2000) and Nayak and Kehily (1997) in the UK; Gilbert and Gilbert (1998) and Martino (2000) in Australia; Quinlivan and Town (1999) in New Zealand; Frank (1987, 1993 in Canada; Deacon *et al.* (1999) in South Africa; and Friend (1993) and Letts (1999) in the US.

4 See, for example, Epstein (1998), Frank (1987), Gilbert and Gilbert (1998), Mac an Ghaill (1994b), Martino (2000), Nayak and Kehily (1997).

5 See, for an early example, Willis (1977) and, more recently, Martino (1999, 2000) and Nayak and Kehily (1997).

6   Section 28 of the Local Government Act 1988 prohibited the 'promotion of homosexuality' by local authorities and the teaching, in publicly maintained schools, of
'pretended family relationships' as equivalent to heterosexual ones.
7   See Epstein and Johnson (1998) for an extended discussion of the politics of Section
28.
8   See, for example, the *Express*, 'Teachers too scared to halt gay insults. Confusing rules
let bullies reign' (7.2.00); the *Guardian*, 'Section 28 helps bullies, study shows'
(2.2.00); the *Independent*, 'The confusion which allows homophobia to flourish in
schools' (10.2.00); *Times Educational Supplement,* 'Nowhere to turn: How teachers
can help gay pupils to beat the bullies' (3.3.00).

References

Butler, J. (1990) *Gender Trouble: Feminism and the Subversion of Identity*, New York and
London: Routledge
Carrington, B. and Short, G. (1989) *Race and the Primary School: Theory into Practice,*
Windsor: NFER
Cohen, P. (1988) 'The perversions of inheritance: studies in the making of multi-racist
Britain' in Cohen, P. and Bains, H. (eds) *Multi-Racist Britain*, London: Macmillan
Deacon, R., Morrell, R. and Prinsloo, J. (1999) 'Discipline and homophobia in South
African schools: the limits of legislated transformation' in Epstein, D. and Sears, J. T.
(eds) *A Dangerous Knowing: Sexuality, Pedagogy and Popular Culture*, London:
Cassell
DfEE (2000) *Sex and Relationship Education Guidance,* London: Department for
Education and Employment
DoE (1988) *Local Government Act 1988*, Department of the Environment
Douglas, N., Warwick, I., Kemp, S. and Whitty, G. (1997) *Playing it Safe: Responses of
Secondary School Teachers to Lesbian, Gay and Bisexual Pupils, Bullying, HIV and
AIDS Education and Section 28*, London: Institute of Education, University of London
Epstein, D. (1993) *Changing Classroom Cultures: Anti-racism, Politics and Schools*,
Stoke-on-Trent: Trentham Books
Epstein, D. (1998) '"Real boys don't work": boys' "underachievement", masculinities and
the harassment of sissies', in Epstein, D., Elwood, J., Hey, V. and Maw, J. (eds) *Failing
Boys? Issues in Gender and Achievement*, Buckingham: Open University Press
Epstein, D. and Johnson, R. (1998) *Schooling Sexualities*, Buckingham: Open University
Press
Epstein, D. and Sealey, A. (1990) *'Where it Really Matters ...' Developing Anti Racist
Education in Predominantly White Primary Schools*, Birmingham: Development
Education Centre
Frank, B. (1987) 'Hegemonic heterosexual masculinity', *Studies in Political Economy*, 24:
159–170
Frank, B. (1993) 'Straight/strait jackets for masculinity: educating for real men', *Atlantis*
18: 47–59
Friend, Richard A. (1993) 'Choices, not closets: heterosexism and homophobia in schools'
in Weis, L. and Fine, M. (eds) *Beyond Silenced Voices: Class, Race, and Gender in
United States Schools*, Albany, NY: State University of New York Press
Frosh, S., Phoenix, A. and Pattman, R. (2002) *Young Masculinities: Understanding Boys in
Contemporary Society*, London: Palgrave

Gaine, C. (1987) *No Problem Here: A Practical Approach to Education and Race in White Schools*, London: Hutchinson

Gaine, C. (1996) *Still No Problem Here*, Stoke-on-Trent: Trentham Books

GALOP (1998) *Telling it Like it is: Lesbian, Gay and Bisexual Youth Speak Out on Homophobic Violence*, London: GALOP

Gilbert, R. and Gilbert, P. (1998) *Masculinity Goes to School*, Sydney: Allen & Unwin

Gooding-Williams, R. (ed.) (1993) *Reading Rodney King/Reading Urban Uprising*, New York and London: Routledge

Hall, S. (1996) 'Introduction: who needs "identity"?' in Hall, S. and du Gay, P. (eds) *Questions of Cultural Identity*, London: Sage

Hey, V. (1997) *The Company She Keeps: an Ethnography of Girls' Friendships*, Buckingham: Open University Press

Letts IV, W. J., and Sears, J. T. (eds) (1999) *Queering Elementary Education: Advancing the Dialogue about Sexualities and Schooling*, Lanham, MD: Rowman & Littlefield

Mac an Ghaill, M. (1994a) '(In)visibility: sexuality, race and masculinity in the school context' in Epstein, D. (ed.) *Challenging Lesbian and Gay Inequalities in Education*, Buckingham: Open University Press

Mac an Ghaill, M. (1994b) *The Making of Men: Masculinities, Sexualities and Schooling*, Buckingham: Open University Press

Mac an Ghaill, M. (2000) 'Rethinking (male) gendered sexualities in education: what about the British heteros?' *The Journal of Men's Studies*, 8, 2: 195–212

Martino, W. (1999) '"Cool boys," "Party animals," "Squids," and "Poofters": interrogating the dynamics and politics of adolescent masculinities in school', *British Journal of Sociology of Education*, 20, 2: 239–263

Martino, W. (2000) 'Policing Masculinities: investigating the role of homophobia and heteronormativity in the lives of adolescent school boys', *The Journal of Men's Studies*, 8: 213–236

Marx, K. (1963) *The 18th Brumaire of Louis Bonaparte*, New York: International Publishers

Nayak, A. (1997) 'Tales from the darkside: negotiating whiteness in school arenas', *International Studies in Sociology of Education*, 7, 1: 57–79

Nayak, A. (1999) 'White English ethnicities: racism, anti-racism and student perspectives', *Race Ethnicity and Education*, 2, 2: 177–202

Nayak, A. and Kehily, M. J. (1997) 'Masculinities and schooling: why are young men so homophobic?' in Steinberg, D. L., Epstein, D. and Johnson, R. (eds) *Border Patrols: Policing the Boundaries of Heterosexuality*, London: Cassell

OFSTED (2002) 'Sex and relationships: a report from the office of Her Majesty's Chief Inspector of Schools', HMI 433, London: OFSTED

Quinlivan, K. and Town, S. (1999) 'Queer as fuck? Exploring the potential of queer pedagogies in researching school experiences of lesbian and gay youth', in Epstein, D. and Sears, J. T. (eds) *A Dangerous Knowing: Sexuality, Pedagogy and Popular Culture*, London: Cassell

Redman, P. and Mac an Ghaill, M. (1997) 'Educating Peter: the making of a history man', in Steinberg, D. L, Epstein, D. and Johnson, R. (eds) *Border Patrols: Policing the Boundaries of Heterosexuality*, London: Cassell

Rivers, I. (1995) 'The victimisation of gay teenagers in schools: homophobia in education', *Pastoral Care*, March: 35–41

Skeggs, B. (1997) *Formations of Class and Gender*, London: Sage

Willis, P. (1977) *Learning to Labour: How Working Class Kids get Working Class Jobs*, Aldershot: Saxon House

Willis, S. and Kenway. J. (2000) 'Gender and the restructuring of work and vocational education in Australia: some perilous possibilities', *Journal of Education Policy,* 11, 2: 239–258

Chapter 8

Masculinities, femininities and physical education

Bodily practices as reified markers of community membership

Carrie Paechter

Introduction

In school, bodies matter, in many different ways. They matter because the people who go to school, children and adolescents, have bodies that are regulated and dispersed through school spaces and times. These bodies are constantly growing and changing, so the relationship between them and the school environment constantly alters to accommodate and deal with this – as the environment itself has to be altered to cope with the changing shapes, sizes and functions of children's bodies (larger furniture, sex-segregated changing rooms, sanitary protection dispensers in the lavatories). These bodies also have relationships with each other, and with the adult bodies of those who supervise them; they are positioned, touched (or not) in various ways at various times, they are analysed, gazed upon and disciplined by peers and teachers, and used in different ways to demonstrate (or not) a range of identities and attributes, some of which are gendered.

This chapter is concerned with bodies and bodily practices within a particular educational context, school physical education and the related worlds of junior sports and playground games. In it I discuss how children often, but not always, encouraged by teachers and by the nature of the curriculum, use their bodies in these contexts as a way of demonstrating particular sexual identities and repudiating others. These different ways in which children and young people use their bodies, particularly in relation to the development and claiming of such identities, have implications for social justice as they have outcomes which serve neither boys nor girls, restricting the future possibilities for both sexes. I will approach this issue through a consideration of how children and young people's bodily practices, alongside other discourses and practices, are used as reified markers of membership of localised communities of masculinity and femininity practice.

Masculinities and femininities as communities of practice

I have argued elsewhere (Paechter 2002) that we can use the idea of communities of practice (Lave and Wenger 1991; Wenger 1998) as a useful way of thinking about the formation and perpetuation of localised masculinities and femininities. Briefly, treating masculinities and femininities as communities of localised practice allows us to deal with the question of the relationship between the conception of gender as performative (Butler 1990, 1993) and the question of how we, as individuals, come to perform particular masculinities and femininities in particular situations. It allows us explicitly to acknowledge that being a man or woman, boy or girl (or an intersex individual of one sort or another) is something that has different meanings at different times and places and is not a once-and-for-all, unitary phenomenon; how we enact masculinities and femininities changes as we move between groups, between places and spaces and through time. Having an understanding of these localised masculinities and femininities as communities of practice also allows us a window of understanding into how masculine and feminine behaviour is developed and learned by children and adults, and a way of seeing why it is that these ways of being are so resistant to change. Furthermore, this approach to the understanding of masculinities and femininities also gives us tools with which to unpick the relationship between bodies and what is usually referred to as gender,[1] and in particular to see how the uses and forms of our bodies are taken up as signs of both our physical and our behavioural sex.

A community of practice, broadly, is a group engaging in a shared practice (Lave and Wenger 1991; Wenger 1998). Novices to that practice are seen as developing expertise through participation in legitimate and acknowledged activities that contribute to but are not central to the practice; gradually these contributions become more complex and important as they progress towards full participation (for example a child might gradually move from making noises alongside family conversation at the dinner table through contributing an anecdote from nursery to discussing the existence of God). Through this they develop not just their expertise in the practice itself but their understanding of and embeddedness in the culture that surrounds it:

> From a broadly peripheral perspective, apprentices gradually assemble a general idea of what constitutes the practice. This uneven sketch of the enterprise (available if there is legitimate access) might include who is involved; what they do; what everyday life is like; how masters talk, walk, work, and generally conduct their lives; how people who are not part of the community of practice interact with it; what other learners are doing; and what learners need to do to become full practitioners.
>
> (Lave and Wenger 1991: 95)

Apprentices are, thus, learning to be part of the community of practice, to be full participants (Lave and Wenger 1991), with all the many and varied social practices that this implies. Thus boys can be seen (broadly) as apprentice men, learning, through observation of the men they encounter and peripheral participation in their activities (being taken to the pub or club, allowed to taste beer or wine, being treated as an increasingly serious participant in football or card games, expected to carry out particular masculine-labelled chores), what it means to be a man in the local communities of practice in which they live. Girls, similarly, can be seen as apprentice women, taking part with adult women in activities pertaining to womanhood in those communities, whether these be 'traditionally' female (helping with cooking, cleaning or childcare) or resistant to the status quo ('take your daughter to work' days).

Much of the literature on gender and education, as well as some of that concerned with gender practice more widely, treats masculinities and femininities in this way, though without explicitly using this theoretical framework. Mac an Ghaill (1994), for example, discusses several communities of adolescent masculinity practice within one school, elaborating in detail the groups' world views, ways of behaving and attitudes to themselves as young men. Skelton (2001) considers two contrasting groups of young boys and the ways in which they practice masculinity within and outside school, relating this clearly to the adult practices that the boys see around them. Some of these boys see themselves very explicitly as apprentice men (more specifically, apprentice 'lads', aspiring to violence, petty theft and car crime) and go to considerable lengths to demonstrate their participation in the lads' community of practice. McRobbie (1991) also gives a detailed account of a community of working-class teenage femininity practice in which the young women's insistence on their legitimate peripheral participation in adult female activities is explicitly described. Consequently, this approach to masculinities and femininities is not a radical departure from the findings of existing studies; it is an alternative theorisation of what is evidenced by those studies. It is my contention, however, that this approach to masculinities and femininities is one that will be important for our understanding of how we learn to participate as males and females in particular social situations and formations.

An important aspect of the theorisation of communities of practice is the use of reified objects such as membership cards, certificates of competence, procedures followed by the group, particular styles of dress, as symbolic markers of inclusion or exclusion. A reified object is, basically, a concept made solid. Wenger (1998) argues that participation in a community of practice and reification of markers of membership form a complementary duality which is fundamental to the negotiation of meaning within the community of practice. Participants negotiate their participation through their shared understanding of the meaning of the reified objects that mark group membership (Wenger 1998: 59). What this means is that certain concepts central to the community become reified as symbolic artefacts and practices; they may then be used not just to focus discussion but as markers of recognition of membership or otherwise of a particular community. Reification can refer to both a process (by which something becomes reified) and a product (the reified object, practice or process), but to be meaningful it must be incorporated into a local practice. In this way, the products of reification are reflections of the practices of a community. Consequently, one way to understand these practices is to examine the reifications associated with it. This is what I am going to do in this chapter, considering how bodies, bodily forms and bodily usages become reified markers of masculinity and femininity in relation to physical education (PE) and sport in schools and related sites such as junior sports clubs.

Bodily forms as reified markers of masculinity and femininity

Of course, and obviously, bodily forms are used as markers of sex in our society. When a baby is born, we look at its genitals and then (except in a few exceptional cases) pronounce it to be male or female. At this point the child is assumed to enter, as a peripheral but nonetheless legitimate participant in the local communities of practice of child and adult masculinity or femininity.

Because an announcement of maleness or femaleness is tied in this way to an announcement of community membership, when we attribute sex using these outward physical markers we are, in some ways, announcing the kind of person the child is on the basis of what she or he looks like. The labelling of an infant as a 'boy' or a 'girl' has enormous ramifications for the way the child is treated, the way she or he is expected to behave, the sort of person she or he is understood to be; it identifies the child as a participant in one set of communities of practice rather than another. Although bodily (or perceived bodily) differences do not in themselves cause behavioural differences between males and females (Connell 2002), they do cause differences in expectations and approaches (Smith and Lloyd 1978; Walkerdine and The Girls and Mathematics Unit 1989), through children's apprentice participation in local communities of masculinity and femininity practice, which in turn affect how an individual turns out.

This classification into two sexes is fundamental to the way most of Western society is ordered (Connell 2002; Fausto-Sterling 1989). Although this is being challenged by academics and those whose bodies or whose relationships with these bodies do not lend themselves to such dichotomous categories (Fausto-Sterling 1993; Fausto-Sterling 2000; Halberstam 1998; Kessler 1998; Namaste 2000), generally we expect people to be male or female, and to have correspondingly masculine or feminine behaviour, although the amount of latitude in what is acceptable masculinity and femininity varies considerably from group to group. Parents of babies whose bodies do not reflect this dichotomy, for example, because they have an enlarged clitoris, a very small penis or external genitals that in other ways do not conform to the expectations of medical norms, are put under enormous pressure to have these genitals altered at an early age so that the sex that is then assigned (which may or may not conform either to the physical structures present at birth or to the baby's chromosomal configuration) can be socially established as early as possible (Kessler 1990) and the range of communities of practice to which they belong made clear.

In everyday life, however, genitals are hidden. This means that we have to attribute maleness or femaleness to individuals whom we encounter on the basis of other things. Once such a categorisation has been made, people are attributed 'cultural genitals', which are the genitals they are assumed to have, in conformity with the attribution already made; this attribution, once achieved, can be so firm that even the discovery of actual genitals that do not correspond to the initial attribution may be ignored (Kessler and McKenna 1978). The initial attribution therefore becomes crucial in giving and sustaining the impression that one is of a particular sex, in a context in which sex is both biologically and socially dichotomous.

These attributions are important because neither maleness and femaleness nor masculinity and femininity are neutral; they are bound up with relations of power (Connell 1987; Connell 2002; Paechter 1998). Most of the world's population lives in societies in which males hold more powerful positions, in which they earn more, in which they do less of the least recognised work (caring for others, housework) and more of that which is highly regarded (managing companies, leading governments). Furthermore, many public arenas are dominated by and organised through masculine ways of working, so that those individuals (male or female) who are comfortable or successful at operating in this way are advantaged in these arenas. Consequently, it becomes necessary for both adults and children to be able to distinguish easily between men and women. This is particularly important for males, who need to protect their dominant position. The hegemony of male dominance is perpetuated through the fostering of a belief (for which there is little actual evidence (Connell 2002)) that differences between males and females are not only widespread, but salient in all aspects of social life. Hence, the enactment or performance of masculinity or femininity (though, for the individual, particularly masculinity) becomes very significant; it demonstrates clearly the communities of practice to which one belongs and, through this, one's position in gendered power relations. The emphasis on behavioural differences, coupled with dichotomous biological and social attribution of sex, also allows members of communities of masculinity and femininity practice that are dominant in a particular context to call into question the validity of that attribution to members of other, subordinate communities.

This enactment of masculinities and femininities, as opposed to an emphasis on bodily features such as secondary sexual characteristics, is particularly salient in the case of children. Before puberty, boys and girls differ outwardly only in terms of their genitals, which are usually covered up. In order to tell girls from boys, they have to rely on such outward and contingent features such as hair length, dress and behaviour. Consequently young children, particularly boys, police and control their peers' permitted masculinities and femininities to enforce conformity to a restricted and stereotypical range of behaviours (Lloyd and Duveen 1992). This results in a situation in which relatively minor items of dress can become important reified markers of community membership; colours, patterns and styles of clothing, as well as haircuts, interests and abilities are imbued with masculinity and femininity. Bem, for example, describes an occasion in which her son went to nursery school wearing barrettes (known in the UK as hairslides):

Several times that day, another little boy had asserted that Jeremy must be a girl, not a boy, because 'only girls wear barrettes'. After repeatedly insisting that 'Wearing barrettes doesn't matter; I have a penis and testicles,' Jeremy finally pulled down his pants to make his point more convincingly. The other boy was not impressed. He simply said, 'Everybody has a penis; only girls wear barrettes.'

(Bem 1998: 109)

For this child, the wearing of barrettes was a more salient marker of membership of the local community of practice of 'girlness' than the presence or absence of particular genitals.

Communities of masculinity and femininity practice within physical education

In physical education (PE), the body is used very explicitly as a reified marker of insider/outsider status with regard to dominant communities of masculinity practices. This is related to the ways in which hegemonic masculinities (Connell 1995) are constructed through particular uses of male bodies and especially through the demonstration of physical prowess and dominance. Studies of the construction of masculinities within PE suggest that the process shares a number of features with the induction into a community of practice described by the concept of legitimate peripheral participation (Lave and Wenger 1991). PE and sporting communities develop and share localised views of what it means to be a man, related in particular to physical toughness and particular body forms.

> ... when boys choose football, they are entering a community of practice that demarcates particular forms of masculinity. Indeed, the self-reproducing cycle of hegemonic masculinity in football is nurtured by a number of forces. Successful footballers ... celebrate their masculinity, coaches act as gatekeepers of dominant forms of masculinity, the media perpetuate the dominant discourses, and junior peer group relationships confirm and conform to made masculinities.
>
> (Fitzclarence and Hickey 2001: 130)

For male children and adolescents, the shared practices of sports and PE, especially of football (in its various national and international forms), become reified as markers of the community of practice of a particular, dominant and to some extent exaggerated, masculinity. Those who do not share these practices are excluded from the community. Boys who are not good at or interested in sports are often explicitly labelled as feminine, and therefore clearly outsiders, using terms such as 'girlie', 'sissy' or 'woman' (Salisbury and Jackson 1996), or as gay, using terms such as 'fag', 'faggot' or 'queer' (Parker 1996), which, in the context of a dominant masculinity also constructed around compulsory heterosexuality likewise signifies complete exclusion. Conversely, those children who by virtue of their genital (or assumed genital) configuration are necessarily excluded from the community of practice of sporting masculinity, i.e. the girls, are not accepted by their male peers as having any interest in, ability at or knowledge about sport (Nespor 1997; Wright 1996); bodily forms are in this way used as reified markers of community boundaries.

The communities of practice of sporting masculinities that are found in schools and in youth sports clubs clearly involve learning processes. Young men learn from their teachers, coaches and older boys what it means to be a man in this context (Fitzclarence and Hickey 2001). They learn together, making their own local compromises and accommodations, using their shared understanding of what is tolerated both by their own community and by the larger local communities of adult masculinities in which they legitimately peripherally participate. These local communities are also related to wider forms of masculinity constructed around sports and sporting prowess; this relationship operates in particular through the mass media and boys' interest in national or local sporting heroes (Nespor 1997). Given that women's sports are virtually ignored in the press (Bryson 1987), this further emphasises the relationship between sports and dominant forms of masculinity.

In this community of practice of masculinity, identity becomes related to sporting competence; such competence confers membership of the community and power within it. The competent body is therefore a clearly reified marker of membership; without such competence one cannot become a full participant in a community of sporting masculinity practice:

> Thus the community of practice associated with football involves definite structural divisions. Ability to play (the beginnings of mature practice) enables access to the inner circle of legitimate participation (the team) or relegation to peripheral participation (the leftovers) … A big part of the sifting and sorting process is associated with the visible display of definable character traits … Because football success is associated with a particular form of masculinity, it brings social power in the hierarchy (the inner circle).
>
> (Fitzclarence and Hickey 2001)

Thus the processes of PE and competitive sport, for boys, form a significant aspect of learning what it means to be a particular sort of man, an important form of legitimate peripheral participation in adult communities of practice of hegemonic heterosexual masculinity. The body that is produced by this activity at the same time becomes a marker of this membership; it is the competent use of the body within the context of the sport that differentiates full from peripheral or nonparticipants. Legitimate peripheral participation in these particular forms of masculinity is a major aspect of identity formation for many boys and young men and thus central to their development as adults. Through the practices and understandings of what it is to be male that take place in communities of practice of PE and sport, they are inducted into a community that goes far beyond this, a local community of masculinity which is in its turn linked to wider forms of masculinity that allow some ways of being men to dominate and others to be subordinated.

Related to this phenomenon and to the symbolic rejection of the feminine in sporting masculinities, is a rejection of the possibility that a female body could display equivalent competence. Women's bodies become symbols of inferiority; less competent boys are seen as 'playing like women' but a woman cannot be regarded as 'playing like a man', however great her expertise. Brown and Rich (2002), for example, discuss a student teacher who is also a highly skilled footballer. They note that 'as a competent performer Christie implicitly challenges the masculine stereotypical orthodoxy of males play football better than females' (91). The boys' reaction to this, however, is to further devalue the competence of their less skilled peers, who are teased for playing 'even worse' than a woman: 'Miss is better than you' (92). 'Christie's feminine physicality is defined in *relation* to and *comparison* with male standards, while the boys compare themselves with a 'women' [*sic*] rather than 'a competent performer' (Brown and Rich 2002: 92).

At the same time, PE, through the practices of PE teachers and the ways that the curriculum is interpreted in schools, is complicit in producing differential bodily forms for boys and girls. This occurs both at the seemingly superficial level of the nature of kit to be worn, and at the level of differentiated activities and the implications these have for bodily use and development. Scraton (1992) notes that female PE teachers impose high standards of dress on girl students, but not on boys, and that this emphasis on appearance is related to stereotypical norms of femininity. Williams and Bedward (2002) point out that in several schools in their study girls were required to wear very short skirts, which made them embarrassed and reluctant to take part, and that the wearing of cycling shorts underneath their skirts, something many girls did because it was less revealing, was strongly discouraged. They also note that this emphasis on wearing feminine rather than practical PE kit led to girls being expected to participate outdoors in dress that could be seen as inadequate for the conditions: 'it was quite common to find students at one school playing netball during November and December in T-shirts and skirts' (Williams and Bedward 2002: 155).

At the curriculum level, activities for boys and girls are strongly differentiated in English secondary schools, where PE, particularly team games, is generally taught in single-sex groups (Penney 2002). These differentiated activities result in boys and girls being encouraged, even required, to use their bodies in different ways, which emphasise particular forms of masculinity and femininity. Harris and Penney (2002), for example, note that recent requirements of the English National Curriculum for PE (Department for Education and Employment 1999) that both boys and girls should gain 'knowledge and understanding of fitness and health' are being interpreted differentially for girls and boys, with the avowed aim of producing differentiated bodies:

The use of the multigym has a different emphasis for boys and girls generally – i.e. strength development v. toning and muscular endurance. In cardiovascular type work, the emphasis tends to be on running activities for the boys and aerobics-type work for the girls.

(Male head of department, state comprehensive school, 2000)

Girls – aerobics and step aerobics. Boys – more work in multigym on strength and power.

(Female head of department, state comprehensive school, 2000)

(Harris and Penney 2002: 139)

In this situation, the different genital configurations of girls and boys are used alongside (one can only assume) unspoken assumptions about the differences between communities of adolescent masculinity and femininity practice, to provide a differential curriculum, the result of which will only serve to further divide the two communities. Boys will become stronger and more powerful, girls more 'toned' (an attribute that is concerned more with appearance than with physical fitness (Paechter 2003)). It is also notable that the activities cited, aimed at 14–16-year-olds, are those characteristic of adult gym users, with men using the multigym and women going to aerobics and step classes. The school is thus complicit in supporting and legitimising adolescents' peripheral participation, in particular restricted forms of adult masculinity and femininity practices as they relate to health and fitness.

The differences between the ways male and female bodies are presented and used in school PE gives an explicit emphasis to the production of masculinities and femininities in which strength and fitness mean different things. Students make choices about whether they take up these masculinities and femininities, and the bodily forms and uses with which they are associated, but whether they do so or not has implications for the physical capital they develop and how they can use it. Many male students are drawn to the forms of masculinity that are promoted through boys' PE, and are happy to develop the sorts of bodies that correspond to this. The costs associated with this position, however, may not be immediately apparent. Shilling (1992) points out that although taking part in sporting activities does develop physical capital, that produced by the activities favoured by working-class boys has less exchange value and is less readily converted into social or cultural capital than that developed in their middle-class peers, while time spent on sports may affect academic performance; this has been and may remain a particular issue for young black men (Carrington and Wood 1983). Furthermore, the forms of masculinity developed through communities of PE and sporting practice, including those in schools, are relatively restricted; too great a commitment to such communities may limit a young man's future choices and life chances, not just in terms of jobs and careers, but in terms of the sort of person he wants to become. On the other hand, rejection of these forms of masculinity will also deliver a double disadvantage as it involves both a stigmatised exclusion from dominant communities of masculinity practice (which even if it is chosen is likely to cause pain (Epstein *et al.* 2001; Parker 1996)) as well as a likely deficit in terms of physical capital (Shilling 1992).

Many dominant teenage femininities have elements that are constructed around a rejection of the physical, of powerful use of one's body, and in particular of organised school PE. This represents a localised view (or constellation of localised views), related to more globalised conceptions, of what it means to be a woman. PE has an important role in the development of the exaggerated femininity characteristic of many adolescent communities of practice because the practices of these communities are often constructed directly through the rejection of PE and sports and of strong, fit, bodily forms – despite the already feminised bodily uses and forms characteristic of secondary school girls' PE. Physical activity for girls, both inside and outside school, emphasises its effects on physical appearance and in particular the ability to match stereotypical standards of feminine beauty and slenderness; the activity is not really taken up for its own sake.[2] Thus PE is important to many dominant adolescent communities of femininity practice mainly because they are constructed in opposition to it, and this opposition is central to group members' construction of their femininity.

Entry to the community of practice as constructed in this way can very much be seen as a learning process. Younger girls do not reject PE or sporting activity (Epstein *et al.* 2001); this develops in adolescence as girls previously engaged by PE and sports gradually withdraw their interest or even attendance (Clarke and Cockburn 2002). As girls become more interested in participating in the local community of practice of adult femininity, they re-align their understanding of themselves so that they understand their bodies not so much as non-physical, but as physical in other, 'feminine' ways, sometimes even using this embodied femininity as a way of avoiding or rejecting participating in PE, for example by claiming that period pains make physical activity impossible on some days. At the same time, a growing awareness of their bodies makes girls more likely to reject PE because of the elements of bodily display involved (Williams and Bedward 2002). Girls who may still be physically bigger than their male peers start to reject the possibility of themselves being physically embodied as strong and fit; they embrace a softer, more physically helpless identity which is strongly related to wider notions of femininity in wider society and in the media (even 'Girl Power' seems more to do with feminised forms of dance and bodily display than with taking a powerful, particularly a physically powerful, stance towards life in general).

In this way, girls learn to reify the soft, feminine body as a marker of community membership; they develop a heterosexualised femininity in which opposition to PE and sport is related to physical weakness (and thus, in the longer term, to dependence on men to perform tasks that require bodily strength). This reification goes alongside strong boundary maintenance through calling into question the heterosexuality, as well as the femininity, of sporty girls. The refusal of this group to position themselves in opposition to PE calls into question their ability legitimately to participate in the community of practice of dominant adolescent femininity. Because this femininity is constructed as heterosexual, one way that community members can deal with the threat to group boundaries, posed by young women who value being fit and strong, is to define them as outsiders by calling their sexual orientation into question (Griffin 1992).

Because communities of femininity practice are local, the form of the female body that is reified at the boundary between full and peripheral or non-participation varies according to the positioning of the community of practice *vis-à-vis* PE and sports. This is particularly clear when we consider differences within the broad (minority) group of girls who are committed to PE and sports. For many of these young women, their strong and fit bodies are a source of contradictory pleasure and embarrassment; while building physical capital through sporting and athletic activities they are at the same time conscious that they may lose cultural and social capital as their bodies cease to conform to conventional dominant notions of femininity; they are concerned that their bodily forms will take them outside the dominant communities of femininity practice. Consequently, they may go to considerable lengths to demonstrate overt femininity, particularly in terms of their physical presentation, outside the PE and sporting arenas. Dewar (1990), for example, describes the operation of the boundary between two communities of practice in a Canadian university PE programme. Given the subject they were studying, all the female participants in this programme had retained a love of sport and a commitment to physical fitness. This was, however, a matter of degree, so that while, in this particular context, the dominant community of practice of femininity valued sports,

> at the same time the sports they participated in were the ones they viewed as suitable for women, or activities that did not tend to be seen as tough, aggressive or 'masculine'… It was important for them to be seen as feminine and athletic.
>
> (Dewar 1990: 93)

Achieving this athletic femininity involved taking part in a restricted range of sports, those that 'would not be viewed as compromising their femininity or heterosexuality' (Dewar 1990: 93), not going all-out for top performance and avoiding the development, and particularly the display, of an overtly athletic body. It was also maintained by drawing a boundary between themselves and the 'women jocks', who openly valued aggression and competitiveness in sport, and whose community of practice was built around an explicit rejection of the stereotypically feminine. These latter women were rendered marginal, or excluded from the dominant community of femininity practice, by their rejection of those students who 'play like girls' (85) and by their less stereotypically feminine mode of dress. Even within this context, then, the dominant community of practice of femininity is partly constructed through a rejection of a total commitment to sports and PE. As one student in Dewar's study, from the majority community, put it:

I think because we don't have our whole identity in what we're doing. You know, we have a lot more other interests. And too is that whole thing of masculinity and femininity I think ... For me I'm not going to go hanging on to my hockey stick wearing sweats all the time because it's not me. That's not what people's conceptions of what a girl is supposed to be and I don't feel good being that.

(Dewar 1990: 92)

In this case, the boundary of the dominant community of femininity practice was drawn in such a place that the loss of physical capital from remaining inside it was insignificant, and indeed the 'women jocks' are likely to have lost some of their potential to translate physical capital into social capital, because of their subordinate form of self-presentation. It is worth noting, however, that this was only possible because of the wider setting of the PE college, and that it may have had knock-on effects on local communities of masculinity practice; Sherlock (1987) points out that female students in PE colleges put pressure on their male colleagues to be more macho, in order to maintain the distinctions between masculinity and femininity practice in that context.

It is clear, then, that for secondary and higher education students, bodily uses and forms become reified markers of membership of localised masculinity and femininity practice, and that school and university PE contributes to this in a variety of ways. For younger children, however, bodies cannot function as reified markers of masculinity and femininity within PE, as the differences between male and female bodies, where they exist, are 'the wrong way round'; there is a period in which girls' bodies are bigger and stronger than those of boys. However, this does not mean that the physical and physical activity have no place in policing the boundaries between local communities of masculinity and femininity practice in younger children. Instead of the bodies produced by sports, the sports themselves become a reified mark of the distinction between the communities; unable to have the actual bodies of sportsmen, boys appropriate the sports, in this way laying claim to a form of symbolic body, or maybe the promise of a sporting body when they get older. Nespor (1997), for example, notes that girls, simply by virtue of their sex, are excluded by their male peers from even the possibility of being interested in or knowledgeable about sports; this would challenge the in many ways tenuous boundary between the communities:

... a public preoccupation with sports was an assertion that a boy was a member of an indisputably male domain, an assertion made plausible by the continuing dominance of men's sports in the popular media and by the boys' refusal to talk with girls about sports, even when girls knew demonstrably more about the subject than the boys did. Actual participation in organized team activity was much less important in establishing masculinity than constant talk about it, in part, perhaps, because girls were as likely to be as active and as proficient as boys in team sports such as basketball.

(Nespor 1997: 147)

The reified practices of both participation in and spectator enjoyment of PE and sport thus act as clear markers of the boundaries of a particular community of masculinity practice (Epstein *et al.* 2001).

Conclusion

PE and sports, particularly within the school context, are clearly important arenas for the development and sustaining of dominant communities of masculinity and femininity practices, through the production (through participation in or resistance to different forms of PE) of particular bodily forms which act as reified markers of community membership. That this takes place not just in schools but in wider society also allows the reverse to happen, with an interest in or knowledge about sports standing in place of the body, particularly as a badge of membership of communities of hegemonic masculinity practice. Because of PE's association with particular bodily forms and usages, and because these forms and usages are closely associated with specific local masculinities and femininities, young men and women will embrace or reject PE according to their positioning with regard to these local communities of masculinity and femininity practice. Whatever their stance, it is likely to have a knock-on effect on their ability to develop physical capital, or to develop it out of proportion to other forms of capital which may have a higher exchange value. This means that the differences in the bodily practices and forms expected of male and female students, and these students' differential reactions to them, have implications beyond PE lessons. A stereotypically feminine body is not a physically healthy body, while the forms of masculinity associated with sporting prowess are potentially psychologically and socially limiting.

Neither young men nor young women are benefited by the current situation. The relationship between bodily forms, PE and dominant communities of adolescent masculinity and femininity practice restricts the future possibilities of both boys and girls. In addressing this, PE has an important part to play, through opening up alternatives to dominant masculinities and femininities and the bodies and bodily practices that are associated with them (Gard, 2001). It cannot do this, however, unless wider social changes also take place. In particular, we need gradually to work within our own local communities of masculinity and femininity practice, and across the boundaries with those of our sons and daughters, to challenge some of the assumptions about male and female bodies that are played out in physical manifestations of masculinity and femininity. PE teachers and teacher educators need to work towards providing a more equal curriculum, and in particular to treating male and female bodies as equal and similar (as they are, after all, for most of compulsory schooling), so that PE does not itself perpetuate differential bodily forms and uses. At the same time, the rest of us need to work towards encouraging and making it possible for young people to take up these more equal opportunities more equally, and to support both boys and girls in treating a wide variety of bodily forms and approaches to exercise, sports and physical fitness as within the boundaries of their communities of masculinity and femininity practice.

Notes

1 I have reservations about the continued use of this term (Paechter 2002) and will
   endeavour to avoid it in this chapter, discussing the issues in terms of masculinity and
   femininity practices, as far as possible, though I am aware that this also perpetuates a
   problematic dichotomy. I am still working on this issue!
2 This is likely to be more the case for young white than for young black women; ideals of
   womanhood are different in different communities. African Caribbean girls are more
   likely to value strength and independence than white girls (Mirza 1992), and their conceptions of femininity are different (Weekes 1997) – they belong to different communities
   of femininity practice.

References

Bem, S. L. (1998) *An Unconventional Family*, New Haven: Yale University Press
Brown, D. and Rich, E. (2002) 'Gender positioning as pedagogical practice in teaching
   physical education' in Penney, D. (ed.), *Gender and Physical Education: Contemporary
   Issues and Future Directions*: 80–100, London: Routledge
Bryson, L. (1987) 'Sport and the maintenance of masculine hegemony', *Women's Studies
   International Forum,* 10, 4: 349–360
Butler, J. (1990) *Gender Trouble: Feminism and the Subversion of Identity,* London:
   Routledge
Butler, J. (1993) *Bodies that Matter: on the Discursive Limits of 'sex'*, London: Routledge
Carrington, B. and Wood, E. (1983) 'Body talk: images of sport in a multi-racial school',
   Multiracial Education, 11, 2: 29–38
Clarke, G. and Cockburn, C. (2002) '"Everybody's looking at you!": girls negotiating the
   "femininity deficit" they incur in physical education', *Women's Studies International
   Forum* 25, 6: 651–665
Connell, R. W. (1987) *Gender and Power*, Cambridge: Polity Press
Connell, R. W. (1995) *Masculinities*, Cambridge: Polity Press
Connell, R. W. (2002) *Gender*, Cambridge: Polity Press
Department for Education and Employment (1999) *Physical Education*, London:
   Department for Education and Employment/Qualifications and Curriculum Authority
Dewar, A. (1990) 'Oppression and privilege in physical education: struggles in the negoti-
   ation of gender in a university programme' in Kirk, D. and Tinning, R. (eds) *Physical
   Education, Curriculum and Culture*: 67–99, London: Falmer Press
Epstein, D., Kehily, M., Mac an Ghaill, M. and Redman, P. (2001) 'Boys and girls come out
   to play: making masculinities and femininities in school playgrounds', *Men and
   Masculinities*, 4, 2: 158–172
Fausto-Sterling, A. (1989) 'Life in the XY corral', *Women's Studies International Forum,*
   12, 3: 319–331
Fausto-Sterling, A. (1993). 'The five sexes: why male and female are not enough', *The
   Sciences*, March/April: 20–24
Fausto-Sterling, A. (2000) *Sexing the Body: Gender Politics and the Construction of
   Sexuality*, New York: Basic Books
Fitzclarence, L. and Hickey, C. (2001) 'Real footballers don't eat quiche: old narratives in
   new times', *Men and Masculinities*, 4, 2: 118–139
Gard, M. (2001) 'Dancing around the "problem" of boys and dance', *Discourse*, 22, 2:
   213–225

Griffin, P. (1992) 'Changing the game: homophobia, sexism and lesbians in sport', *Quest*, 44: 251–265

Halberstam, J. (1998) *Female Masculinity*, Durham: Duke University Press

Harris, J. and Penney, D. (2002) 'Gender, health and physical education' in Penney, D. (ed.), *Gender and Physical Education: Contemporary Issues and Future Directions*: 123–145, London: Routledge

Kessler, S. (1990) 'The medical construction of gender: case management of intersexed infants', *Signs: Journal of women in culture and society*, 16, 1: 3–26

Kessler, S. (1998) *Lessons from the Intersexed*, New Brunswick: Rutgers University Press

Kessler, S. and McKenna, W. (1978) *Gender: an Ethnomethodological Approach*, New York: John Wiley and Sons

Lave, J. and Wenger, E. (1991) *Situated Learning: Legitimate Peripheral Participation*, Cambridge: Cambridge University Press

Lloyd, B. and Duveen, G. (1992) *Gender Identities and Education: the Impact of Starting School*, Hemel Hempstead, Herts: Harvester Press

Mac an Ghaill, M. (1994) *The Making of Men: Masculinities, Sexualities and Schooling*, Buckingham: Open University Press

McRobbie, A. (1991) *Feminism and Youth Culture*, Basingstoke: Macmillan Education

Mirza, H. S. (1992) *Young, Female and Black*, London: Routledge

Namaste, V. K. (2000) *Invisible Lives: the Erasure of Transsexual and Transgendered People*, Chicago: University of Chicago Press

Nespor, J. (1997) *Tangled up in School*, Mahwah, New Jersey: Lawrence Erlbaum Associates

Paechter, C. F. (1998) *Educating the Other: Gender, Power and Schooling*, London: Falmer Press

Paechter, C. F. (2002) 'Physical education, gender identity and gender role: some thoughts'. Paper presented at the British Educational Research Association Seminar: Social Justice, Education and Identity, Institute of Education, London, March

Paechter, C. F. (2003) 'Power, bodies and identity: how different forms of physical education construct varying masculinities and femininities in secondary schools', *Sex Education* 3, 1: 47–59

Parker, A. (1996) 'The construction of masculinity within boys' physical education', *Gender and Education,* 8, 2: 141–157

Penney, D. (2002) 'Gendered policies' in Penney, D. (ed.) *Gender and Physical Education: Contemporary Issues and Future Directions*: 103–122, London: Routledge

Salisbury, J. and Jackson, D. (1996) *Challenging Macho Values: Practical Ways of Working with Adolescent Boys*, London: Falmer Press

Scraton, S. (1992) *Shaping Up to Womanhood: Gender and Girls' Physical Education*, Buckingham: Open University Press

Sherlock, J. (1987) 'Issues of masculinity and femininity in British physical education', *Women's Studies International Forum*, 10, 4: 443–451

Shilling, C. (1992) 'Schooling and the production of physical capital', *Discourse*, 13, 1: 1–19

Skelton, C. (2001). *Schooling the Boys: Masculinities and Primary Education*, Buckingham: Open University Press

Smith, C. and Lloyd, B. (1978) 'Maternal behavior and perceived sex of infant: revisited', *Child Development*, 49: 1263–1265

Walkerdine, V. and The Girls and Mathematics Unit (1989) *Counting Girls Out*, London: Virago

Weekes, D. (1997) 'Shades of Blackness: young Black female constructions of beauty' in Mirza, H. S. (ed.), *Black British Feminism: a Reader*: 113–126, London: Routledge

Wenger, E. (1998) *Communities of Practice: Learning, Meaning and Identity*, Cambridge: Cambridge University Press

Williams, A. and Bedward, J. (2002) 'Understanding girls' experience of physical education: relational analysis and situated learning' in Penney, D. (ed.), *Gender and Physical Education: Contemporary Issues and Future Directions*: 146–159, London: Routledge

Wright, J. (1996) 'The construction of complementarity in physical education', *Gender and Education*, 8, 1: 61–79

Chapter 9

Science education for social justice

Michael J. Reiss

Not another aim for science education?

The question as to the whole purpose of school science education has been widely debated in recent years in the science education community. Increasingly it has been agreed that school science education should serve the needs of the whole school population (e.g. Millar 1996). For this reason, scientific literacy, however this term is understood, is seen as the prime aim of science teaching (see also Layton *et al.* 1993; Irwin and Wynne 1996; Hodson 1998). Generally, scientific literacy is seen as being a vehicle to help tomorrow's adults to understand scientific issues (Gräber and Bolte 1997). In the UK, for example, it might be hoped that a good school science curriculum that took scientific literacy seriously would help pupils to understand the uncertainties around genetically modified foods, global warming and the radiation from mobile phones.

My contention here is that while the scientific literacy movement has much to commend it, it still offers too narrow a vision of what science education might achieve. I would like to explore what a science curriculum might be like that took as its premise the notion that science education should aim for social justice. This is not to suggest that this should be the only aim of school science; rather, that it is an aim that has been very greatly underplayed. I aim to build on the work of a number of authors including Longbottom and Butler (1999), Longbottom (1999), Rodriguez (1998) and Barton (1998, 2001), all of whom have extended the debate about the aims of school science. Situating science education within a framework of social justice brings it alongside certain other components of the curriculum. For too long the science education debate has been conducted without reference to the wider aims of schooling.

John Longbottom explores the nature of science teaching if science education is justified in terms of socio-political goals. He argues that science education should 'contribute to the advancement of democracy, and so improve the quality of human existence' (Longbottom 1999: 4). Alberto Rodriguez explores the potential of science education to serve as a platform for resistance – a notion only recently beginning to be explored in science education writing, though well established in, for example, anti-racist education (Ahmed *et al.* 1998). Angie Barton, who has worked with homeless children in the USA to develop more appropriate science learning, has shown that active participation in science lessons, and real learning about science, take place when children believe that their work can effect improvements for themselves, their friends and their families.

The nature of scientific knowledge

But first I need to address the argument that scientific knowledge is value-free and that, by extension, science education should be too. This, of course, is a two-part argument. Even if it were accepted that scientific knowledge is value-free, it would not necessarily follow that science education is too, just as even if some (or perhaps all) aspects of mathematics are value-free, this does not mean that there are no such things as feminist and/or anti-racist mathematics education.

In fact, the issue as to the nature of scientific knowledge, including the extent to which it is or is not value-free, is still a topic of heated debate among philosophers of science and science educators (e.g. Reiss 1993; Ogborn 1995; Chalmers 1999; Donnelly 2002). Side-stepping this particular debate, it can be asserted that, even if we accept a characterisation of science as open-minded, universalist, disinterested and communal (Merton 1973), all scientific knowledge is formulated within particular social contexts (e.g. Fuller 1997). At the very least this means that the topics on which scientists work – and so the subject matter of science itself – to some extent reflect the interests, motivations and aspirations both of the scientists that carry out such work and of those who fund them. There is no doubt that the majority, almost certainly the great majority, of the funding provided for scientists, both currently and for some considerable time past, has been provided with the hope/expectation that particular applied ends will be met. These might be the production of a new vaccine, the development of a new variety of crop, the synthesis of a new chemical dye, the construction of a better missile detection system, and so on.

The point is that it can be argued that values are inevitably and inexorably conflated with science in most cases. Both the scientists and those who fund them hope that production of a new vaccine will lead to more lives being saved (presumed to be a good thing), that the development of a new variety of crop will lead to increased food yields (presumed to be a good thing), that the synthesis of a new chemical dye will lead to greater cash flows, increased profits, improved customer satisfaction or increased employment (all presumed to be good things), that the construction of a better missile detection system will lead to increased military security (presumed to be a good thing) and so on. In each of these cases, the science is carried out for a purpose. Purposes can be judged normatively; that is they may be good or bad. Indeed, just beginning to spell out some of the intended or presumed goods (increased crop yields, increased military security, etc.) alerts us to the fact that perhaps there are other ways of meeting these ends or, indeed, that perhaps these ends are not unquestionably the goods that may have been assumed (Reiss 1999).

It can further be argued that the separation of science from values in general, and ethical considerations in particular, is a relatively recent, Western and secular phenomenon (cf. Cobern 1998; Ogunniyi *et al.* 1995; Haidar 1997). In particular, Islamic science has been described as a science whose processes and methodologies incorporate the spirit of Islamic values (Sardar 1989). Early classifications of Islamic science included metaphysics, within which was knowledge of non-corporeal beings, leading finally to the knowledge of the Truth, that is, of God, one of whose names is the Truth (Nasr 1987). To this day Islamic science 'takes upon a more holistic human-centred approach that is grounded in values that promote social justice, public welfare and responsibility towards the environment' (Loo 1996: 285).

Social justice in the science classroom

I mostly wish to concentrate on how school science education might contribute to promoting justice outside the classroom – i.e. in the wider world. But first it is worth mentioning that, as every teacher knows, pupils differ in all sorts of ways. They arrive at school with different ways in which they prefer to learn and learn best; they arrive knowing different amounts as a result of their lives to date; and they arrive expecting to learn different amounts that day (Reiss 2000a).

Recent years have shown a greater acknowledgement within professional associations, textbook authors, publishers, awarding bodies, individual teachers and other science education professionals of the diversity among pupils that exists in science lessons as in all subjects (Thorp *et al.* 1994; Cobern 1996; Guzzetti and Williams 1996). No longer is it implicitly assumed, for instance, that physics is an activity undertaken predominantly by white middle-class males interested chiefly in car acceleration and the motion of cricket balls. More generally, a greater number of teachers realise that the content of what they teach and the way they teach can turn pupils on to science or off it.

What is a teacher of science to do faced with this pupil diversity? To what extent are different curricula, resources and teaching approaches needed for different categories of pupils? Should, for example, the same science resources be provided for a pupil with a physical disability (such as severe sight impairment) and a pupil without such a disability? Surely not. But should both pupils receive exactly the same science curriculum? The question is a harder one. And what of girls and boys? Should they receive identical teaching approaches? The issue is hotly contested.

Even when answers to such questions are clear, much remains to be done. In the UK, for example, differences in educational attainments in science and other subjects are still strongly related to class and economic position (Croxford 1997; Robinson and White 1997; Strand 1999) while certain pupils from certain ethnic backgrounds continue to underperform (Gillborn and Gipps 1996). Whereas gender inequalities in the UK are considerably less than in many other countries (Harding and McGregor 1995), girls continue to be several times less likely than boys to continue with the physical sciences once they have the option, while boys are more likely than girls to leave school with no qualifications.

Social justice beyond the classroom through science education

Despite the widespread tendency in just about all countries to keep on lengthening the period of full-time education, students in such full-time education still spend most of their hours outside school, college or university and there comes the time eventually when most people (academics and teachers excepted) leave these formal educational institutions. How might school science lessons prepare people for social justice beyond the science classroom?

Gaell Hildebrand (2001) has argued in favour of what she terms 'critical activism' in science education. She urges that there should be both participation in science (doing science) and participation in debates about science (challenging science). I agree. It is in doing science that pupils better understand how scientific knowledge is formed. It is in enabling pupils critically to discuss scientific issues that they not only become better able to understand the scope of science but more able to appreciate its potential for good and bad.

For we live, surely, in an age when the power of science has never been more manifest. At the same time it is fortunate that, while many secondary students, and their parents before them, have unhappy memories of much of their school science education, both students and parents almost universally consider science education to be important. In the UK, for example, science is seen as a prestigious subject and valued for the understanding it offers (Osborne and Collins 2000; Reiss 2000b).

To illustrate more concretely what science education for social justice beyond the classroom might consist of, here are three instances:

- food – for 8- to 11-year-olds
- nuclear power – for 12- to 14-year-olds
- individual differences – for 15- to 16-year-olds.

In each case suggestions for classroom activities are given with outline teacher notes in square brackets alongside.

Food

Here are some possible classroom activities for pupils aged 8 to 11 to tackle when learning about food.

- Find out about the different ways in which different cultures preserve food (e.g. salting, drying, pickling, curing, cooking, freezing, canning, making into jam). Research jam recipes and try making jam. What happens if the jam ends up too watery or is made without adding sugar? [All cultures have ways of preserving foods. There is no universal 'best' way. Suitable ways depend on such things as climate, availability of resources and custom. Such multi-cultural activities should include traditional English activities – hence jam making. It isn't easy to make jam that won't go mouldy!]

- List different foods eaten by pupils in the class. Find out where these foods come from (by looking at packets, asking parents, etc.) and produce a world map of where our food is grown. [Some foods are produced locally; others far away. Obtaining all our food locally has benefits in terms of reducing the cost (financial and environmental) of transport but our diets would be less diverse and food exports are important for many countries.]
- Carry out a survey to see how much of the cooking is done by different people in a family. Are all families the same? [In many cultures cooking is a gender-specific activity but the extent to which this is the case varies considerably between cultures and across the generations. Some instances of cooking – e.g. barbecues – may show gender reversal.]
- Keep food diaries to record which foods are eaten at what times of the day. [Can relate to balanced diets. Some pupils may need to be helped to avoid making culturally-specific judgements about what constitutes an inappropriate diet.]
- Make both unleavened and leavened 'breads'. Investigate factors that affect how much leavened bread rises. [A classic primary science activity that links with religious education.]
- Research what leads to famines. What caused the Irish potato famine of 1845–9? [In one sense it was the small organism *Phytophthera infestans* (rather like a fungus). Out of a population of nine million people, over a million starved to death and about one and a half million emigrated to the USA. However, throughout these years Irish farmers continued successfully to produce cereals, cattle, pigs, eggs and butter. Enough food was produced to ensure that no one in Ireland needed to starve. Farmers had to export these crops to England to get the money they needed to pay the rents they 'owed' their English landlords. Farmers who failed to export their produce were evicted from their farms, and had their cottages razed to the ground.]
- Examine the place of food in different religious festivals (e.g. Eid, the Passover, Christmas, the Chinese New Year). [Foods have both literal and symbolic worth.]
- Find out what is meant by organic food. Why do people buy it? [Foods produced without artificial fertilisers and pesticides. Reasons include fears over human health, a wish for food to be more natural and concerns over animal welfare.]

Nuclear power

Here are some possible classroom activities for pupils aged twelve to fourteen to tackle when learning about nuclear power.

- Research the roles played by such scientists as Henri Becquerel, Ernest Rutherford, Marie Curie and Lise Meitner. [Lise Meitner played a crucial role in the discovery of nuclear fission but was not awarded the Nobel Prize with Otto Hahn in 1944 for this research.]
- Plot a map of the distribution of nuclear power stations around the globe and suggest reasons for the results observed. [Nuclear power stations are expensive to build and require considerable engineering expertise. In some countries public support for new nuclear power stations is lacking.]
- Plot graphs of the decrease in radioactivity in vegetation in Cumbria in the years after Chernobyl and compare the results with government predictions. [It is taking orders of magnitudes longer for the radioactive levels to return to safe levels than had been predicted. Science is not always a certain subject.]
- Explain how carbon dioxide emissions from electricity-producing stations in France fell by two-thirds from 1980 to 1987. [Expansion of the French nuclear power industry. Over two-thirds of French electricity is generated in this way, a higher percentage than in any other country.]
- Write to both pro- and anti-nuclear power organisations asking them the same specific questions, e.g. 'How safe is nuclear power?' and 'How important is nuclear power for electricity generation?' [Helps pupils to consider the significance of sources of scientific knowledge and enables them to consider the extent to which such knowledge is value-free.]
- Examine the medical evidence for and against an increase in the incidence of leukaemia around certain nuclear power stations. [Controversial. Can help students to appreciate how difficult it may be to see if technologies are safe or not. In addition, to what should the safety of nuclear power stations be compared?]
- Design and use a questionnaire to investigate fellow pupils' knowledge of and attitudes towards nuclear power. [A good learning experience, developing and reinforcing knowledge about nuclear power. The work on attitudes can introduce pupils in science lessons to both quantitative and qualitative approaches to the gathering and interpretation of data.]
- Role-play a Cabinet meeting trying to decide whether to extend a country's nuclear power programme or to scrap it. [Role plays don't appeal to all teachers and pupils and can polarise arguments. Alternatives include discussion in small groups. Done well, though, role plays can enhance empathy and understanding of the position of others, especially if one role-plays a view different from one's own. Should be followed by de-briefing.]
- Write an imaginary letter from one of the service persons or indigenous people on test islands such as Bikini Atoll. [Too little writing in science is in such

a genre. Also helps pupils realise that issues of sickness and death resulting from nuclear explosions aren't restricted to Japan in the Second World War. Note the controversy over use of depleted uranium shells in the Gulf War.]

Individual differences

Here are two possible areas for students aged fifteen to sixteen to study, both to do with learning about individual differences between people. In each case the idea is that students would research the issue using information from books, articles and the Internet, draw on their own life experiences and then be aided by their teachers in analysing and discussing the issues. One outcome might be a long (say, 1,000-word) report of the sort that is currently uncommon in science education for students in this age group to produce.

•   Is there a genetic basis to differences between people in their intelligence (based on Reiss 2000c)?

   [Many people argue that the very notion of a simple measure of 'intelligence' is deeply problematic: some question the very concept of intelligence; some argue that there are intelligences rather than intelligence; some admit the existence of intelligence but maintain that the problems in measuring it are insurmountable. Then there are arguments that, while they accept the notion of simple measures of intelligence, deny the academic worth of research programmes concerned with the genetics of intelligence. Such arguments may point out the extent to which we live in an age that inappropriately reifies the gene, or assert that no methodology can untangle the relative contributions made by the genes and the environments in which each of us has lived. Then there are the arguments from history. Attempts by previous generations, and more recently, to measure intelligence have all too often led to unwarranted prejudice and discrimination against black people, women, working-class people and others.

   Even if one accepts that the notion of intelligence has meaning and that there may be an inherited component to it, possible reasons can be suggested for why it might be preferable for us not to know about the genetics of intelligence. Suppose, for example, the results of such research show, appear to show or are widely taken as showing that there is an inherited component to intelligence with consistent and statistically significant (even if minor) differences between the average intelligences of different racial groups. Suppose further that these racial differences correlate (at least on average) with the possession of certain alleles. Might not such knowledge lead, on the one side (those with high intelligence), to racism or greed (the 'It's not worth educating them' viewpoint) and on the other side (those with low intelligence) to people becoming disheartened, envious or bitter ('However hard I work, I'm not going to pass my exams/get a well-paid job')?]

- Why do females and males differ in behaviour?

  [Students could start by looking at, for example, clothing or the way people carry objects such as books. Are there (i) absolute differences (i.e. no overlap between the behaviours of females and males); (ii) differences between the average behaviours of females and males (e.g. what percentage of each population wears trousers or carries books held across their chest?); (iii) no differences between females and males?

  Students could then consider why there are or are not differences in such behaviours, looking at the importance of cultural expectations (e.g. how one is brought up by one's parents, how one's peers would react if one suddenly behaved differently).

  Students could then go on to look at generalisations about males and females, for example with regard to which sex is more athletic, which more aggressive, which more caring and which more interested in sex? Are there absolute differences or are there only differences on average? Where do such differences, if they occur, come from? Are some differences biological in the narrow sense? Are others cultural? What role do genes, hormones, upbringing, the media and so on play? How much choice does each of us have as an individual about how we behave? Are we autonomous beings or the prisoners of our genes and environment?]

What would it mean for social justice to be sought through science education and should it be?

The above examples illustrate what science classrooms might perhaps look and feel like if they had the pursuit of social justice as their aim. But what, more fundamentally, would it mean for social justice to be sought through school science, and should it be?

Social justice is about the right treatment of others (what Gewirtz (1998) characterises as the relational dimension of social justice) and the fair distribution of resources or opportunities (the distributional dimension). Of course, considerable disagreement exists about what precisely counts as right treatment and a fair distribution of resources. For example, some people accept that an unequal distribution of certain resources may be fair provided certain other criteria are satisfied (e.g. the resources are purchased with money earned, inherited or obtained in some other socially sanctioned way – such as gambling in some, but not all, cultures). At the other extreme, it can be argued that we should ensure either that all resources are distributed equally or that all people have what they need. Such distributions might be achieved through legislative coercion, social customs or altruism on the part of those who would otherwise end up with more than average.

One would not expect school science lessons to go into much depth attempting to resolve such debates held among ethicists. However, these fundamental questions are perfectly accessible to even quite young children and good school science not only provides but requires opportunities for debates about such issues as the fair distribution of resources like food, clean water and energy.

Traditionally, ethical questions concerning justice have concentrated mainly upon actions that take place between people at one point in time. In recent decades, however, these considerations have widened in scope in two important ways. First, intergenerational issues are recognised as being of importance (e.g. Cooper and Palmer 1995). Second, interspecific issues are now increasingly taken into account (e.g. Rachels 1991). These issues go to the heart of 'Who is my neighbour?' (Reiss, 2003).

Interspecific issues are of obvious importance when considering biotechnology and ecological questions. Put at its starkest, is it sufficient only to consider humans or do other species need also to be taken into account? Consider, for example, the use of new practices (such as the use of growth promoters or embryo transfer) to increase the productivity of farm animals. An increasing number of people feel that the effects of such new practices on the farm animals need to be considered as at least part of the ethical equation before reaching a conclusion. This is not, of course, necessarily to accept that the interests of non-humans are equal to those of humans. While some people do argue that this is the case, others accept that although non-humans have interests these are generally less morally significant than those of humans.

Accepting that interspecific issues need to be considered leads one to ask 'How?'. Need we only consider animal suffering? For example, would it be right to produce, whether by conventional breeding or modern biotechnology, a pig unable to detect pain and unresponsive to other pigs (Reiss 2002)? Such a pig would not be able to suffer and its use might well lead to significant productivity gains: it might, for example, be possible to keep it at very high stocking densities. Someone arguing that such a course of action would be wrong would not be able to argue thus on the grounds of animal suffering. Other criteria would have to be invoked. It might be argued that such a course of action would be disrespectful to pigs or that it would involve treating them only as means to human ends and not, even to a limited extent, as ends in themselves. More generally, the whole environmental movement has broadened its focus to non-sentient organisms (e.g. plants) and to even broader considerations (e.g. ecosystems, wildernesses).

Intergenerational as well as interspecific considerations may need to be taken into account. Nowadays we are more aware of the possibility that our actions may affect not only those a long way away from us in space (e.g. acid rain produced in one country falling in another) but also those a long way away from us in time (e.g. increasing atmospheric carbon dioxide levels may alter the climate for generations to come). Human nature being what it is, it is all too easy to forget the interests of those a long way away from ourselves. Accordingly, a conscious effort needs to be made so that we think about the consequences of our actions not only for those alive today and living near us, about whom it is easiest to be most concerned.

These issues lead more generally to the question of what might actually be the aims of teaching ethics in science, for there are other valid aims in addition to striving for greater justice. Based on Davis (1999), at least four aims can be suggested (Reiss 1999).

First, teaching ethics in science might intend to heighten the ethical *sensitivity* of participants. For example, a chemistry teacher might encourage their students to think of what happens to household cleaners when they are poured down the sink.

Second, teaching ethics in science might increase the ethical *knowledge* of students. The arguments in favour of this are much the same as the arguments in favour of teaching any knowledge – in part that such knowledge is intrinsically worth possessing, in part that possession of such knowledge has useful consequences. For example, appropriate teaching about the issue of rights might help students to distinguish between legal and moral rights and to understand something of the connections between rights and duties.

Third, teaching ethics in science might improve the ethical *judgement* of students. As Davis, writing about students at university, puts it:

> The course might, that is, try to increase the likelihood that students who apply what they know about ethics to a decision they recognize as ethical will get the right answer. All university courses teach judgement of one sort or another. Most find that discussing how to apply general principles helps students to apply those principles better; many also find that giving students practice in applying them helps too. Cases are an opportunity to exercise judgement. The student who has had to decide how to resolve an ethics case is better equipped to decide a case of that kind than one who has never thought about the subject.
> (164–5)

Fourth, and perhaps most ambitiously, teaching ethics in science might make students *better people* in the sense of making them more virtuous or otherwise more likely to implement normatively right choices. For example, a unit on renewable and non-renewable resources might lead students to re-use and recycle materials more. There is, within the field of moral education, an enormous literature both on ways of teaching people to 'be good' and on evaluating how efficacious such attempts are (e.g. Wilson 1990; Carr 1991; Noddings 1992). Here it suffices to note that while care needs to be taken to distinguish between moral education and moral indoctrination, there is considerable evidence that moral education programmes can achieve intended and appropriate results (e.g. Straughan 1988; Bebeau *et al.* 1999).

Conclusions

Much school science education has been narrow in its aims, all too often serving only to train those in full-time education for possible science studies at the next age level. The scientific discourse is a tremendously powerful one and pupils and students need to be helped to examine it critically. A science education that takes seriously the search for social justice as one of its aims would be a richer education and an education more likely to satisfy students interested in fairness and human concerns. It would, though, be an education that would make new demands on science teachers in terms of aims and pedagogy.

References

Ahmed, J., Gulam, W. A. and Hapeshi, D. (1998) 'Brickbats, survival and resistance', *Multicultural Teaching*, 16, 3: 7–14

Barton, A. C. (1998) 'Teaching science with homeless children: pedagogy, representation, and identity', *Journal of Research in Science Teaching*, 35: 379–394

Barton, A. C. (2001) 'Science education in urban settings: seeking new ways of praxis through critical ethnography', *Journal of Research in Science Teaching*, 38: 899–917

Bebeau, M. J., Rest, J. R. and Narvaez, D. (1999) 'Beyond the promise: a perspective on research in moral education', *Educational Researcher*, 28, 4: 18–26

Carr, D. (1991) *Educating the Virtues: an Essay on the Philosophical Psychology of Moral Development and Education*, London: Routledge

Chalmers, A. F. (1999) *What is this Thing Called Science?*, 3rd edn, Buckingham: Open University Press

Cobern, W. W. (1996) 'Constructivism and non-western science education research', *International Journal of Science Education*, 18: 295–310

Cobern, W. W. (ed.) (1998) *Socio-cultural Perspectives on Science Education: an International Dialogue*, Dordrecht: Kluwer

Cooper, D. E. and Palmer, J. A. (eds) (1995) *Just Environments: Intergenerational, International and Interspecies Issues*, London: Routledge

Croxford, L. (1997) 'Participation in science subjects: the effect of the Scottish curriculum framework', *Research Papers in Education*, 12: 69–89

Davis, M. (1999) *Ethics and the University*, London: Routledge

Donnelly, J. F. (2002) 'Instrumentality, hermeneutics and the place of science in the school curriculum', *Science and Education*, 11: 135–153

Fuller, S. (1997) *Science*, Buckingham: Open University Press

Gewirtz, S. (1998) 'Conceptualizing social justice in education: mapping the territory', *Journal of Education Policy*, 13: 469–484

Gillborn, D. and Gipps. C. (1996) *Recent Research on the Achievements of Ethnic Minority Pupils*, London: HMSO

Gräber, W. and Bolte, C. (eds) (1997) *Scientific Literacy: an International Symposium IPN 154*, Kiel: Institut für die Pädagogik der Naturwissenschaften an der Universitität Kiel

Guzzetti, B. J. and Williams, W. O. (1996) 'Gender, text and discussion: examining intellectual safety in the science classroom', *Journal of Research in Science Teaching*, 33: 5–20

Haidar, A. H. (1997) 'Arab prospective science teachers' world view: presuppositions towards nature', *International Journal of Science Teaching*, 19: 1,093–1,109

Harding, S. and McGregor, E. (1995) *The Gender Dimension of Science and Technology*, Paris: UNESCO

Hildebrand, G. M. (2001) 'Con/testing learning models'. Conference paper presented at the Annual Meeting of the National Association for Research in Science Teaching, St Louis, 25–28 March

Hodson, D. (1998) *Teaching and Learning Science: Towards a Personalized Approach*, Buckingham: Open University Press

Irwin, A. and Wynne, B. (eds) (1996) *Misunderstanding Science? The Public Reconstruction of Science and Technology*, Cambridge: Cambridge University Press

Layton, D., Jenkins, E., Macgill, S. and Davey, A. (1993) *Inarticulate science? Perspectives on the Public Understanding of Science and Some Implications for Science Education*, Driffield: Studies in Education

Longbottom, J. (1999) 'Reconceptualising science education'. Conference paper, Second International Conference of the European Science Education Research Association, Kiel, 31 August–4 September

Longbottom, J. E. and Butler, P. H. (1999) 'Why teach science? Setting rational goals for science education', *Science Education*, 83: 473–492

Loo, S. P. (1996) 'The four horsemen of Islamic science: a critical analysis', *International Journal of Science Education*, 18: 285–294

Merton, R. (1973) *The Sociology of Science*, Chicago, IL: University of Chicago Press

Millar, R. (1996) 'Towards a science curriculum for public understanding', *School Science Review*, 77, 280: 7–18

Nasr, S. H. (1987) *Science and civilisation in Islam,* 2nd edn, Cambridge: Islamic Texts Society

Noddings, N. (1992) *The Challenge to Schools: an Alternative Approach to Education*, New York: Teachers College Press

Ogunniyi, M., Jegede, O., Ogawa, M., Yandila, C. and Oladele, F. (1995) 'Nature of world view presuppositions among science teachers in Botswana, Indonesia, Japan, Nigeria, and Philippines', *Journal of Research in Science Teaching*, 32: 817–831

Ogborn, J. (1995) 'Recovering reality', *Studies in Science Education*, 25: 3–38

Osborne, J. and Collins, S. (2000) *Pupils' and Parents' Views of the School Science Curriculum: a Study funded by the Wellcome Trust*, London: King's College London

Rachels, J. (1991) *Created from Animals: the Moral Implications of Darwinism*, Oxford: Oxford University Press

Reiss, M. J. (1993) *Science Education for a Pluralist Society*, Milton Keynes: Open University Press

Reiss, M. J. (1999) 'Teaching ethics in science', *Studies in Science Education* 34: 115–140

Reiss, M. J. (2000a) 'Science in society or society in science?' in Warwick, P. and Sparks Linfield, R. (eds), *Science 3–13: the Past, the Present and Possible Futures*: 118–129, London: RoutledgeFalmer

Reiss, M. J. (2000b) *Understanding Science Lessons: Five Years of Science Teaching*, Buckingham: Open University Press

Reiss, M. J. (2000c) 'The ethics of genetic research on intelligence', *Bioethics*, 14: 1–15

Reiss, M. J. (2002) 'Introduction to ethics and bioethics', in Bryant, J. A., Baggott-Lavelle, L. M. and Searle, J. F. (eds), *Bioethics for Scientists*: 3–17, New York: Wiley Liss

Reiss, M. J. (2003) 'How we reach ethical conclusions' in Levinson, R. and Reiss, M. J. (eds), *Understanding Bioethics: De-coding the Problems*, London: RoutledgeFalmer

Robinson, P. and White, P. (1997) *Participation in Post-compulsory Education*, Twickenham: Centre for Education and Employment Research, School of Education, Brunel University

Rodriguez, A. J. (1998) 'What is (should be) researcher's role in terms of agency? A question for the 21st century', *Journal of Research in Science Teaching*, 35: 963–965

Sardar, Z. (1989) *Explorations in Islamic Science*, London: Mansell

Strand, S. (1999) 'Ethnic group, sex and economic disadvantage: associations with pupils' educational progress from Baseline to the end of Key Stage 1', *British Educational Research Journal*, 25: 179–202

Straughan, R. (1988) *Can We Teach Children to be Good? Basic Issues in Moral, Personal and Social Education, 2nd edn*, Milton Keynes: Open University Press

Thorp, S., Deshpande, P. and Edwards, C. (eds) (1994) *Race, Equality and Science Teaching*, Hatfield: ASE

Wilson, J. (1990) *A New Introduction to Moral Education*, London: Cassell

Chapter 10

The development of young children's ethnic identities

Implications for early years practice

Paul Connolly

Introduction

There is now a colossal research literature on the development of racial prejudice among young children (for overviews see Milner 1983; Aboud 1988). Studies first pioneered in the 1920s and 1930s and repeated in a variety of formats since then have consistently shown that children have the capacity to recognise racial differences and to develop negative attitudes and prejudices towards certain groups from the age of three onwards. While this body of work has undoubtedly played an important role in highlighting the reality of racism in the lives of young children, it has attracted a significant amount of criticism over recent years most notably from a number of social psychologists (Billig 1985, 1987; Reicher 1986; Potter and Weatherall 1987; Condor 1988) and, more recently, sociologists (Troyna and Hatcher 1992; Connolly 1996, 2001; Van Ausdale and Feagin 1996, 2001). A central focus of the criticism has been the dominance of structured, experimental designs within the research to date and their tendency to encourage rather crude and simplistic understandings of the nature and influence of 'race' in young children's lives.

Moreover, in failing to study young children's behaviour within its 'natural settings', it has been argued that the research has tended to reify the concept of 'race'. Thus rather than studying the particular processes that encourage children to develop and reproduce racial categories, those categories have often simply been taken for granted (Reicher 1986; Condor 1988). As a consequence, as Billig (1985, 1987) has argued, such work has also tended to reproduce the view that racial prejudice is natural and inevitable. Without an understanding of social context, much of the research has tended to explain the development of young children's racial prejudices as an inevitable result of normal perceptual processes of categorisation. What is needed instead, Billig contends, is for this way of thinking to be turned on its head. Thus rather than examining how people's 'natural' tendency to categorise leads on to racism, researchers should be focusing on how racism, and the particular structures and relations associated with it, lead people to then categorise others in certain ways. This is precisely what some researchers have recently begun to do (see Holmes 1995; Van Ausdale and Feagin 1996, 2001;

Connolly 1998). Using qualitative, ethnographic methods they have attempted to problematise the notion of 'race' and draw attention to the specific ways in which it is constructed and re-constructed by young children in the development of racial boundaries and identities. In doing so, such work has also drawn attention to the complex, context-specific and contradictory nature of racism in young children's social worlds.

However, another problem with this existing body of research that has attracted less attention to date has been its tendency to focus on physical rather than cultural markers of difference. Overwhelmingly, the research has tended to focus on children's awareness of and attitudes towards groups defined primarily in terms of skin colour. At present there are, literally, only a handful of studies that have attempted to explore young children's ethnic identities and prejudice in contexts where difference is marked by cultural factors rather than skin colour (see Jahoda and Harrison 1975; Cairns *et al.* 1980; McWhirter and Gamble 1982; Andereck 1992; Bar-Tal 1996; Royle *et al.* 1999).

This represents an important limitation in our understanding, especially given the shifts that have taken place over recent decades in popular racist discourses. The rise of what Barker (1981) originally termed the 'new racism' has tended to replace crude biological arguments with ones that focus on cultural factors in an attempt to construct difference. This can be seen most notably in relation to the growing centrality of nationalism and religion in contemporary discourses on 'race' (see also Reeves 1983; Donald and Rattansi 1992; Anthias and Yuval-Davis 1992; Gillborn 1995; Cohen 1999). As Short and Carrington (1996, 1999) have argued, such developments have significant implications for how racism can be most effectively addressed through education. Their own research on children in their middle years (aged 8 to 11) has shown that they are already developing an awareness of this new racism and appropriating and using it in relation to their own perceptions of difference. As Short and Carrington conclude from this, a need therefore exists for schools to complement conventional anti-racist education with a critical multiculturalism that can help children to reflect upon their attitudes and misconceptions and to understand the open, fluid and complex nature of cultural identities (see also Gillborn 1995, 1996; Kinchloe and Steinberg 1997; May 1999).

This chapter aims to complement the work of Short and Carrington and others by extending the focus to children in their early years and examining their awareness of cultural markers of difference and how these tend to inform their own ethnic identities and also their attitudes towards others. It draws upon data from two separate studies that I have recently directed (see Connolly *et al.* 2002; Connolly and Healy 2003) that have focused on the development of ethnic awareness and prejudice among young Catholic and Protestant children in Northern Ireland. As will be demonstrated, this provides a valuable case study, given the complex ways in which ethnic identities and divisions in Northern Ireland are formed so strongly in the absence of any physical markers. Following an outline and discussion of the main findings, the chapter will conclude with a consideration of the implications of these findings for challenging young children's racial and ethnic prejudices more generally.

Conceptualising 'race' and ethnicity

Before discussing the two studies and the data arising from them, it is important first to clarify how the concepts of 'race' and ethnicity are being used in this chapter and what the relationship is between them. This is particularly important given the problems associated with previous research on racial prejudice and young children and its tendency to reify the concept of 'race' as highlighted above. For the purposes of this chapter, and in line with Jenkins (1997), racism and the racial categorisations that are associated with it are to be understood as a particular form of the broader social phenomenon of ethnicity. In this sense ethnicity, and more specifically the concept of ethnic group, is usefully defined as follows:

> An ethnic group is not one because of the degree of measurable or observable difference from other groups; it is an ethnic group, on the contrary, because the people in it and the people out of it know that it is one; because both the *ins* and the *outs* talk, feel, and act as if it were a separate group. This is possible only if there are ways of telling who belongs to the group and who does not, and if a person learns early, deeply, and usually irrevocably to what group [he or she] belongs. If it is easy to resign from the group, it is not truly an ethnic group.
>
> (Everett Hughes 1994: 91, quoted in Jenkins 1997: 10)

As can be seen, ethnic groups are not objectively defined. Rather, they are socially constructed through a process that identifies and gives significance to a number of particular traits (whether physical and/or cultural) and uses these as a basis upon which to decide group membership. Racism manifests itself specifically when physical characteristics are signified and used as a means of distinguishing between groups. Such an approach to conceptualising 'race' has three main advantages. First it stresses the socially constructed nature of 'race' and avoids the tendency to reify the concept. In this sense there is nothing natural or inevitable about the identification and development of racial groups. Rather, treating 'race' as a specific form of ethnicity encourages an analysis of the particular social contexts and processes that have given rise to certain groups identifying and racially categorising others. Second, in making use of Barth's (1969) concept of 'boundary maintenance' that has come to underpin modern approaches to the study of ethnicity, it also allows a recognition of the fact that racial groups and identities are not static and fixed but are the product of negotiation and struggle and are likely to change between one context and the next and over time. Finally, this approach provides the analytical space for understanding how constructions of 'race' and the racialisation of particular groups within the population are likely to draw upon a combination of social markers, including physical but also, crucially, cultural ones. This, in turn, provides the basis for a more comprehensive analysis of what has been termed the new racism as discussed earlier.

As Jenkins (1997) has argued, however, conceptualising 'race' as a particular element of the broader social phenomenon of ethnicity in this way does not imply that 'race' and ethnicity are simply inter-changeable concepts that mean the same thing. The consequences of evoking and employing racial markers of difference – because of their emphasis on biologically-rooted and fixed differences in innate ability and temperament – tend to result in particular forms of inter-group relations based upon inequality, dominance and exploitation. While relations between particular ethnic groups may also take this form, they need not inevitably do so. In fact it is quite possible for relations between particular ethnic groups to be free from conflict or, even if conflict is a characteristic of these relationships, this need not inevitably lead onto inequalities and patterns of domination and exploitation. Moreover, by the very fact that racial signifiers imply innate biological differences, people are much more likely to be ascribed racial group membership and will often have very limited opportunities to avoid or resist this ascription. In contrast, membership of ethnic groups marked by cultural factors is, by definition, likely to present greater opportunities for individuals to re-define themselves and successfully cross group boundaries, at least in theory.

With these definitions in place, the remainder of the chapter will now examine some of the findings arising from the two case studies. Following a brief outline of the two studies, the chapter will attempt to draw out three main themes arising from these: the ways in which ethnicity first tends to manifest itself in young children's lives; the consequent development of children's ethnic awareness and identities with age; and children's increasing social competence in understanding and reproducing ethnic identities and prejudices. The implications of these three themes for practice in the early years will then be considered.

Methodology

Before discussing the details of the two case studies, a little detail regarding the background to the current situation in Northern Ireland is necessary. Since the island of Ireland was partitioned in the early 1920s and the Northern Ireland state created, the region has experienced sustained, and at times extremely violent, ethnic division and conflict. At its most basic level it is a conflict between two main ethnic groups: Protestants who are the majority in Northern Ireland and tend to regard themselves as British; and Catholics who are the minority and tend to see themselves as Irish. Ultimately, it is a conflict about nationality with the majority of Protestants wanting Northern Ireland to remain part of the United Kingdom and the majority of Catholics wanting it to be re-united with the Republic of Ireland. Politically these divisions have been reflected in the fact that the major political parties in the region tend either to be Unionist (i.e. Protestant) or Nationalist (i.e. Catholic). The violent nature of the conflict has also led to the emergence of armed paramilitary groups that also reflect this broad dualism with Loyalists such as the UDA and UVF arising from the Protestant side, and Republicans, most notably the IRA and INLA, arising from the Catholic side.[1] Since 1969 the conflict has resulted directly in the deaths of over 3,600 people (Fay *et al.* 1999).

This is, inevitably, a very crude summary of what is an extremely complex situation. It is generally recognised, for example, that there are significant divisions and a range of differing perspectives and experiences within both the Protestant and Catholic 'communities' (O'Connor 1993; Shirlow and McGovern 1997; Coulter 1999). However, it still remains the case that these two groups represent the fundamental axis of ethnic division within Northern Ireland, resulting in high levels of geographical and social segregation. It has been estimated, for example, that 75 per cent of people living in the region live in areas that are predominantly Catholic or Protestant. Moreover, the vast majority of schools (95 per cent) are also segregated, being either Catholic-maintained or Protestant-controlled schools. Ethnic division, therefore, is a fact of life in Northern Ireland. However, in the absence of physical cues to mark out difference between Catholics and Protestants, a complex range of cultural markers has emerged over the years to differentiate one community from the other. It is quite common, for example, to see the entrances to housing estates marked out with either the British Union Jack or Irish Tricolour flags to establish whether they are Protestant or Catholic areas respectively. Kerbstones, lamp-posts and railings are also often painted similarly to mark out areas as Protestant (painted red, white and blue) or Catholic (painted green, white and orange). In addition a particularly noticeable feature of certain areas in Northern Ireland has been the painting of wall murals often depicting images of and support for particular paramilitary groups.

At an interpersonal level ethnic differences can be marked in a number of ways including: a person's name (first names and surnames can sometimes indicate whether a person is Catholic or Protestant); what sports a person likes and plays; and what football team's shirt a person wears (Protestants tending to wear Rangers shirts and Catholics tending to prefer Celtic shirts – both football teams in the Scottish Premier league). Given all of these differing ways in which ethnic identities and divisions are signified in Northern Ireland, the two studies that form the focus for this chapter have attempted in differing ways to understand when young children first come to develop an awareness of these ethnic markers and, consequently, when they begin to identify themselves with one of the two main communities and also when and to what extent do they begin to hold negative (known as 'sectarian') attitudes towards those from the other community.

The first study (see Connolly *et al.* 2002) adopted a broadly quantitative approach, randomly selecting 352 children aged between three and six from across Northern Ireland. The children were accessed through primary schools and nurseries and the written consent of parents gained before they were interviewed.[2] The aim was simply to gather some baseline data on the general nature and extent of young children's ethnic awareness and how this tends to develop with age and vary in terms of factors such as gender, social class and religion. Mindful of the criticisms of existing structured and experimental studies on young children's racial attitudes, however, we devised a research instrument that collected the children's qualitative comments and then consequently coded and statistically analysed these. In essence children were shown a range of photographs and items reflecting events and symbols most commonly associated with the two main ethnic groups in Northern Ireland and were simply asked if they knew what each of these were and, if so, what they could tell us about them. The items included: the British Union Jack and Irish Tricolour flags; Celtic and Rangers football shirts; photographs of a police armoured Land Rover, an Orange March and an Irish dancer; and particular colour combinations (i.e. red, white and blue and also green, white and orange).

The children were given no information or prompts regarding any of the items and their responses were simply recorded verbatim. As will be described in more detail below, these responses were then analysed and coded in relation to:

- whether they expressed a preference for one item or event over another;
- whether they could demonstrate some awareness of that particular item or event;
- whether through their comments they demonstrated a tendency to identify with one of the two ethnic groups;
- whether they made any unsolicited sectarian comments.

An extensive pilot study was carried out prior to the main fieldwork to ensure that the items used reflected the full potential range of young children's awareness and experiences.

While such a quantitative approach is necessary to enable generalisations to be developed regarding the overall picture in relation to young children's ethnic awareness in Northern Ireland, it is clearly limited in terms of helping to uncover and explain the particular social processes and contexts within which such an awareness develops. With this in mind the second study to be reported here adopted a much more in-depth, qualitative and ethnographic approach (see Connolly and Healy 2003). It focused on three age groups of children – three to four, seven to eight and ten to eleven – chosen from four different areas in Belfast: two adjoining working-class estates, one Protestant and the other Catholic, both with a history of sectarian violence; and two suburban middle-class areas, again one Catholic and the other Protestant. Access was gained via a local primary school and nursery in each of these four areas and, as before, written parental consent was gained before each child was interviewed. Alongside observations of the children in the nurseries/schools the research also included largely unstructured interviews with small friendship groups of between two and four children at a time. Other than asking general questions to stimulate conversation regarding what the children liked to do and who they played with, the interviewer restricted her role to simply asking for clarification and/or asking children to expand upon or explain what they had said in a little more detail. A more detailed discussion of the methodology underpinning this approach is available elsewhere (see Connolly 1996, 1997).

The foundations of an 'ethnic habitus'

The definition of ethnic group offered by Hughes and quoted earlier is useful in the stress it gives to the way that ethnicity tends to be experienced as a natural and given part of a person's life. It is, as he argues, more than just an identity that can be worn and disregarded with ease. Rather, ethnicity is much more fundamental than this. In this sense we can borrow and develop one of Bourdieu's (1977, 1990) concepts and talk of an 'ethnic habitus' as representing a particular set of predispositions and ways of behaviour (i.e. 'habits') that are learnt and internalised over time and that tend to structure the way people think about and interact with their social world.

In understanding ethnicity in this way, it is not suggested that ethnic identities are actually fixed and engrained. As stressed earlier, they tend to evolve and change over time and from one context to the next; they are not empirically distinctive and objectively defined but they are, rather, contingent and contradictory. However, and this is the point, at any particular time a person's ethnic identity is *experienced* as a fundamental and permanent aspect of their sense of self. The task for research is therefore to understand how ethnic identities are constructed and experienced in such a core and powerful way as this. From the present two studies, it is clear that the period of early childhood is a critical one within which an individual tends to internalise the key parameters of their ethnic habitus. This is certainly evident from the findings of the broader survey of three- to six-year-olds. In a social context characterised by division where those divisions are continuously marked and reinforced through a range of ritualised events and symbols, it is not surprising that even the youngest of children begin to pick up and reproduce the cultural preferences of their family and local community.

This is evident from the findings presented in Table 10.1 that focus simply on the attitudes of the three-year-olds. During each interview, and where appropriate, after the children were asked to say what they knew about a particular item, they were asked either if they liked it (in the case of single items such as photographs of Orange Marchers, policemen, Irish dancers) or whether there was one item they preferred and, if so, which one (in the case of two related items such as the British and Irish flags and also the Celtic and Rangers football shirts). Even at the age of three, significant differences were emerging in relation to Protestant and Catholic children's tendencies to dislike or prefer certain cultural events or symbols over others. As can be seen from Table 10.1, such differences tended to reflect those found between Catholics and Protestants more broadly.

Table 10.1 Differences in cultural preferences between Catholic and Protestant three-year-olds

	Catholics	Protestants
Percentage of children who:		
Do not like Orange Marchers[a]	18% (22)	3% (35)
Do not like the police[b]	34% (35)	15% (33)
Prefer the British Union Jack flag[c]	36% (31)	60% (37)
Prefer the Irish Tricolour flag[c]	64% (31)	40% (37)

Notes
Total numbers of children who expressed a preference and thus to which each percentage relates are given in parentheses. Significance of differences (directional hypotheses): [a]$p = 0.023, \chi^2(1) = 3.964$; [b]$p = 0.035, \chi^2(1) = 3.317$; [c]$p = 0.025, \chi^2(1) = 3.882$.

For example, Orange Marches are a central and ritualised event associated with Protestants and, over the years, have caused much antagonism and conflict as Catholics tend to resent what they feel are triumphalist and invasive marches through their areas while Protestants tend to feel that they have a right to march wherever they wish in their own country. At times particularly contested marches have provided the catalyst for widespread and serious disorder. As can be seen from Table 10.1, such ethnic divisions are already coming to structure the world views of three-year-olds with nearly one in five Catholic children stating that they do not like Orange Marchers compared to a negligible proportion of Protestants. Similarly, 98 per cent of the police force are Protestants and it has therefore been regarded by many Catholics as a partisan organisation whose aim has been to protect the Northern Ireland state and the dominance of Protestants over Catholics. Again, from Table 10.1 it can be seen that such perceptions are also beginning to shape the attitudes of children even as young as three with twice as many Catholic children compared to Protestants at this age stating that they dislike the police.

The other area where significant differences were found among three-year-olds, as also illustrated in Table 10.1, related to the children's preferences for particular flags. As can be seen, quite noticeable differences were evident in terms of Catholic children's tendency to prefer the Irish Tricolour flag and Protestant children's tendency to prefer the British Union Jack. While the three-year-olds did not show any significant differences in terms of their preference for other events and symbols – such as Celtic and Rangers football shirts, different colour combinations and particular first names – these differences were certainly found to emerge among the older children in the sample and were all evident among the six-year-olds whose preferences, generally, were more defined and differentiated than among the three-year-olds (see Connolly *et al.* 2002).

What is particularly interesting about the findings described above in relation to the three-year-olds is the fact that such preferences were not generally accompanied by any clear understanding of the cultural or political significance of the choices made. Of all the children who stated that they either did not like the police

Table 10.2 Average number of events/symbols of which children could demonstrate some cultural and/or political awareness by age

Age	Average number of events/symbols	Standard deviation
3	0.82	1.09
4	1.42	1.13
5	2.14	1.44
6	2.65	1.83

or did not like Orange Marchers, none of them offered any comments to suggest that they had any awareness of the political significance of their views. Similarly, in relation to the flags, when the three-year-olds were shown each flag and asked both what it was and what they knew about it, only 16 per cent could offer any knowledge that would indicate any awareness of the cultural or political significance of one or both of the flags.[3] What this tends to highlight, therefore, is that there is evidence for the beginnings of an ethnic habitus at the age of three. As has been shown, while the children may not have much awareness of the cultural choices or preferences they make at this age, they are already beginning to develop habits or predispositions that reflect the ethnic characteristics associated with the communities within which they are growing up.

Such preferences can be seen, in turn, as providing the key parameters within which a child's awareness is consequently developed and thus their ethnic habitus is consolidated over the following few years. It is certainly the case that the children's awareness of the cultural and political significance of the particular events and items they were shown increased significantly with age ($r = 0.457$, $p<0.0005$). This is illustrated in Table 10.2 that shows the mean number of separate items of which each age group of children could demonstrate some cultural/political awareness. As can be seen, while three-year-olds, on average, could only demonstrate awareness of just under one item, this was approaching three items for six-year-olds.

The development of ethnic identities and prejudices

A child's increasing awareness of particular ethnic symbols and events does not necessarily imply that they are more likely to acquire a particular ethnic identity. Moreover, there is no necessary relationship between the acquisition of an ethnic identity and the tendency to develop ethnic prejudices. A child can identify strongly with either the Protestant or Catholic 'community' without having to hold negative attitudes towards the other. From the data of the first study, it is useful therefore to gain some understanding of the nature and extent of these three processes among three- to six-year-olds. The findings are outlined in Table 10.3 which sets out the proportions of children in each group who: can demonstrate awareness of the cultural/political significance of at least one of the items they

Table 10.3 Overall levels of ethnic awareness, group identification and prejudice among young children by age (%)[a]

| Age | Percentages of children demonstrating | | |
	Ethnic awareness[b]	Ethnic identity	Ethnic prejudice
3	51	5	I
4	75	7	3
5	88	13	7
6	90	34	15

Notes
a   Total children in the sample is 352, split evenly across the four age groups.
b   Defined in terms of demonstrating at least some awareness of the cultural and/or political significance of one or more of the symbols/events shown.

were shown; show a tendency to identify with one of the two main ethnic groups (i.e. to see themselves as being Catholic or Protestant); and, finally, make unsolicited negative (sectarian) comments about the other ethnic group.

A child was counted as identifying with a particular group if in their comments they did one or more of the following: a) claimed group membership directly (i.e. 'I'm a Catholic/Protestant' or 'I'm British/Irish'); b) inferred the existence of a particular group and also their membership of it indirectly (i.e. 'That's *our* colours' or 'That's *my* flag'); and/or c) stated that they liked or disliked something because it was associated with a particular group (i.e. 'I like that flag because it's British' or 'I like Celtic because they're Catholic'). The following provide some illustrations of group identification:

Responses to question: 'What is a Catholic/Protestant?':

• 'I'm a Catholic' (Catholic boy, aged 6)
• 'Yes that's what we are – Protestants' (Protestant girl, aged 6)
• 'We are all Catholics and we don't like the Prods' (Catholic boy, aged 6)

Responses to question: 'Why do you like that flag the best?':

• 'That's our flag' (Catholic girl, aged 4)
• 'It's the one of our country' (Protestant boy, aged 4)
• 'Because it's a good flag. Because I'm Catholic and it's a Catholic flag' (Catholic girl, aged 6)
• 'It means that it's a Northern Ireland flag. It's on lamp-posts outside my house. It's to tell people that this is Northern Ireland' (Protestant boy, aged 6)

Similarly, a child was counted as making a sectarian statement if they did one or more of the following: a) used an explicitly sectarian term (i.e. 'Fenian', 'Taig' or 'Prod'); b) offered a negative stereotype about the other group (i.e.

Catholics/Protestants) or a group of people explicitly associated with them (i.e. Orangemen or Irish dancers); and/or c) made a statement that s/he 'didn't like' or 'hated' a particular event, symbol or group of people because they were associated with the other group. Some examples of children's comments that were counted as explicitly sectarian are provided below:

Responses to question: 'What do you know about Protestants/Catholics?':

- 'They [Catholics] rob' (Protestant girl, aged 4)
- 'It's a bad person [Protestants] because they want to kill all the Catholics' (Catholic girl, aged 6)
- 'Catholics are the same as masked men, they smash windows' (Protestant girl, aged 4)
- 'Catholics don't like Protestants and that's why they don't like them – they're bad' (Catholic boy, aged 6)

Responses to question: 'Why do you like that flag the best?':

- 'Has my two fave colours on it [green and orange] and that one's just yucky [referring to Union Jack]. I hate English and I love Irish' (Catholic boy, aged 6)
- 'It's the Fenian flag [Irish Tricolour]. It's only bad people that have that colour of flag and that's all I know about that flag' (Protestant girl, aged 6)

Overall, two key themes emerge from these findings. First, they confirm the general point made earlier about the relationship between awareness, group identity and prejudice. Only a small proportion of those who expressed some ethnic awareness went on to identify with a particular ethnic group. Similarly, not all those who regarded themselves as belonging to one group then made negative sectarian statements about the other. Second, it can be seen that while children at the ages of three and four are capable of developing ethnic group identifications and prejudices, these do not significantly emerge until the next couple of years where such tendencies seem to increase exponentially. Certainly by the age of six, the findings in Table 10.3 suggest that a third of children identify with one of the two main ethnic groups and nearly one in six (15 per cent) hold ethnic prejudices.

Children's ethnic competence

It is evident from some of the quotes used above that the nature of the five- and six-year-old children's ethnic identities and the types of ethnic prejudices they held were relatively limited. Thus while the general parameters of their identities and beliefs were being set in place, there was still a fair amount of work required to fill these in and build them up. As was shown, their actual cultural/political awareness of particular events and symbols (the essential blocks to be used to build these identities and beliefs further) were generally quite limited. However, it can be also seen that the early years appear to represent a time where the building of ethnic identities and prejudices takes place at an increasingly intense rate; witnessed by what seems to be an exponential growth in the proportions of children beginning to identify with a particular ethnic group and make sectarian comments between the ages of three and six. To complete the picture being constructed in this chapter regarding the early years, it is therefore useful to examine briefly the experiences and perspectives of seven- and eight-year-old children as highlighted in the second, more qualitative, ethnographic study mentioned earlier. Because of the limited space available, the following discussion will restrict itself to the interviews with the working-class children.[4]

As the working-class children in this study grow older they are likely to spend much more of their time outside and thus to increase their exposure to the various cultural symbols found in their local areas (including flags, murals and painted kerbstones). Moreover, for those children living in areas experiencing high levels of sectarian tensions and violence, they are also likely to develop an acute sense of awareness of the continual threat posed by those 'on the other side'. It is through these processes that children begin to fill in and build upon the ethnic parameters they had already learnt and internalised. As can be seen from the discussion with Louise and Aine (both Catholic) during one group interview, the broader cultural symbols they had increasingly become aware of (in this case Rangers football shirts) were now providing an ideal language for representing and making sense of this threat. The girls had begun discussing people living in the neighbouring Protestant housing estate.[5]

Louise:	Protestants support Rangers.
Interviewer:	Why is that?
Louise:	Because Rangers are Protestants.
Interviewer:	So what are Protestants, what does that mean?
Louise:	It's bad to be a Protestant and/
	[...]
Interviewer:	What was that Louise?
Louise [quietly]:	Protestants come down and shoot ye.
Interviewer:	Do they?
	[...]
Aine:	They shot a man down our way.
Interviewer:	Why did they do that?
Aine:	I don't know.

The generally tense atmosphere that is associated with what are called 'interface' areas between Protestant and Catholic communities is evident in the following discussion that took place between Chloe, John and Mandy (all Protestant). It demonstrates how broader social processes and relations provide the central dynamics through which ethnic identities are forged and developed:

Interviewer:	Do you ever go over there [*across the peaceline*] to play?
Chloe:	Aye and get my head bricked in!
Interviewer:	Why would that happen?
Chloe:	Cos they're bad.
Interviewer:	They're bad?
John:	They are Catholics.
Interviewer:	And does that mean that they're bad?
All:	Yes.
Chloe:	They throw bricks and all over at us.
Interviewer:	Why?
Chloe:	I don't know.
Mandy:	Ivor got chased by the Fenians [*derogatory term for Catholics*] in three cars.
Interviewer:	Who's Ivor?
Mandy:	My brother.
Interviewer:	Oh dear, who chased him?
Mandy:	The Fenians.
Interviewer:	Who are they?
Mandy:	Catholics. Bad people, throw bricks at all our houses.
Chloe:	My wee friend got her windows put in by one of them. [...]
Interviewer:	So why do they throw bricks in at your houses?
Mandy:	Cause they're bad and because we don't support Celtic.
Interviewer:	Is that the only reason?
Mandy:	Yeah.

Again, the use of particular cultural symbols (i.e. Celtic in the latter case with Mandy) that the children had already become acquainted with at an earlier age to symbolise and represent ethnic divisions is clear in the above. For those living in areas such as these where low-level violence has become an almost routine aspect of their lives, it is not surprising that some will positively identify with the local paramilitary groupings. For these children they can come to represent their natural 'defenders'. This is particularly true for some of the boys as illustrated in the discussion below with Phil and George (both Protestant) who, as can be seen, are fantasising about membership of particular loyalist organisations:

Phil:	The UDA, they're men and they have guns. [...]
George:	I work for the UDA [laughs].
Phil [*singing*]:	We all work for the UDA! We all work for the UDA!
George:	They're good.
Phil:	Sometimes they're good and sometimes they're bad.
Interviewer:	What good things do they do?
George:	Hundred guns in your head!

Phil:	I don't know.
George:	I know something good they do, they won't blow up this school.
Interviewer:	Will they not?
George:	Cos we're all Protestants.
Phil:	Cos we're all Prods, everyone here in this here whole estate is all Prods.
Interviewer:	Why is that?
Phil:	Just is, I don't know.

Implications for early years practice

As has been stressed throughout this chapter, ethnic groups are not objectively defined or natural. Rather, they are socially constructed with the particular physical and/or cultural markers that are afforded significance and used to differentiate one group from the next, being the product of specific social and economic processes and practices. The history of ethnic groups, therefore, is one characterised by a continuous defining and re-defining of boundaries and constant struggles over identity, representation and belonging. Where physical markers are used, as in the case of 'race' and racism, then the construction of particular ethnic groups is usually also accompanied by relations of domination and exploitation between these groups.

While ethnic groups are therefore not fixed and static but are rather characterised by contradiction and contingency, the power of ethnicity is precisely in its ability to encourage individuals to experience and believe that their membership of and sense of belonging to a particular group is natural, fundamental and fixed. The evidence provided in this chapter suggests that one of the key reasons for this strength of feeling attached to ethnic identities is the fact that they are learnt and internalised at a very early age. From the age of three, many children are already assimilating the key parameters of an ethnic habitus within which their identities will be built and secured over the coming years. Only in a matter of a few years do such identities provide the potential for the development of negative attitudes and prejudices towards other ethnic groups.

The usefulness of the case studies used in this chapter relates to the fact that the strong ethnic identities being developed by some of these children do not rely, in any sense, on physical differences. Rather they are based upon a range of complex and often subtle cultural markers. Given the significance of the new racism with its emphasis on cultural differences, the case studies therefore provide important insights into the social competence of young children and the possible ways in which the new racism can be impacting upon their social worlds. While the findings presented here have immediate implications for working with young children in Northern Ireland (see Connolly *et al.* 2002), they therefore also carry important lessons for attempting to address racism and ethnic prejudice among young children more generally. Three particular points are worth drawing out in conclusion. The first is the need to extend the type of critical multiculturalism advocated elsewhere (see Short and Carrington 1996; Kinchloe and Steinberg 1997; May 1999) into the early years and to think carefully about what this means in practice. Given the central importance of the early years to the production of ethnic identities, it is important that young children are not only encouraged to understand and experience a range of different cultural events and symbols but, more importantly, they are helped to begin to develop a critical reflexivity with which they can challenge existing stereotypes and prejudices and also develop a more grounded appreciation of their own identities and also those of others. In this sense, the challenge is more than simply fostering a learning environment that is non-discriminatory, free from stereotypes and which is multicultural (although this is still extremely important, see Siraj-Blatchford 1994; Millam 1996), it is also about conceiving of appropriate means of engaging young children more critically in the ways they are encouraged to think about and experience identity, difference and diversity. All of this is particularly important in nurseries/schools that are largely mono-ethnic (whether in terms of religion in Northern Ireland and/or 'race' elsewhere). In such environments it can be that much easier for children to come to regard their own ethnic identity as 'natural' and inevitable and thus to view others as strange and/or inferior.

Second, there is clearly also a need to develop a more proactive approach to dealing with expressions of racism and ethnic prejudice among young children. Certainly by the ages of five and six, existing qualitative research has shown that children are already socially competent in the ways they appropriate and make use of a variety of racist discourses (see Van Ausdale and Feagin 1996, 2001; Connolly 1998). In relation to the present study, ethnic prejudice among the children in the form of sectarianism was found to increase significantly among this age and, by the time the children are seven and eight, they are also able to talk extremely confidently and knowledgeably about their own experiences and their attitudes towards others. A need exists, therefore, for researchers and practitioners to think about how best to challenge young children's behaviour and to encourage them to appreciate the negative effects and consequences of that behaviour for others. At the beginning of the early years, for example, research has shown that young children are capable of learning that certain forms of behaviour are right or wrong and also to begin to empathise with others and to understand the consequences of their actions. Similarly, they are also able to respond positively to attempts to model out alternative, more positive and prosocial behaviours (Eisenberg and Mussen 1989; Wittmer and Honig 1994; Honig and Wittmer 1996). Moreover, as children move through the early years the evidence presented in this chapter, and from the qualitative studies on racism and young children more generally, suggests that a greater emphasis can be placed on encouraging children to discuss, think through and reflect upon their behaviour.

Finally, the way that ethnicity is lived and experienced at such a fundamental level in people's lives also has important implications for early years practitioners, parents and local communities. It certainly cannot be taken for granted that they will all be committed to the goals of encouraging young children to reflect upon their identities and recognise and value difference and diversity. Early years practitioners will only be able to achieve this successfully with their children if they are willing to do it themselves. A need exists therefore for training that can not only provide practitioners with the knowledge and skills to address these issues with young children but also the space within which they can explore and reflect upon (and be challenged about) their own attitudes and identities. In relation to parents and the local community, especially in areas where racial and/or ethnic tensions exist, it is likely that there will be some opposition to nurseries/schools explicitly encouraging young children to understand and value difference and diversity. In this sense, any educational strategy cannot simply be imposed but needs to be developed in partnership with parents and the local community. While this will represent a significant challenge for those working in particular areas, it is clear that without the support of parents and the local community any strategy aimed at addressing ethnic/racial prejudice and discrimination among young children will have limited success.

Notes

1 UDA (Ulster Defence Association); UVF (Ulster Volunteer Force); IRA (Irish Republican Army) and INLA (Irish National Liberation Army).
2 For both research projects, it is reasonable to hypothesise that gaining parental consent for the children to be interviewed would have been difficult given the potentially sensitive nature of the focus of the research. This, however, was not found to be the case. A letter was sent through each school/nursery to all parents of the children selected explaining the nature of the research, asking permission for their child to be interviewed and including a tear-off slip for the parents to sign and return. The letter also invited parents to contact one of the researchers should they have any questions. None of the parents contacted in relation to both studies refused permission for their child to take part, although some did telephone a researcher to clarify the nature of the interviews. These parents were generally satisfied once it was explained to them that the anonymity of their child would be guaranteed and/or also that the interviews would be non-directive and that they were simply aiming to gain an insight into the children's views. The willingness of parents to allow their children to take part may be the result of a number of factors including: the fact that the schools were clearly supporting the research; the fact that the research possibly gained legitimacy because the first study was funded jointly by the Community Relations Council and the television company Channel 4, and the second study by the Office of the First Minister and Deputy First Minister; and the opportunity that was provided for parents to discuss any concerns they may have had with a member of the research team.
3 Given the limitations of space it is not possible to explain here how children's awareness was measured and codified from the comments they made. Details on this are, however, available elsewhere (see Connolly et al. 2002).
4 At the time of writing, the fieldwork relating to the middle-class children had just been completed and the interviews were being transcribed and analysed. It was not at this stage possible to engage in a comparative analysis. It is worth stressing, however, that the seven- to eight-year-old working-class children to be discussed here are from areas that have experienced high levels of sectarian tensions and violence over the years. It would therefore be wrong to attempt to generalise from their views and experiences to the population of children as a whole in Northern Ireland. Rather, the point of focusing on these children is simply to demonstrate what children of this age are capable of understanding and their ability to develop particular attitudes and identities.
5 A key to the transcripts is provided on page 182.

Key to transcripts

/   Indicates interruption in speech.

[…]   Extracts edited out of transcript.

…   A natural pause in the conversation.

[*italic text*]   Descriptive text added to clarify the nature of the discussion.

[normal text]   Text added to help clarify the point the child is making.

References

Aboud, F. (1988) *Children and Prejudice*, Oxford: Basil Blackwell

Andereck, M. (1992) *Ethnic Awareness and the School: an Ethnographic Study*, Newbury Park, CA: Sage

Anthias, F. and Yuval-Davis, N. (1992) *Racialized Boundaries: Race, Nation, Gender, Colour, Class and the Anti-Racist Struggle*, London: Routledge

Barker, M. (1981) *The New Racism: Conservatives and the Ideology of the Tribe*, London: Junction Books

Bar-Tal, D. (1996) 'Development of social categories and stereotypes in early childhood: the case of "the Arab" concept formation, stereotype and attitudes by Jewish children in Israel', *International Journal of Intercultural Relations*, 20, 2/4: 341–370

Barth, F. (ed.) (1969) *Ethnic Groups and Boundaries: the Social Organisation of Cultural Difference*, London: Allen & Unwin

Billig, M. (1985) 'Prejudice, categorization and particularization: from a perceptual to a rhetorical approach', *European Journal of Social Psychology*, 15: 79–103

Billig, M. (1987) *Arguing and Thinking: a Rhetorical Approach to Social Psychology*, Cambridge: Cambridge University Press

Bourdieu, P. (1977) *Outline of a Theory of Practice*, Cambridge: Cambridge University Press

Bourdieu, P. (1990) *The Logic of Practice*, Cambridge: Polity Press

Cairns, E., Hunter, D. and Herring, L. (1980) 'Young children's awareness of violence in Northern Ireland: the influence of N.I. television in Scotland and Northern Ireland', *British Journal of Social and Clinical Psychology*, 19: 3–6

Cohen, P. (ed.) (1999) *New Ethnicities, Old Racisms?*, London: Zed Books

Condor, S. (1988) '"Race stereotypes" and racist discourse', *Text* 8: 69–89

Connolly, P. (1996) '"Seen but never heard": rethinking approaches to researching racism and young children', *Discourse: Studies in the Cultural Politics of Education*, 17, 2: 171–185

Connolly, P. (1997) 'In search of authenticity: researching young children's perspective', in Pollard, A., Thiessen, D. and Filer, A. (eds) *Children and Their Curriculum*, London: Falmer Press

Connolly, P. (1998) *Racism, Gender Identities and Young Children*, London: Routledge

Connolly, P. (2001) 'Qualitative methods in the study of children's racial attitudes and identities', *Infant and Child Development*, 10, 3: 219–233

Connolly, P., Smith, A. and Kelly, B. (2002) *Too Young to Notice? The Cultural and Political Awareness of 3–6-Year-Olds in Northern Ireland*, Belfast: Community Relations Council

Connolly, P. and Healy, J. (2003) 'The development of children's attitudes towards "the troubles" in Northern Ireland', in Hargie, O. and Dickson, D. (eds) *Researching the Troubles: Social Science Perspectives on the Northern Ireland Conflict*, Edinburgh: Mainstream Publishing

Coulter, C. (1999) *Contemporary Northern Irish Society*, London: Pluto Press

Donald, J. and Rattansi, A. (eds) (1992) *'Race', Culture and Difference*, London: Sage

Eisenberg, N. and Mussen, P. (1989) *The Roots of Prosocial Behaviour in Children*, New York: Cambridge University Press

Fay, M., Morrisey, M. and Smyth, M. (1999) *Northern Ireland's Troubles: the Human Costs*, London: Pluto Press

Gillborn, D. (1995) *Racism and Antiracism in Real Schools*, Buckingham: Open University Press

Gillborn, D. (1996) 'Re-asserting and refining anti-racism: facing up to contemporary racisms', *Education Review*, 10, 1: 15–20

Holmes. R. (1995) *How Young Children Perceive Race*, London: Sage

Honig, A. and Wittmer, D. (1996) 'Helping children become more prosocial: ideas for classrooms, families, schools, and communities', *Young Children*, 51: 62–70

Hughes, E. (1994) *On Work, Race and the Sociological Imagination*, Chicago: Chicago University Press

Jahoda, G. and Harrison, S. (1975) 'Belfast children: some effects of a conflict environment', *Irish Journal of Psychology*, 3: 1–19

Jenkins, R. (1997) *Rethinking Ethnicity: Arguments and Explorations*, London: Sage

Kinchloe, J. and Steinberg, S. (1997) *Changing Multiculturalism*, Buckingham: Open University Press

May, S. (ed.) (1999) *Critical Multiculturalism: Rethinking Multicultural and Antiracist Education*, London: Falmer Press

McWhirter, L. and Gamble, R. (1982) 'Development of ethnic awareness in the absence of physical cues', *Irish Journal of Psychology*, 5, 2: 109–127

Millam, R. (1996) *Anti-Discriminatory Practice: a Guide for Workers in Childcare and Education*, London: Cassell

Milner, D. (1983) *Children and Race: Ten Years On*, London: Ward Lock Educational

O'Connor, F. (1993) *In Search of a State: Catholics in Northern Ireland*, Belfast: Blackstaff Press

Potter, J. and Wetherall, M. (1987) *Discourse and Social Psychology: Beyond Attitudes and Behaviour,* London: Sage

Reeves, F. (1983) *British Racial Discourse: a Study of British Political Discourse about Race and Race-Related Matters*, Cambridge: Cambridge University Press

Reicher, S. (1986) 'Contact, action and racialization: some British evidence', in Hewstone, M. and Brown, R. (eds) *Contact and Conflict in Intergroup Encounters*, Oxford: Basil Blackwell

Royle, R., Barrett, M. and Takriti, Y. (1999) 'Religious identity in Egyptian Muslim and Christian children aged 6–13 years', *Arab Journal of Psychiatry,* 10, 2: 120–127

Shirlow, P. and McGovern, M. (1997) *Who are 'The People'? Unionism, Protestantism and Loyalism in Northern Ireland*, London: Pluto Press

Short, G. and Carrington, B. (1996) 'Anti-racist education, multiculturalism and the new racism', *Educational Review*, 48, 1: 65–77

Short, G. and Carrington, B. (1999) 'Children's constructions of their national identity: implications for critical multiculturalism' in May, S. (ed.) *Critical Multiculturalism: Rethinking Multicultural and Antiracist Education*, London: Falmer Press

Siraj-Blatchford, I. (1994) *The Early Years: Laying the Foundations for Racial Equality*, Stoke-on-Trent: Trentham Books

Troyna, B. and Hatcher, R. (1992) *Racism in Children's Lives*, London: Routledge

Van Ausdale, D. and Feagin, J. (1996) 'Using racial and ethnic concepts: the critical case of very young children', *American Sociological Review*, 61, 5: 779–793

Van Ausdale, D. and Feagin, J. (2001) *The First R: How Children Learn Race and Racism*, Lanham, MD: Rowman & Littlefield

Wittmer, D. and Honig, A. (1994) 'Encouraging positive social development in young children', *Young Children*, 49: 4–12

Chapter 11

Special educational needs and procedural justice in England and Scotland

Sheila Riddell

Introduction

Much work in the field of social policy tends to ignore issues of identity, assuming that individuals experience particular social policy regimes in very similar ways. This idea has been subject to criticism by writers such as Hughes (1998), Hughes and Lewis (1998) and Saraga (1998), who maintain that social welfare is experienced differently by different individuals and groups. The implication of these ideas is that future welfare regimes must deliver services which accommodate, rather than curb, individual difference, whilst retaining some notion of collective entitlement. Within recent sociological theory, on the other hand, there has been a focus on individualism and difference, to the extent that the power of structural forces has often been underplayed. Within postmodernity, the self is construed as performative and reflexive, constantly defined and redefined in varying social contexts. Writers like Beck (1992), Beck, Giddens and Lash (1994) and Lash and Urry (1993) emphasise the ability of the individual to self-define through patterns of consumption, thus bypassing the forces of social determination.

This chapter explores the impact of specific regimes of procedural justice on the identities of parents and professionals in the field of special educational needs (SEN). Having outlined some of the key differences in models of procedural justice at national levels, case studies are used to examine the ways in which different regimes of procedural justice are experienced and negotiated at local authority level by parents and professionals. The chapter aims to illustrate the high level of complexity within policy systems. Whilst broad differences may be identified between approaches to special needs policy (and education policy) in Scotland and England, parents and professionals at local authority level respond differently, exploiting the range of trade-offs between competing policy frameworks to negotiate a range of identities. It is argued that such an analysis enables us to combine understandings from sociology and social policy. Individuals negotiate identity with significant others within contexts which are not entirely determined by overarching external forces, but at the same time allow only a certain amount of room for individual negotiation.

Procedural or administrative justice relates to a particular aspect of social justice and concerns the ways in which policies are implemented in practice. Different models of procedural justice have different modes of decision making, legitimating goals, forms of accountability and characteristic remedies. They exist with each other in a state of tension, although one model may dominate at any one time. There are both positive and negative trade-offs between the different models of procedural justice. In the following section, we describe the version of procedural justice which tended to dominate in the post-war period within the field of SEN. Subsequently, we suggest a more complex model which emerged as an outcome of our analysis of change within this field.

Research methods

This chapter draws extensively on work carried out during the course of the ESRC-funded project 'Justice Inherent in the Assessment of Special Educational Needs in Scotland and England', conducted between 1997 and 2000 by researchers at Glasgow and Edinburgh Universities. On the basis of a preliminary analysis, we chose four case study authorities, two in Scotland and two in England. These differed in relation to their use of mainstream schools to educate children with SEN and also in relation to their rate of appeals by parents against local authority decisions regarding provision. Fifty-nine case studies were conducted with families involved in the process of opening a Record or Statement of Needs.[1] In selecting case studies, efforts were made to include children with a range of difficulties and to maintain a balance between 'contested' and 'non-contested' cases. Case studies consisted of interviews with parents, professionals, education officers and, where appropriate, the child. Some meetings between parents and professionals were observed. In the two English authorities, 120 interviews and six observations were conducted and in the two Scottish authorities, seventy-four interviews and nine observations were carried out. Finally, a long 'pen portrait' was written for each family.

Models of procedural justice within the field of special educational needs

Mashaw's (1983) analysis of the operation of the disability insurance system in the USA in the 1970s suggested that three models of procedural justice were evident (see Table 11.1).

Using this framework, we have argued elsewhere (Riddell et al. 2000) that until the early 1980s the dominant SEN policy frameworks in both Scotland and England were based on professionalism and bureaucracy, with legality becoming increasingly important following recent legislation in both countries. In England during the 1980s and 1990s, following the 1993 Education Act which made provision for the Code of Practice (DfE 1994) and the Special Educational Needs Tribunal, there was a growth in the influence of different

Table 11.1 Policy frameworks adapted from Mashaw's study of disability insurance in the USA

Policy framework	Decision-making mode	Legitimating goal	Nature of accountability	Characteristic remedy
Bureaucracy	Applying rules	Accuracy	Hierarchical	Administrative review
Profession	Applying knowledge	Service	Interpersonal	Complaint to a professional body
Legal system	Weighing up arguments	Fairness	Independent	Appeal to a court or tribunal

policy frameworks based on managerialism, consumerism and markets. In Scotland, the Education (Scotland) Act 1980 (as amended) continued to provide the basic legal framework. Various policy documents (e.g. SOEID 1996; 1998) made recommendations about good practice, but professionalism remained the dominant policy framework. Systems in both England and Scotland are undergoing change at the moment, with the White Paper *Modernising Government* (Cabinet Office 1999) signalling a growing emphasis in both countries on managerialism within mixed economies of welfare. In addition, the SEN and Disability Act 2001 (now part 4 of the Disability Discrimination Act), which covers England, Wales and Scotland, makes discrimination against disabled pupils and students unlawful. This is likely to boost policy frameworks based on legality and consumerism in both England and Scotland.

Whilst it is important to identify the broad thrust of public policy at national level, in translating policies from the statute book to the local level there are many opportunities for subversion and transformation. In the following sections we first explore the nature of parent and professional relationships and identities which have emerged in modern welfare states, before discussing the SEN policy frameworks in play in two local authorities, one in England and one in Scotland. Finally, we present four case studies of parents and professionals to illustrate some of the negotiated identities evident in each context.

SEN decision making and professional identity

The expansion of the welfare state after World War Two produced a growing number of public sector professionals. The role of such professionals has traditionally been both to work for the greater social good and to deliver efficient public services (Cole and Furbey 1994). McPherson and Raab (1988) argued that professional autonomy was greater in Scotland than in England because Scottish semi-independence rested on the autonomy of its professionals. Before devolution, the Scottish Office acted as the central state in Scotland, especially in areas such as education where Scotland has traditionally been most distinctive. According to Humes (1986) and McPherson and Raab (1988), the agenda of Scottish education in the twentieth century was set by Scottish Office officials who enjoyed a particularly powerful position. Professionals were able to defend this power on the basis that they were the bulwark against creeping anglicisation. In Whitehall, the presence of ministers prevented professionals from occupying such a dominant position, although they were still expected to fulfil the potentially conflicting tasks of achieving social amelioration whilst at the same time delivering services in a dispassionate manner.

One of the problems of bureaucratic systems pointed out by Weber was that, whilst there is a need for professional expertise, there is a danger that professionals will become ungovernable and self-serving. During the 1970s and 1980s, attacks on professionals came from two distinct quarters. Those on the left suggested that, whilst pretending to operate as benign agents, professionals were reinforcing social inequalities and extending their empires (Weatherley 1979; Lipsky 1980; Wilding 1982). The benign humanitarianism of professionals was subject to particular criticism by those working in the field of special educational needs (Tomlinson 1982; Armstrong 1995). However, an even stronger attack was mounted by those on the right, who wished to reduce expenditure on welfare. Adopting the arguments of the left, it was suggested that professionals, far from being neutral, were driven by ideology and self-interest. Furthermore, it was argued that their system of self-regulation resulted, not only in poor value for money, but also in corruption and inefficiency (Deakin 1994). To bring these wayward professionals into line, it was maintained they needed to be subjected to the disciplines of managerialism and the market. Within the context of the market (Le Grand 1991; Glennerster 1991), professionals should be responsive to rational client choices and should adapt their services to meet client needs. Managerialism dictated that professional performance should not be judged by internal standards, but by externally imposed and objectively measured targets. As the collection of papers edited by Exworthy and Halford (1999) demonstrates, the response of professionals to managers and managerialism has varied, and in different contexts there is evidence of collaboration, co-option and resistance.

SEN decision making and parental identity

The position of professionals and parents in education is interactive; changes in the position and identity of one group have inevitable knock-on effects on the position of the other. National and local policies provide the framework in which these positions are negotiated, but are interpreted differently by individual parents and professional actors. Vincent (2000) identified the following three positions which parents may adopt in relation to state education: partner/client, consumer or citizen. Most current education policies recognise that parents have a distinctive role to play in their children's education and many education policies today seek to develop partnerships. However, Vincent is critical of the notion of partnership

since it implies an equal relationship, when in fact parents' relationship to education is structured by social class, gender and 'race'. Mordaunt (2001) also casts
doubt on the idea of equal partnerships between parents and professionals in the
field of SEN. In this sense, the idea of partnership may be used as a legitimating
device by schools to justify their aims and practices.

The position of parents as consumers of education has developed more
recently as a key element in the Conservatives' agenda of marketisation and managerialism. School choice policies allowed parents to exercise the power of exit,
described thus by Hirschman as 'widely held to be uniquely powerful by inflicting
revenue losses on delinquent management' (1970: 210). The power of parental
exit has had a strong influence on the composition of schools, leading to greater
social polarisation in urban areas (Adler *et al.* 1989; Gewirtz *et al.* 1995). Schools
have sought to attract high-achieving pupils by focusing on their public image and
the improvement of performance measured by national tests and examinations.

Whilst schools have had to alter their product to maintain their market share,
Vincent (2000) commented that this does not necessarily lead to greater parental
involvement in the day-to-day educational processes, although a number of measures, such as the creation of governing bodies (England) and school boards
(Scotland) has given them some new means of doing this. Vincent also considers
the extent to which parents are adopting the position of active citizen, exploiting
opportunities for engaging in deliberative democratic processes either as members of school governing bodies or school boards (although the phenomenon of
co-option is well known here) or as members of small local parents' organisations
operating around educational issues. She concludes that local groups – an example would be the support groups for parents of children with SEN – are valuable
for participants, and may even be powerful locally, but are unlikely to bring about
radical social change because of the limited range of parents they attract and the
difficulty of focusing on general rather than individualised issues.

A key concern of this chapter is to consider the position of parents of children
with SEN and professionals within specific social welfare regimes in England
and Scotland. To what extent do SEN professionals in Scotland enjoy greater
power than their English counterparts and to what extent has 'commercialised'
professionalism replaced the traditional model of social democratic professionalism in the two countries? Do parents of children with SEN operate as
partners/clients, consumers or citizens and what national/regional differences are
apparent? How do the positions of professionals and parents interact with one
another? In considering these questions, we bear in mind Vincent's reminder that
professionals are not a homogeneous group and neither are parents. Whilst Fabian
ideas of professionalism have been challenged by new regimes of performativity,
individual actors accept or reject these ideas to different degrees, each fashioning
their own subject position within a given structure. In the same way, whilst
national or local systems might encourage parents to operate either primarily as
clients or consumers, individual parents will differ in their relation to education
professionals.

A typology of approaches to procedural justice

As noted earlier, in developing our thinking on special educational needs policy, we have drawn on the work of a number of commentators including Kirp (1982) and Mashaw (1983). Kirp suggested that 'the way in which a policy problem gets defined says a great deal about how it will be resolved'. Policy frameworks co-exist with each other in a state of dynamic tension:

> They are pursued by different policy actors for different reasons. They have distinctive potentialities and equally distinctive pathologies, and tend to fall in and out of favour with policy makers over time. Choosing among these policy frameworks affects the policy system and, vitally, the supposed bene-ficiaries.

> (Kirp 1982: 138)

As illustrated in Table 11.2, each policy framework is characterised by specific forms of decision making, legitimating goal, nature of accountability and charac-teristic remedy.

The first three policy frameworks in Table 11.2 were those which have domi-nated the field of SEN until very recently. Bureaucracy uses rules as the basis for decision making. It promises accuracy and consistency, is hierarchical and if there is evidence of malfunction then administrative review is the remedy which is

Table 11.2 Six normative models of procedural justice

Model	Mode of decision making	Legitimating goal	Mode of accountability	Characteristic remedy for user
Bureaucracy	Applying rules	Accuracy	Hierarchical	Administrative review
Professionalism	Applying knowledge	Public service	Interpersonal	Second opinion: complaint to a professional body
Legality	Weighing up arguments	Fairness	Independent	Appeal to a court or tribunal (public law)
Managerialism	Managerial autonomy	Efficiency gains	Performance measures	Management sanctions; complaint to ombudsman
Consumerism	Active participation	Consumer satisfaction	Consumer charters	'Voice' and/or compensation through charter
Markets	Price mechanism	Private sector – profit; public sector – efficiency	Commercial viability	'Exit' and/or court action (private law)

likely to be applied. The professional policy framework operates by applying professional judgement; it seeks legitimacy through claiming to place the client's interests above those of the practitioner; accountability is to clients and other professionals and if there is dissatisfaction then a client may complain to a professional body. A policy framework based on legal principles weighs up arguments to determine fair outcomes. It claims to be independent (hence the depiction of Justice as blind) and appeal is to a court or tribunal.

Other policy frameworks, specifically managerialism, consumerism and markets, became increasingly important during the 1990s, particularly in England (see below for further discussion). As noted earlier, managerialism refers to new attempts to regulate public services with a view to increasing efficiency, effectiveness and value for money (Clarke and Newman 1997). To achieve efficiency gains, performance measures are used to assess whether individuals and services have attained pre-specified outcomes. If targets are not met, management sanctions may be applied, which are likely to involve financial penalties or the loss of contracts. Dissatisfied users may complain to the ombudsman. Consumerism, which flourished in the 1990s, was based on the view that service users should have the major say in the nature and delivery of public services. Citizenship was seen increasingly in terms of individual members of the public adopting the role of critical consumer. Consumer charters were intended to provide information on the nature and quality of services people had a right to expect. Complaints procedures had to be in place and compensation paid to those who had a legitimate grievance with regard to service quality. Finally, markets were seen by the New Right as the ultimate means of raising standards and achieving better value for money. People were increasingly given the power to choose between existing services. Those which were more popular were expected to expand and flourish, whilst unpopular services were intended to wither and die. The mode of accountability within this version of procedural justice is commercial viability and the characteristic remedy for those dissatisfied with services is to exercise their power of exit by choosing a different service.

Policy issues are not usually expressed in terms of a single policy framework, indeed they are more commonly described in terms of composite policy frameworks. Interest groups may suggest that their perspective reflects superior values to those of other contenders, but in practice policy frameworks have different strengths and weaknesses and trade-offs are made between them. Thus, for example, the professional policy framework emphasises service and the need to provide individual solutions to particular problems, but provides few opportunities for legal recourse if the service user disagrees with the professional's perception of the problem. A policy framework based on legality promises to judge individual claims for resources fairly, but the negative trade-off might be that parents who are poor and inarticulate may not be in a position to claim their rights. Such a policy framework has no concern for systemic equity and collective justice. A bureaucratic policy framework might score highly on sticking to agreed procedures, but may be inflexible and unable to meet individual needs. Kirp's analysis thus makes clear that establishing the dominance of a policy framework is a highly political activity, since proponents of different frameworks are in competition with each other. Below, we discuss two local authority case studies, one in England (LA3) and one in Scotland (LA1) in the light of our typology of models of procedural justice.

Local authority case studies

Demographic characteristics

LA3 was a small English metropolitan authority in the heart of an old northern coalfield serving a relatively homogeneous and largely disadvantaged community. There were few people from minority ethnic backgrounds and a low proportion of people moving into or out of the area. Unemployment in the area was high (12.8 per cent compared with 7.4 per cent nationally). Education had traditionally had a low profile among the aspirations of the community, signalled by the low proportion of students remaining in education after the age of 16 (53 per cent as opposed to 70 per cent nationally). The 1991 census showed that higher education qualifications were held by only 7.5 per cent of the population, compared with a national figure of 13.5 per cent. According to a 1999 OFSTED report, standards in schools were low compared with national averages and those of similar LEAs. The authority was criticised by OFSTED for having done little to raise the profile of education and levels of pupils' achievements, and was seen as having complicated and inefficient internal management arrangements.

LA1 was a Scottish city which had experienced a long period of industrial decline. Forty-two per cent of the city's population lived in an area of deprivation. In 54 per cent of city schools more than half the children were entitled to free school meals. The city had an unemployment rate of 11.6 per cent, the highest of any council area in Scotland and 29 per cent above the UK level. Forty-one per cent of children in the city were in families dependent on income support. The city had a high and increasing number of single-parent households and a relatively high minority ethnic population.

SEN provision

In LA3, 3.8 per cent of the school population had a statement of needs. Most statemented children (83.5 per cent) were educated in mainstream schools and the authority had only three special schools, four units attached to mainstream and one stand-alone unit. This high use of mainstream schools was not as a result of a major policy change, but rather because special schools had never been built in this area. Some mainstream schools had been adapted to accommodate pupils with physical disabilities while the units attached offered specialised teaching to children with hearing impairments, specific learning difficulties, autism and behaviour problems. LA3 had very low rates of appeals. According to the Special Educational Needs Tribunal Annual Report, two appeals were registered with the SENT in 1998–99 and five in 1997–98. During this period there was one complaint of maladministration to the Commission for Local Administration in England.

Scottish LA1 had a relatively high proportion of children with a record of needs (2.8% of the school population), indicative of the high levels of social deprivation in the area. Due to a major building programme in the 1950s and 1960s, LA1 had a large amount of special provision for children with SEN (31 special schools and three special units attached to mainstream) and as a result had a low proportion of children with a record in mainstream schooling (18.5 per cent). This was a reversal of the position in LA3.

SEN policies and procedures

In terms of its SEN policy, LA3 was characterised as a benign bureaucracy, but a range of competing policy frameworks were evident and these are summarised in Table 11.3.

In line with English national policy, many features of SEN policy and procedure in LA3 were geared towards assisting parents to play an active role in the assessment and statementing of their children and to seek legal redress where appropriate. However, many parents experienced structural disadvantage and were therefore unable to exploit fully the options available. For example, with the initial letter announcing the commencement of statutory assessment procedures, parents were given a DfEE booklet explaining the process of drawing up a statement. However, many parents interviewed did not find this booklet accessible. For a time, a senior officer had hand-delivered all initial notices of the authority's intention to begin the process of statutory assessment. However, this practice was discontinued because of changes in personnel. It was felt that whilst it had been very worthwhile for some parents in terms of demystifying the process, for others it was 'a waste of time because you go and you can tell they're not listening to you' (Education Officer, LA3). Instead of providing parents with more help, this officer concluded that there was no point in trying to secure greater involvement because parents lacked understanding and motivation, thus locating the fault with them rather than the system of communication.

Within our typology, Scottish LA1 was characterised as an example of bureaucratised professionalism (see Table 11.4), indicating the extent to which professionals had been co-opted into bureaucratic systems. Like English LA3, the policy framework included elements of bureaucracy, professionalism and legal/consumerist systems.

Whilst procedures in LA3 sometimes mitigated against parental involvement, this was even more evident in LA1. Practice in this authority was often in direct contravention of advice in the Scottish Executive's *Manual of Good Practice* (SOEID 1998). For instance, the Scottish Executive advised that parents should be

Table 11.3 Model features of English LA3*

Model	Features	
Bureaucracy	Decision on who gets a statutory assessment made by committee. Members: 8 officers, 2 professionals and 1 administrative assistant. This most important decision. Committee works to criteria when deciding whether to begin a statutory assessment. Decision on who gets a statement (of lesser significance) made by sole officer. Underpinned by system of internal monitoring. Formulaic allocation of EP time to schools	NB: Most of the members of this committee have been practising teachers. Distinction between officers and professionals is blurred
Professionalism	EPs generally perceived to have most influence. In some cases MO/psychiatrist. EPs see themselves as working on behalf of the child	NB: EPs hold no gate-keeper role when decision made to begin a statutory assessment. EPs stressed they have no more power or influence than any other report writer when decision is made on who gets a statement. EPs valued working in this way
Legality	Regulations within the Code of Practice give parents clear grounds for appeal/complaint if procedures not followed. Rights to appeal to SENT are set out in the Education Act 1996	Very low rate of appeal to SENT or complaint to ombudsman
Managerialism	Performance indicator of time taken to open a statement of needs published. Concern to adhere to recommended timescales. Recent OFSTED report recommended more tightly regulated systems to raise standards in schools and to improve administration of SEN, including budgetary control	NB: Evidence of local authority subjecting systems to tighter scrutiny – research seen as element in this
Consumerism	If parents make firm representation at the draft statement stage, generally seen to have most power. Parent Partnership Officer seeking to engage with parents	NB: Few parents informed of their rights beyond the legal minimum. Parents tend to trust professionals to do the right thing. Parents did not indicate they had used LEA-initiated pamphlets. Named Person little used. Evidence of heads acting in that capacity or *(continued)*

Model	Features	
		suggesting Named Person not needed, thereby counteracting the independent nature of the role. Schools used this ploy to protect own level of support hours. At the draft statement stage, evidence of some schools using parents to fight for support hours to mean one-to-one rather than small group hours, even when parents not in agreement
Markets	Parents given list of schools from which to choose	NB: Choice of school restricted to mainstream because of lack of special schools

* See page 206 for key to Table

invited to attend all statutory assessments, but case study parents were routinely invited to attend only the medical assessment. Whereas local authorities were advised to give parents copies of all assessment reports, these were only distributed when specifically requested. This meant that parents often turned up at the case conference without having seen any assessment reports which professionals had had time to digest. Parents in LA1 were given two tightly printed sides of A4 at the start of the statutory assessment process explaining procedures. This document minimised the legal significance of the record, stating:

> It gives you something in writing about your child's difficulties and how the education authority and others are going to help. It helps to make sure that you are fully involved in the process of assessment and also gives you certain rights to object if things are not going as you want them to.

No mention was made of the authority's obligation to provide resources to meet the needs specified in the record, and parents were not told what to do if 'things are not going as you want them to'. Furthermore, the Named Person was described as 'someone to whom you can talk and can help you' instead of a technical adviser and advocate as suggested in Scottish Executive guidance. Only one parent in our LA1 case studies used a Named Person as an advocate. Parents were told that the letters 'may seem very formal and may take a long time'. No attempt had been made by the authority to write the letters in an accessible manner whilst conveying the necessary legal advice. Finally, no mention was made of the recommended time for the opening of a record (i.e. six months). In 1998–99, LA1 took on average 43 weeks to open a record (average time in Scotland was 34 weeks).

Table 11.4 Model features of Scottish LA1*

Model	Features	
Bureaucracy	Local Authority stipulates particular phrases to be used where extra resources are implicated, LA also edits final copy of Record. EPs see themselves as working on behalf of the Local Authority but are often resentful of their professional status being compromised. Coincidence of interest between EPs and education officers	NB: EP in sole charge of bureaucratic process until draft RoN stage when local authority sends copies to parents and other professionals prior to sending final version of RoN
Professionalism	EPs generally perceived to have most influence – have absolute control over RoN process and outcome Decision to commence assessments with regard to opening a RoN made by EP. Parents, schools and other professionals can initiate recording but this rarely happens. On completion of assessments EP recommends to Senior Education Officer if RoN should be opened. EP's decision rarely if ever questioned	NB: EPs hold vital gate-keeping role with regard to commencing assessments leading to RoN. EPs conscious of privileged position in RoN process – best qualified to guide the process
Legality	Parents may object to school nominated on the RoN, but little understanding of the process or their power within it	NB: Parents unaware of the potential of the RoN document to challenge the EA. Knowledge of process restricted to EP's explanation and 2-page description. Procedures within LA Appeal Committee seriously flawed No data available on SEN placement appeals or appeals to Scottish ministers
Managerialism	Accounts Commission for Scotland publishes information of time taken to open Record. No other PIs published nationally	NB: EA takes much longer to open Record than the 6 months recommended time
Consumerism	Little local support available to parents. ISEA offers advice to parents on SEN procedures and rights	NB: Few opportunities for parents to exercise 'voice'. Sparse information available. System not 'user friendly'. Named Person little used – often presented to parents by EP as next of kin or family friend rather than advocate
Markets	Information not routinely provided on possible schools	

* See page 206 for key to Table

In LA1 it was evident that the desire to control spending on special educational needs was of major concern. An education officer explained that she instructed educational psychologists to write the record in general terms without committing the authority to any specific expenditure:

> I do have a certain expectation in terms of content. For example, special needs auxiliary, we now have as a standard phrase in the record 'Access to special needs auxiliary as determined by the Individualised Educational Plan', or if it's transport, 'Transport has to be kept under review'.
>
> (Education Officer)[2]

Communication between professionals and parents

LA3 officers sometimes marginalised parents in the statementing process. For example, parents were routinely given copies of all assessment reports with the draft statement, but did not receive them at the same time as the professionals and therefore had a shorter period of time to consult and consider the need for further action (e.g. requesting a second medical opinion). In addition, as required by law, parents were given a list of all the possible schools which their child might attend. However, the LA almost always recommended that the child should be placed in the local mainstream school, thus closing down rather than opening up discussion of alternatives. Educational psychologists were invited to comment on the relatively low levels of appeal. It was suggested by a senior official that 'there is quite a lot of effort goes into conciliation'. In addition, the passivity of the local community was seen as a problem, rather than the failure of the local authority to support and encourage the use of legal redress procedures.

On the face of it, parents in LA3 were given all the information they needed to appeal. They were informed of their right to appeal, and after the delivery of the draft statement were offered two meetings with a senior official in addition to access to a Parent Partnership Officer. If a resolution was not reached after these meetings, parents were told that they could begin appeals proceedings. However, it was evident that few parents found the appeal route particularly attractive. Unlike more socially advantaged authorities, in LA3 there were few support groups or voluntary organisations and parents lacked the back-up necessary to launch a successful appeal. Parents did have access to a Parent Partnership Officer, but the worker in this post concentrated on explaining what the local authority was doing, rather than suggesting alternatives. Very few parents appointed a Named Person to act as independent advocate.

Psychologists in Scottish LA1 found themselves pulled in different directions by the conflicting expectations that they could both act as honest brokers, giving parents the best possible advice about their children's needs, and also as agents of the authority, chairing the meetings and drafting the record in terms of the resources available to the authority. It was acknowledged by psychologists that they were told not to quantify resources on the document. As a result, whilst a lot of resources were devoted to assessing the child's needs, the record was often bland and meaningless. In contrast, whilst noting that the SEN budget was constantly overspent, an education officer insisted that resourcing in this area was 'needs-led'.

Not surprisingly, parents were somewhat confused about the purpose of the record and their role within the process:

> ... I thought they wanted, like, my input on it, but it wisnae, it was just if I agreed with what they wrote, then you didn't have to write anything, just sign it. But if I didnae agree, then write whit I didnae agree on. I didnae know – cause it was all mumbo-jumbo ... I thought it [the record of needs] was nonsense an' awe for the whole time it took and I was like, 'Whit the hell is this?' It's rubbish, pure absolute rubbish that's in it. I don't know if it's awe there, or if that's even the kind of copy I got. I never really opened it.

> (Ben's mother)

Views like this were typically understood by educational psychologists as evidence that the process was too bureaucratic and difficult for parents to understand. However, this parent's perception that the record had no clear purpose was borne out by the conflicting statements by the educational psychologists and education officers.

Relationship between education officers and psychologists

In LA3, educational psychologists described themselves operating as independent agents. They provided important advice to the LEA officers, but did not make the final decision on whether to open a statement, nor did they draft the statement itself. Despite this independence, a large number of appeals would undoubtedly have added to the EPs' workload and therefore it was not in their interests to encourage parents to appeal, but rather to accept a place in their neighbourhood mainstream school. This was in line with existing local authority provision, thus conflict between officers and educational psychologists was avoided.

In LA1, there was a greater degree of conflict between professionals and managers. Whilst educational psychologists complained about the 'raging ambiguity of our position', an education officer felt that since educational psychologists were employed by the authority, then it was quite reasonable that they should comply with the authority's guidelines on SEN provision.

Overall, LAs 1 and 3 were similar with regard to their high levels of poverty and social disadvantage. Whereas English national policy gave considerable power to parents in assessment and statementing procedures, parents in LA3 were by and large disengaged from the process and did not make use of their legal rights of appeal. Whilst formal systems existed to empower parents, educational psychologists and officers were, to some extent, complicit in parental passivity.

Scottish SEN policy provided fewer opportunities for parental engagement in the process, and in LA1 professionals downplayed opportunities for involvement even further. The process of opening a record tended to be seen as a formality, with no commitment on the authority's part to provide any resources. Tensions between educational psychologists and education officers were apparent, the former resenting their co-option into a bureaucratic system over which they had no control.

We now present four case studies which illustrate the ways in which parents interacted with the policy frameworks in the English and Scottish authorities.

Negotiating parent and professional identities within particular procedural justice regimes

Sarah – Scottish LA1: parent as uneasy client

Sarah lived at home with her mother and father in a three-bedroomed council flat in a deprived area of the city. Sarah's father worked full time in a factory and her mother was not employed outside the home. Sarah was a premature baby and subsequently developed speech and language problems, learning difficulties and behavioural difficulties. A younger child in the family also appeared to have speech and language difficulties.

Sarah's record of needs was opened more than a year after she started primary school. An effect of delaying the opening of the record until this point was to cut down opportunities for discussion of school placement, since this decision had already been made. Sarah's case illustrates the difficulties experienced by working-class parents in understanding and contributing to a process which is regarded somewhat cynically by key professionals as a bureaucratic exercise. According to the educational psychologist who worked on Sarah's case:

> The record of needs is neither a detailed piece of literature, nor is it a productive active thing to work upon. It's meant to be something that's understandable to the parents and that is a summary of the child's needs. However, it is not. It's too locked in time to have any long-term significance ... What it does do is that it names the school, it summarises the needs, it suggests in very bland terms how the authority might meet those needs. But really, you're only saying things that the authority is going to be willing to provide.
>
> (Educational psychologist, Scottish LA1)

According to the educational psychologist, the authority insisted that the record should contain a range of prescribed statements in relation to resources that had been approved by the legal department, and committed the authority to as little as possible. Choice between mainstream and special settings was also constrained, because very little additional support was available in mainstream. Her main advice to Sarah's mother had been that a language unit would not be an appropriate placement and that one of the authority's special schools offered better education than the one which was closest to home.

Sarah's mother was initially enthusiastic about the opportunity afforded by a record of needs to improve the quality of education available:

> I had never heard of a record of needs before. But it was a nursery school teacher that Sarah got in the last year she was there. She was a relief teacher, and she had a wee boy that had problems and she advised me – she was the first wan that mentioned the record of needs. She went, 'If it ever crops up that Sarah needs a record of needs, go for it because it's the best thing and it really helps you if you've got any problems or anything like that. If you've got one you'll really get the help'.
>
> (Sarah's mother)

Sarah's mother mentioned this to a range of professionals and as a result it was decided to open a record. However, as the process continued Sarah's mother became increasingly disenchanted. She was told that Sarah would not be given a place at a language unit and later felt that her involvement was not really required. When she phoned the educational psychologist to ask what she should write on Part 7 of the record (the parents' account of the child's difficulties and educational requirements), she was told that a written contribution was not really necessary.

Because Sarah's father was working full time, it was not possible for him to attend any of the meetings and Sarah's mother found it difficult to explain to him what the process was about:

> Sometimes they use language that you can understand but sometimes there are so many people talking at the wan time, know like. I've never had a meeting wan to wan with anybody, there's always been a few and it's just too much – I cannae remember who said this and who said that. I mean it's a bit hard trying to explain to Sarah's daddy when he comes in and goes, 'Right, what happened?' and I go, 'I don't know. Too much at the wan time when you're trying to take it all in' and then they want feedback from you, it's just too much for me.
>
> (Sarah's mother)

Ultimately, Sarah's family accepted the educational psychologist's recommendation of a particular special school and the draft record was duly signed and returned with no parental statement attached. However, both the educational psychologist and the parents felt there had been little purpose in the exercise. The educational psychologist felt constrained by the LA's insistence that the document must commit as few resources as possible. Whilst supporting the principles of inclusion, she felt that so little support was available in mainstream that a special school placement would suit the child better. Having been hopeful that a record of needs would ensure that the required resources were in place, Sarah's parents became gradually disillusioned with the process. Starting out with clear views about the type of education they wished their child to receive, they gradually accepted the role of uneasy client.

Ben – Scottish LA1: the transgressive parent

Most parents in Scottish LA1 adopted the position of passive recipient of services, even if this was at first resisted. However, there were examples of parents who vigorously contested the authority's control, using the legal rights available to them to challenge professional autonomy. Because parents were expected to accept the views of the educational psychologist and senior education officer, there was considerable consternation when these were challenged and no conciliation system was in place to defuse the situation.

Ben was six years old at the time of the research and had two brothers. The family lived in a deprived area of the city in local authority accommodation. All three children had special needs. Before starting nursery, Ben was diagnosed as autistic with language and communication, social and behavioural difficulties.

Ben's mother was an assertive single parent who wished to get the best for her children and felt she was being manipulated into acquiescence by the authority. She was aware that all her children had special needs, and felt that they should be educated in the same school to maintain the strong bond between them. The authority felt that the children had different needs and therefore should be educated in different locations.

The process of assessment and recording began just before Ben was due to start school. At first, Ben's mother felt confused by the procedures, although she did not like the authority's approach. For example, she turned up at a meeting which she believed was to review Ben's progress only to discover that the meeting was to discuss the draft record of needs. She discovered that whilst the professionals in attendance had all been given copies of the assessment reports, she did not have these documents. After this meeting, she decided to seek independent advice: '... so that was when I said to ISEA [Independent Centre for Special Education Advice] "Can I send you this draft copy, can you have a look at it and tell me what's missing?" and she said "Everything".'

Ben's mother was told by ISEA that she was entitled to see all assessment reports and at this point she began a telephone and letter-writing campaign aimed at forcing the authority to share all information about her child with her. Many requests were necessary to get all assessment reports from the authority. Subsequently, she queried the terms of the record. For example, in Part 5 (measures proposed by the authority to meet the child's special educational needs), under the 'Other Services' heading, the record stated:

- Community medical officer and links with hospital service
- Access to physiotherapy and occupational therapy according to changing needs
- Speech and language therapist as part of a multi-disciplinary team.

According to Ben's mother, she was forced to ask the ISEA representative to explain what the record meant:

And I said to her ... what is this [record] supposed to have, because the psychologist hisnae told me and I thought that's what she was there for, to take us through this and what each part meant and everything. But it disnae even say on this that he needs speech and language therapy and how many times a week he is going to get it. Em, his physiotherapy, I mean they just say that it will be deemed appropriate, but as far as I'm concerned that is not right. He was supposed to get occupational therapy when he started school in August, and he's never been assessed in school yet. So ... if they say he needs occupational therapy and it's been deemed appropriate ... they should agree that he either needs it or he doesn't need it and when he was going to get it and how much he would get.

She also pointed to the lack of clarity in the summary of impairments section, suggesting that it was not enough simply to describe a child as 'autistic', without specifying how this manifested itself. At one point, Ben's mother had taken her children out of school in protest and the case had featured in the local press.

The response of the education authority was first to question the purpose of the record: 'I think there's pressure from people who assume the document brings all sorts of additional resources when in fact it doesn't. It is not a resource document' (Educational Psychologist). In addition, doubt was cast on the motives of Ben's mother:

I would not underestimate the power of the media in that she has got into that sort of groove if you like matched perhaps with an aspect of her own personality that has become rigid and rather tunnel visioned. She is having to go down a route and I don't think she is thinking clearly about the rights – the needs of her children ... She is an articulate lady and she is taking other people along with her and I think the needs she is expressing is filling a need in herself.

(Educational Psychologist)

It was evident that the case was causing considerable consternation to the education officer involved in the case, who said that she had never had her judgement questioned in this way before. Ben's mother was aware that the authority was concerned that she would make a formal appeal on both the school placement and the terms of the record. The nature of the authority's reaction, particularly when compared with the routine nature of appeals in many English authorities, indicates that appeals are regarded far more seriously in Scotland, perhaps because they are so rare. Most authorities do not have conciliation procedures, and therefore as soon as a parent embarks on an appeal it is likely that it will be taken to the education authority appeal committee and subsequently to Scottish ministers. If a Scottish parent adopts the position of consumer, then many local authorities in Scotland treat this as an aberration. Lacking conciliation procedures, education officers feel extremely vulnerable and uncertain about how to respond.

Rose – English LA3: parent as (tentative) consumer

Rose was aged six and a half at the time of the research and was attending a mainstream infants school. She lived with her father, mother and two older sisters in a terraced house. This case study illustrates the development of a consumer identity, as parents use enhanced opportunities within the English system to operate as consumers of services with an awareness of their rights.

From an early stage in her development, Rose's mother felt that her daughter was not developing normally and was frustrated when first the health visitor and then the school appeared unwilling to take her concerns seriously. She instigated the process of assessment, lobbied for the acceleration of the school-based stages of support and obtained independent assessments to challenge the local authority's view of Rose's needs. Keeping careful notes, Rose's mother had written to and telephoned the local authority, taken her daughter to the dyslexia unit in another town for assessment, asked for help from the school nurse, approached the Independent Panel for Special Education Advice (IPSEA), sought additional medical assessments including a brain scan and engaged an active Named Person. Throughout the process, Rose's mother was frustrated by the local authority's inefficiency. One of her letters, requesting the commencement of a statutory assessment, was 'mysteriously lost', giving the local authority additional time to draft the statement.

On her statement, Rose's special needs were described as 'deficits in attention, motor control and perceptions' (DAMP), an unusual diagnosis perhaps reflecting the wide range of professionals drawn into the assessment at the parents' insistence. Rose's mother made it clear that she perceived herself to be fighting for her child's rights and challenging the complacency of the LEA:

> I have felt involved because I've made myself involved … You do it for your child; at the end of the day I'll do anything for my children. And it motivates me to fight for her because she was so unhappy at that point at school.
>
> (Mother)

The written contribution to the assessment made by Rose's mother reminded the LEA of its legal duties and chided them for their impersonal approach :

> As Rose's parents, it is our responsibility to see Rose gets the education, by law, she is entitled to. She is our daughter and we love her very much. We feel very strongly about her receiving help quickly. She can get stressed and I am afraid of this affecting her physically making her ill. I will not allow this.
>
> …
>
> I would just like to add how very disappointed I am at your very poor response to my letters. The two letters I have received from you have been standard letters. I even asked for comments from you on my last letter and yet

still no response. I understand that you are very busy but this is no excuse for common courtesy.

(Parental contribution to statutory assessment)

Ultimately, this case was not taken to appeal, although at various stages it was evident that this might have happened. In her statement, Rose was allocated 17.5 hours of support per week individually or in a small group to be delivered by a curriculum support assistant under the direction of the class teacher. Rose's mother had initially requested additional support from a trained teacher, but eventually accepted this compromise. Clearly positioning herself as service consumer and rejecting the position of client, Rose's mother was simply concerned to get the best possible provision as she saw it for her child. Whilst drawing on the expertise of voluntary organisations, Rose's mother did not wish herself to become involved in discussion or action beyond her immediate concerns.

Jane – English LA3: the disengaged parent

The second case study in the English authority illustrates the limits of a consumer or partnership approach. Jane was six years of age at the time of the research. She lived at home with her parents and two older siblings. One of Jane's elder siblings had been excluded from school. The family lived in poor quality local authority housing.

Jane had epilepsy and the statement noted that she had poor language development and difficulty in relating to her peers. Her parents were concerned about her slow progress at school. Her mother commented: 'I just want her to get as much help as she can 'cos she's behind. And like I say, it's not fair her being so behind in the class.' The parents' contribution to the assessment, written by the head teacher on their behalf, noted: 'We just can't understand why she is not making any progress in school, when she seems to be trying.'

According to the school, the assessment had proceeded normally and they were satisfied with the outcome of '12.5 hours of support per week from a Curriculum Support Assistant who will work with her individually or in small group situations'. However, it was clear that the parents had been unable to engage in the process. There was concern that Jane had not been presented at a medical assessment and the Educational Welfare Officer had intervened to tell the parents that they were obliged to do this and legal action would be taken if they did not comply. LEA officers were clear that the statement and all reports had been sent to the parents, and the draft statement had been signed by Jane's mother, but she insisted that she had never seen any of these papers. Jane's parents said that if dissatisfied with their daughter's education, they would 'take things further', but were not clear about what course of action this might involve. Jane's mother said she found it easier to communicate with her GP than the school.

Clearly, these parents were regarded as passive recipients of welfare services by the professionals who worked with them. The parents' response was to opt out of the process entirely, denying any knowledge of assessments and correspondence and refusing to take their child for a medical assessment until compelled to do so. Professionals were perceived as punitive rather than benign agents of the state. In order for them to be more actively involved as service consumers or as active citizens, far greater support from the LEA would be necessary to overcome the effects of poverty and exclusion. Professionals, however, felt that they had taken all reasonable steps to engage with this family and, whilst they were concerned about the family's lack of engagement, did not know what else they could do, particularly given the multiple pressures on their time. This case exemplifies the danger of making individual professionals responsible for counteracting the effects of deep-rooted social and economic exclusion.

Conclusion

This chapter has illustrated the tensions between different policy frameworks in local authorities in England and Scotland. In England, traditional forms of bureaucracy and professionalism had been challenged by legality, consumerism, managerialism and marketisation. There was evidence that English professionals found this system pressurising and they used a variety of tactics to minimise the extent to which parents could operate as critical consumers. In Scotland, professionalism was still the dominant motif, although in LA1 educational psychologists appeared to be operating as 'bureau-professionals' (Newman and Clarke 1994) rather than independent advisers of parents and children. Whilst Scottish professionals enjoyed a considerable amount of power, they were nonetheless aware of the contradictions within their position, as they attempted to act as local authority agents and to discharge their responsibility to act in the best interest of their client. Despite the fact that parents were actively deterred from adopting the position of consumer, there were fears at authority level that the system was becoming too 'adversarial'. A recent proposal that mediation services and a Special Educational Needs Tribunal should be established in Scotland has been criticised by some educational psychologists and education officers. Even though SEN professionals in Scotland have considerably more autonomy than their English counterparts, they are highly resistant to emerging consumer identities among parents. This is in line with McPherson and Raab's thesis, discussed earlier, that professional autonomy has been particularly important in Scotland, standing as a symbol of resistance to English policy incursions.

Policy formation and implementation are clearly dynamic processes. Politicians attempt to implement policy objectives which accord with their broader goals, and these are transformed as they are implemented at local levels. Within each of our case study local authorities, elements of professionalism, bureaucracy and consumerism could be observed. Whilst efforts have been made at national levels to encourage parents to develop consumer identities, particularly in England, our case studies illustrate the factors which prevent parents from exercising control. Professionals may resist attempts to regulate their actions and parents may be unable to adopt the role of critical consumer because of structural constraints.

There is also evidence within both the English and the Scottish systems of considerable variation in the experiences of individual families. Many families of children with SEN in local authorities 1 and 3, like those of Jane and Sarah, experienced high levels of social disadvantage and were disengaged from the process of assessment and statementing/recording. Rather than empowering such parents, these procedures were experienced as a 'disciplinary mechanism' (Foucault 1977) and parents actively resisted the imposition of a consumer identity. However, in both the English and the Scottish authorities, there were families like those of Rose and Ben who were highly engaged in the process and resisted the identity of passive consumer.

Overall, it is evident that parents and professionals are involved in an iterative process of identity formation, and that management of scarce resources is a driving force in this process. If all parents were to adopt the position of active consumer, the system would collapse under the pressure. Whilst some parents, particularly those who speak the same language as professionals, are empowered to claim their rights, it is in the interests of professionals to discourage most parents from active engagement and challenge. Social class clearly plays a key role in determining which parents will be cooled out of the system. Where socially excluded parents perceive that this is taking place, their response may be to avoid all co-operation, thus mounting a challenge to the illusion of consensus. Whilst the actions of professionals in the field of special educational needs have long been characterised in terms of 'benign professionalism' (Tomlinson 1982) they may also be understood as a rational response to the pressures of inadequate resourcing. Finally, our study illustrates the importance of charting the emergence of contrasting national policies following devolution, but also shows the importance of examining fine-grained experience at local level, as parents and professionals negotiate identities in relation to each other.

Acknowledgements

I would like to thank warmly the colleagues with whom I collaborated on this study. They are Professor Mike Adler and Dr Enid Mordaunt, Department of Social Policy, University of Edinburgh and Alastair Wilson, Strathclyde Centre for Disability Research, University of Glasgow.

Key to Tables 11.3 and 11.4

EP = Educational Psychologist
MO = Medical Officer
SENT = Special Educational Needs Tribunal
OFSTED = Office for Standards in Education

RoN = Record of Needs
ISEA = Independent Centre for Special Education Advice
LA = Local Authority

Notes

1 A statement of needs is a document which summarises the educational needs of children with SEN and the ways in which the local authority proposes to meet these needs.
   A Record of Needs is the equivalent Scottish document. There are some important technical and legal differences between statementing and recording which are discussed in
   the text. A Named Person may be appointed in Scotland at the request of the parent to
   provide advice and support throughout the process of assessment and recording. These
   terms are discussed in more depth in Riddell, S. (2002) *Policy and Practice in
   Education: Special Educational Needs*, Edinburgh: Dunedin Academic Press.
2 Quotations are reproduced here using the precise words and inflection of the speaker.
   We believe this is important in order to convey, as closely as possible, the precise meaning which the speaker wished to convey. Editing the speaker's language and grammar
   would have been at the cost of authenticity. Occasionally, a few words have been missed
   out of a quotation to make the meaning clear. This is indicated in the text by three dots.

References

Adler, M., Petch, A. and Tweedie, J. (1989) *Parental Choice and Education Policy*,
    Edinburgh: Edinburgh University Press
Armstrong, D. (1995) *Power and Partnership in Education*, London: Routledge
Beck, U. (1992) *Risk Society: Towards a New Modernity*, London: Sage
Beck, U., Giddens, A. and Lash, S. (1994) *Reflexive Modernization*, Cambridge: Polity Press
Cabinet Office (1999) *Modernising Government*, London: The Stationery Office
Clarke, J. and Newman, J. (1997) *The Managerial State*, London: Sage
Cole, I. and Furbey, R. (1994) *The Eclipse of Council Housing*, London: Routledge
Deakin, N. (1994) *The Politics of Welfare: Continuities and Change*, London: Harvester
    Wheatsheaf
Department for Education (1994) *Code of Practice on the Identification and Assessment of
    Special Educational Needs*, London: DfE
Exworthy, M. and Halford, S. (1999) (eds) *Professionals and the New Managerialism in the
    Public Sector*, Buckingham: Open University Press
Foucault, M. (1977) *Discipline and Punish*, London: Penguin
Gewirtz, S., Ball, S. J. and Bowe, R. (1995) *Markets, Choice and Equity*, Buckingham:
    Open University Press
Glennerster, H. (1991) 'Quasi-markets for education?', *Economic Journal*, 101: 1,
    268–1,267
Hirschman, A. (1970) *Exit, Voice and Loyalty*, Cambridge MA: Harvard University Press
Hughes, G. (ed.) (1998) *Imagining Welfare Futures*, London: Routledge
Hughes, G. and Lewis, G. (eds) (1998) *Unsettling Welfare: the Reconstruction of Social
    Policy*, London: Routledge
Humes, W. (1986) *The Leadership Class in Scottish Education*, Edinburgh: John Donald
Kirp, D. (1982) 'Professionalisation as policy choice: British special education in compara-
    tive perspective', *World Politics*, XXXIV, 2: 137–174

Lash, S. and Urry, J. (1993) *Economies of Signs and Space*, London: Sage

Le Grand, J. (1991) 'Quasi-markets in social policy', *Economic Journal*, 101: 1,256–1,267

Lipsky, M. (1980) *Street-level Bureaucrats*, New York, NY: Russell Sage

Mashaw, J. L. (1983) *Bureaucratic Justice: Managing Social Security Disability Claims*, New Haven and London: Yale University Press

McPherson, A. and Raab, C. D. (1988) *Governing Education*, Edinburgh: Edinburgh University Press

Mordaunt, E. (2001) 'The nature of special educational needs partnerships' in Riddell, S. and Tett, L. (eds) *Education, Social Justice and Inter-Agency Working: Joined-Up or Fractured Policy*, London: Routledge

Newman, E. and Clark, J. (1994) 'Going about our business?' in Clarke, J., Cochrane, A. and McLoughlin, E. (eds) *Managing Social Policy*, London: Sage

Riddell, S., Adler, M., Mordaunt, E. and Wilson, A. (2000) 'Special educational needs and competing policy frameworks in England and Scotland', *Journal of Education Policy*, 15, 6, 621–635

Saraga, E. (ed.) (1998) *Embodying the Social*, London: Routledge

Scottish Office Education and Industry Department (1996) *Assessment of Children with Special Educational Needs* (Circular 4/96), Edinburgh: SOEID

Scottish Office Education and Industry Department (1998) *A Manual of Good Practice in Special Educational Needs*, Edinburgh: HMSO

Tomlinson, S. (1982) *A Sociology of Special Education*, London: Routledge and Kegan Paul

Weatherley, R. (1979) *Reforming Special Education*, Cambridge, MA: MIT Press

Wilding, P. (1982) *Professional Power and Social Welfare*, London: Routledge and Kegan Paul

Vincent, C. (2000) *Including Parents? Education, Citizenship and Parental Agency*, Buckingham: Open University Press

Chapter 12

Social justice, identity formation and social capital

School diversification policy under New Labour

Eva Gamarnikow and Anthony Green

> At the heart of our reforms is the planned transformation of secondary edu-
> cation. The core values remain the same; that every child is of equal worth
> but the model of comprehensive schooling that grew up in the 1960s and
> 1970s is simply inadequate for today's needs ... The secondary school of the
> future will be specialist, not simply in the technical sense but with a charac-
> ter and ethos that is distinctive to each school and which focuses on the
> individual talent and potential of each child ... It means every secondary
> school on a ladder of improvement ... It means a new focus on the leadership
> of Heads ... greater career opportunities for teachers ... radical intervention
> to deal with failure in schools and LEAs ... using our best schools to raise the
> standards of the rest ... (and) a relentless drive against poor behaviour, indis-
> cipline and truancy ... Only in this way can we fulfil the original
> comprehensive ideal – every child being of equal worth.
>
> (Morris 2002)

The focus of this chapter is on understanding and interrogating educational policies, institutions and practices as state-sponsored contexts of identity formation in
which it is recognised that the point of the education system is *not* to produce a
pattern of equal identities – it is *difference and distinction* that count. While each
child may be, in the words of the former Secretary of State for Education, 'of
equal worth', that is at best nominal, and a credentialing system of normalised
horizontally diverse and vertically unequal identities is the material and ideological *raison d'être* of the system. There are, of course, winners and losers and the
prize for governmentality in New Labour mode is to promote belief in the myth,
or at least acquiescence to the rhetoric, of excellence for all – everyone's a winner.

We develop this theme by exploring concepts of social justice, drawing on the
work of Rawls (1973) and postmodern developments (Fraser 1997; Gewirtz 1998,
2000) which link social justice and identity. We then open up a brief connective
analysis of the concept of social capital to establish a rationale for focusing upon
its pivotal role in New Labour social policy with respect to the dynamics of identity formation and social justice. Having established the theoretical parameters of
the argument, we then examine current New Labour education policy discourse,

focusing on the relationships between the institutionalisation of both the horizontalist *specialisation* and verticalist *beaconisation*, with *trust* and *social capitalist professionalist* networks as the key components of educational reform.

Social justice

Here we are drawing on two broad perspectives on social justice, each of which is arguably compatible with capitalist forms of liberal social programmes, Rawlsian (Laborde 2002; Rawls 1973) and postmodernist (Fraser 1997; Gewirtz 1998, 2000; Young 1990). Rawls's theory of distributive justice is concerned with establishing the parameters of social justice in unequal societies. His key argument, for our purpose, is that social inequalities can only be justified if they benefit the worst off. The political power of this principle can be seen in the different ways in which it has been used to justify various policies over time. In the social democratic era, the welfare state of Marshall's (1950) social citizenship constituted a critique of classical economic markets that were seen as responsible for massive social inequalities, but which could be attenuated by de-marketisation and more equal distribution of social goods such as education, health, housing, etc. In the subsequent neo-liberal era, the Rawlsian principle also found resonance in the notion of the 'trickle-down' effect – an incongruously classical justification for feeling comfortable with increasing social inequalities by reference to their supposed beneficial effects for the worst off. The New Labour policy vision is, by contrast, less direct and more confused and confusing (Blair 1998, 2002; Driver and Martell 1998; Giddens 1998; Powell 1999). The disadvantaged and 'excluded' are the focus of 'opportunity' policies, to ensure that access to education, health, housing etc. are more equally distributed. However, the emphasis is not so much on equalisation, but on more equitable distribution of opportunities to become, or to identify with being, unequal yet included. Here the supposed merits of meritocracy lie in providing more equal opportunities for the worst off, while allowing the hierarchical opportunity structure itself to remain fixed and unequal. In their different ways, therefore, various policy perspectives have addressed the classic Rawlsian social justice issue of legitimation and governmentality (Dean 1999; Foucault 1991).

A difficulty with the Rawlsian perspective on social justice is the overwhelming focus on economic inequalities within an assumed society of culturally identical citizens. More recent theories (Fraser 1997; Gewirtz 1998, 2000; Young 1990) add two other dimensions to social justice that more directly problematise the issue of cultural identity and the realities of participation (see also Cribb and Gewirtz, this volume). Here social justice also includes relational and associational aspects – recognition and esteem of difference as cultural justice and equity of participation in social and political life. Thus, linking these to the issue of identity, following Rawls's principle of justice, a system of differentiated educational outcomes – individuals' credentialed identities – requires legitimation as fostering the publicly recognisable interests of the least esteemed and least advantaged.

Thus, social justice is also about recognition and authenticity of identity and equity in participation.

Turning to current school diversification policy, there are three main themes with regard to what is problematic about the social justice implications for education. First, there is a requirement to evaluate policy in terms of assessing outcomes aimed at feasible relative social opening versus social closure and social class consolidation. Will current policy provide greater opportunities for social mobility? Second, there are the Rawlsian distributive justice considerations, which address the likely effects of institutionalised, systemic diversification of credentialed educational identities. Third, there is the question of policy discourse as obfuscation of the mechanisms of power through its accounts of systems of distribution of educational opportunities in which all parties seem committed, rhetorically at least, to equality of opportunity.

The bottom line of apparent or assumed policy agreement is that equality of opportunity is a social good to be aspired to and that any policy development should be assessed against this, whether policy is coming from old-style social democracy, neo-liberalism or Third Way formulations. The question is, however, not so much this ideal as a distant target, but the policies, processes and procedures promulgated to move in the direction of its realisation. Thus our first consideration is about feasible policy under any model of progressive capitalism that can be assessed as moving in the direction of equalising opportunities. That is to say, over time a progressive policy in these terms would be presentable in a graphic model in which, while everyone in the system is showing signs of improving, no matter from which position they start, those best placed are improving at slower rates than those who start from a lower position in the system of opportunities. Thus their respective graphs of attainment of social goods over time – in this case significant educational credentials which are exchangeable in the market for life chances – tend to converge, as the downsiders improve more rapidly than the upsiders. Thus everyone is winning, an oxymoronic proposition left as such, but rendered reasonable if the less well off are indeed doing better than the well off (for examples of this form of argument see Coleman 1990; and more recently, Gillborn and Youdell 2000; Wolf 2002). The issue then becomes whether we can be confident that this is systematically happening, or likely to happen as a consequence of contemporary education policy. We argue that it is unlikely.

The second consideration picks this issue up as a matter of distributive justice and focuses on how current policy fares in relation to Rawls's basic model as it might apply to the circumstances of current English state education. In recognition of the argument that opportunities are systematically and unequally distributed, the problem shifts to whether the continuing systematic inequality can be rationalised in Rawls's terms. Thus, so far as educational institutionalised identity formation is concerned, every student should have an equal opportunity to attend a school that has parity of esteem of institutional identity with every other school in the system of available schools. Similarly, within each school parity of both opportunities to achieve and respect for students' achievements should prevail. This implies horizontal differentiation with vertical equality or different but equal, a highly contestable, perhaps essentially contradictory policy aspiration, encapsulated in Estelle Morris's 'every child of equal worth'. However, in Rawls's terms, where hierarchy does manifest itself in the educational system, giving rise to patterns of differentially credentialed identities, to be progressive it must operate in the name of fostering the best interests of the least well placed, the least esteemed identities. We argue that current policy does not measure up well in these terms, indeed it obfuscates the issues. This takes us to our third main consideration, namely, that social capital theory is importantly, though not solely, implicated in these policy obfuscation processes. Thus the modes and mechanisms of social capitalism are implicated as ideology so far as the state's role in identity formation is concerned.

Social capital theory

There are many different variants of social capital theory (Coleman 1988; Putnam *et al.* 1994; Putnam 2000; Fukuyama 1995; Bourdieu 1983) which we have discussed elsewhere (Gamarnikow and Green 1999a, 1999b). Although the specificities of focus and emphasis vary between, in particular Coleman, Putnam and Fukuyama, and Bourdieu, all agree about the traditionally recognised ingredients: norms of trust and reciprocity, networks, civic engagement. Social capital theory is fundamentally concerned with two aspects of the social. First, it concerns the benefits which accrue to individuals from being located in social networks. In this context, social capital theory views social structures and social relations as tactical and strategic resources at the personal level. The second aspect flows from the first and is concerned with the collective benefits which derive from social networks. Social capital theorists argue that generalising the trust and reciprocity embedded in networks can lead to increased economic productivity (Fukuyama 1995), greater participation by citizens (Putnam 1994, 2000), more educogenic parenting (Coleman 1988), etc. In simple terms, a society with high levels of social capital is a cohesive, well-functioning society, with improving socially desirable outcomes and fewer negative ones, such as crime and social exclusion.

As far as social policy is concerned, social capital ideas are highly favoured and in post-socialist, post-welfarist, late modern societies they have become a standard policy instrument (Office of National Statistics 2001), though only rarely named as such. The take-up of these ideas is global (Giddens 1998, 2001; Castells 1996): the World Bank, for instance, has a dedicated social capital website and promotes anti-poverty and development strategies which focus on social capital building (Fine 1999; World Bank 2000).

From the perspective of critical policy analysis, social capital theory is interesting in that it draws attention to the social as both a *topic* for policy development and a *resource* in policy implementation. Sociologists (for example, Baron *et al.* 2000; Morrow 2001) have argued that social capital theory has useful heuristic properties in drawing attention to social networking, informal structures, communities etc. In this sense, social capital is neither intrinsically good nor bad; it is simply a way of conceptualising aspects of the social. Difficulties arise, however, if, as we argue below, social policy draws upon social capital mechanisms when these have the *ideological* effect of both obscuring and reinforcing structures of inequality and social injustice. This tendency to ignore or mis-recognise structures of inequality can arise from particular forms of social capital theory itself, most notably theories drawing on Putnam's (1994, 2000) functionalist model of a plurality of equivalent networks which supposedly secure democratic participation. However, ignoring or mis-recognising structures of inequality can also be related to the socially constitutive processes of governmentality which propose vision for creating social integration. Bourdieu's (1983) approach, by contrast, regards the social capital of networks as linked to other unequally distributed capitals, cultural, symbolic and, of course, economic. We are relatively sympathetic to his approach. In particular, links between social justice, identity and social capital as resources can be found in contexts where the role of social networks is to produce and reproduce differential advantages in social and cultural recognition and the positional consequences of forming differential esteem of identity. Thus, social identity is vital for *whom you know* and has consequences for structures of opportunities for both *what you can do*, and *what you can be*.

New Labour and current education policy

So far as social justice is concerned, New Labour's approach is characterised by distinct rhetorical shifts from Old to New, accompanied by fundamental continuities of purposes and procedures with the neo-liberal agenda for education and identity formation. Central are continuities of complexification, diversification and choice, while in reality the state has by no means withered away. However, policy is clearly marked by re-focusing on the social with notions of partnership and community, dynamic images of co-operation in which policy issues are recognisably complex and solutions require joining up networks of potential capacity, linking local state, voluntary and community interests in re-modelled forms of association for a new civil society (Balloch and Taylor 2001; Glendinning *et al.* 2002). In education, for instance, EAZs[1] , Excellence in Cities[2] and the new diversification express these dynamics in differing forms of social capitalisation. It is the social that is ambiguously to partner, and provide opportunities for, the economic, in place of prioritising the role of economic revival to provide trickle-down possibilities for enhancing justice in the social.

In more detail, currently New Labour education policy perspectives are shifting radically away from the initial (Blunkett era) 'standards not structures' (DfEE 1997). In 2002, policy aims continue with the emphasis on improving the quality of all institutions, but particularly of those falling below minimum standards. The new element is to re-focus on structures, on the system of educational provision and do so by identifying diversification of educational institutions as the mechanism for achieving higher quality education (DfEE 2001; DfES 2001; DfES 2002). At the heart of this lies the rhetorical move from Old to New Labour on education, symbolised in the critique of 'one size fits all' comprehensives (Blair 2002; DfES 2002; Morris 2002), and immortalised in recent education history's new 'discourse of derision' (Ball 1990) as the 'bog-standard' or 'bargepole' comprehensive,[3] which carries with it the concomitant push for further diversification of secondary provision. According to the policy rationale, diversification is intended to support individual students' different abilities and talents, satisfy parental demands for quality education, and to institutionalise and celebrate diversity of credentialed educational identities.

There are a number of distinct, and potentially contradictory, mechanisms for achieving these policy aims, as set out in Estelle Morris's quotation (cited above), which merit attention in the present discussion. In an attempt to inject a measure of clarity into current policy discourse on diversification as identity formation, we highlight two oscillating dimensions in this policy of diversification: *specialisation* and *beaconisation*. Specialisation is concerned with increasing the horizontal diversity of schools and institutionalised school identities. The 'one size fits all' comprehensive is to be superseded by the specialist post-comprehensive. Beaconisation, by contrast, is about recognising an explicit and unambiguous hierarchy of schools, identified and ranked on the basis of excellence, managerial and/or pedagogic, as well as 'results'.

We turn first to specialisation. Here every school is to develop 'distinction'. The aim is to create a range of specialist schools, as well as a collection of specialisms, from having a distinctive 'ethos', through to adopting one of the (increasingly extending list of) officially designated specialist statuses. The former of these forms of specialisation is presented as an unproblematic plethora of unique, distinct nominal institutional identities, where each school is to develop its special(ist) ethos or mission. This type of horizontal diversity is available to all schools (DfEE 2001: 47).

Specialist schools have their origin in the Conservatives' City Technology College programme, initiated in 1987 (Whitty *et al.* 1993). The specialist school policy was further developed in the early 1990s in the wake of *Choice and Diversity* (DFE 1992) focusing on four specialisations: in science and technology, the arts, sport and languages. The Green Paper (DfEE 2001) added three more to this list, engineering, science, and business and enterprise. The White Paper (DfES 2001) added maths and computing. The Birmingham Specialist Schools Network, Technology Colleges Trust, etc., constitute starring elaborations of the whole system.

New Labour's discursive contribution to egalitarian organic solidarity in a system of diversity in institutional ethos, mission and identity, appears to offer a wide range of justifications for these innovations. These include references to benefits to schools, benefits to individual students, cultural justice in recognition of diversity, plus intolerance for institutional racism. From the social justice perspective outlined earlier, this form of egalitarian, horizontal diversity of specialised institutional identity can be justified if it benefits the worst off, as Coleman (Coleman *et al.* 1982; Coleman and Hoffer 1987; Coleman 1990) argued in relation to the relatively higher educational achievement of African-American and Hispanic students in (fee-paying) Catholic, as opposed to public (state-provided) schools in the USA. However, it will do nothing of the sort if it disguises hierarchy in a mist of complexity.

We argue that hierarchy is disguised in the current specialist schools policy by combining it with the second dimension of the policy of diversification, namely beaconisation. Beaconisation is radically different from specialisation. Here there is a hierarchy of school types, ranging from the leading lights, the beacons or advanced specialist schools at the top, to schools 'facing challenging circumstances' and/or in special measures (formerly known as 'failing' or 'sink' schools). In this context, beacon schools, first established in September 1998, specialise in designated forms of excellence.

The rationale here is to capitalise on fundamentally hierarchical or vertical differences in identities between schools in the form of a ladder of improvement. A school's position on any rung of the ladder both specifies its identity in relation to excellence (or otherwise) and establishes an improvement agenda for 'upward social mobility' to acquire a more prized institutional identity. As in all stratification systems, movement up or down the structure consolidates the legitimacy of the system of inequality of identities by reproducing that structure itself.

Diversification in its two forms, specialisation and beaconisation, is thus a complex and problematic device for linking reform of structures with reform of the system: extension of specialist status to all schools (horizontal diversity of identity) and expansion of a graduated hierarchy of excellence/weakness (vertical differentiation of status). What links these two moments of horizontal and vertical diversification is the requirement to develop new social capital in the form of professionalist partnerships or networks to share good practice between officially designated diverse schools. Thus, in contexts of horizontal specialisation, schools are to become communities clustered around a shared normative consensus, represented by a distinct ethos for each school, and, increasingly, the development of networks of professionals and schools sharing good practice, or rather, exchanging distinct specialist skills and knowledges, i.e., state-sponsored networks of diversely formed professionality. Beaconisation, by contrast, promotes reform and improvement of weaker schools by means of professional partnerships or federations with stronger schools, i.e., state-sponsored networks of unequally formed professionality. Here location towards the top of the hierarchy is linked to a requirement to develop the social capitalistic professional inter-school partnerships promoting curricular and managerial excellence and/or improvement as an intrinsic aspect of beacon identities.

The fundamental principle is social capitalist, namely to encourage co-operative networks of schools, to share potentially equally esteemed specialisms but, explicitly, unequally distributed excellence. The aim is to improve the performance of the underachieving schools by building on and developing the social capital of education professionals. Thus, the engine driving this new policy of improving the quality and outcomes of education is a state-sponsored rediscovery and rebuilding of teacher professionalism (Morris 2002).

What we detect here is systematic fudging and ambiguity in the policy discourse. On the one hand, it focuses on horizontal diversity, spawning egalitarian networks of professional trust and institutional co-operation. On the other hand, the policy discourse constructs a hierarchical system of professional clientelist relations, masquerading as professional partnerships of equals, where the weak are led by and learn from the strong. Or, quite possibly, this policy discourse is invoking both at the same time. It all revolves around the elusive idea, prize and practice of *trust* as we will elaborate below.

Specialisation/beaconisation: institutional identity, social capital and social justice

In our view, this policy of combined specialisation and beaconisation is a fascinating example of New Labour policy-making fudge on social justice. Both aspects of the policy appear to be about diversification and improvement in the quality of education for all. What is obfuscated is the distinction between specialisation and beaconisation, and the overlapping between a system of schools fostering a diversity of 'equal but different' institutionalised identities and a hierarchical system of school identities managed and improved by networks of professionals led by the high achievers. Thus diversification becomes a discursively complex and oscillating duality of specialisation/beaconisation.

Turning to the mechanisms for identity formation and their implications for social justice in education, specialisation/beaconisation is clearly not a form of traditional social democratic redistribution from the strong to the weak, from the rich to the poor. Neither is it about extending unfettered neo-liberal market relations in which the weak/poor go to the wall and the strong/rich get stronger/richer. Instead, specialisation/beaconisation is an ideological mechanism containing a number of elements. First, specialisation/beaconisation reasserts the policy of greater autonomy for the good/successful, as a form of distinction and material reward. Second, distinction as responsible autonomy and additional funding carry with them the apparently benign Christian charitable approach to professional relations, adapting the Matthew principle: to those that have shall be given ... *provided they are prepared to share it.* Third, in terms of social capital mechanisms, the effect of the policy formulation is to present an unproblematic image of improvement through professional co-operation and partnership. For this to work, the state must capitalise upon already existing forms of trust and networks. Fourth, state policy appears to be creating and institutionalising new professional identities, that of civic entrepreneurial heads (Leadbeater 1997; Leadbeater and Goss 1998), the integrators of these new social capital mechanisms. Their role is to identify resources of already existing trust between colleagues (DfES 2001: 38–9) and to mobilise and enhance them for the common good of the network – but not to capitalise on behalf of their own school. Finally, what is the status of some schools not in the beaconised partnership networks and not esteemed specialists?

The delicate point of tension in these policy developments is that everything revolves around the question of trust, a vital aspect of the social. Trust seems to be the *sine qua non* of social capitalism (Fukuyama 1995). However, social capital theory is highly ambiguous about 'trust'. If trust exists then social capital relations work and are lubricated by that trust. However, in this context relations of trust are not created by the state. So far as policy formulation and implementation are concerned, the state can take advantage of extant trust and social capital, but can it create trust? The key question is: where trust is a problematic matter, somehow it has to be created for there to be *any* social capital to be mobilised, worked with and through. It requires the potentially co-operating partners to identify themselves as being in some ways similar, equal, having a common problem, perhaps even a common enemy. In this context New Labour seems to be proceeding wisely to the extent that they are encouraging the producers, the educationalists, to work things out for themselves. In the latter respect, for instance, Thatcherism inadvertently encouraged the spontaneous development of networks of resistive educational partnerships between schools unwilling to be drawn into competitive relations they saw as, in principle, antithetical to the education service.

Weaker players in the education market, however, may co-operate, not primarily because of trust, but because *there is no alternative* (TINA). Where the weak schools are in a TINA crunch of funding and other pressures there are likely to be consequent effects on professional morale. Thus, New Labour seems to be relying, in this respect, on the good will of the professionals or on what might constitute a new educationist guild ethic, to hold together the weak Cs and Fs, to borrow from Basil Bernstein for a moment (Bernstein 1996), of radically diversified education market relations, while keeping all involved on the same ladder of improvement.

Social policy, social justice and ideology

Our argument is that the evolution from Old to New Labour represents complex shifts in policy discourse on social justice in/through education. Old Labour was characterised by recognition of rights to opportunities to express talents, and by comprehensive social mixing as a means to bring beneficial effects for all (Thrupp 1999). New Labour's approach is concerned with the effects of this educational (and social) exclusion on human capital development. Here New Labour has turned to social capital, both as a real problem to be addressed for social cohesion and also as the magical solution to the problem of creating a just and efficient system of relations between education markets and human capital production.

As will have become evident in what is our ideology/critique (Eagleton 1991; Malesevic and MacKenzie 2002; Thompson 1984) of the current turn in New Labour education policy, we assume a strong role for the state in every aspect of policy formulation and implementation. We are not contemplating a radically devolved model of power, though the rhetorical imagery of governmental discourses might suggest otherwise, particularly the notion of the *enabling* state (Giddens 1998; Secretary of State for Social Security 1999). The grip of the state on the reins of power has not slackened radically since the 1980s, despite claims to rolling back, of transformations from provider to regulator state models, and the more recent mobilisation of social capital in education. Both marketisation in education and social capitalistic notions of partnerships, compacts and networking are powerfully framed in order to deliver the appearance of meeting social and economic targets in the face of pressures of globalisation to localise and regionalise, apparently devolving government both upwards towards the transnational and downwards from central government to the local. Thus, while more modes of state control may be indirect, deploying managerialist targeting and accountability (Clarke *et al.* 2000; Gewirtz 2001), it is nevertheless *control* and its object is securing governmentality, in spite of Blair's professed view that the current reforms place 'power in the hands of the professionals' (Blair 2002).

The educational profession may well be being repositioned, as it is being redesigned, to be the emerging state-sponsored educational producers' guild in this strategy. Under New Labour, the social capitalistic strategy of networking has been revalidated, and is now seen as part of the solution, in the name of recognising and asserting the role of civil society in governance. Up to the 1980s, by contrast, a central consideration in the genesis of social division and injustice was the unfair networking of the well placed.

Social justice, identity formation and schools

As ideology/critique our argument focused on lines of potential contestation and antagonism, as well as on obscuring mechanisms, so far as the identification and realisation of social interests in education policy are concerned. In this respect, on a broader note, the discursive strategy of abstraction is an important moment in power and empowerment, in power/knowledge, in Foucault's (1980) terms, as well as in several other traditions of ideology analysis, where the social, as distinct from, say, the economic, the political, the personal, etc., is discursively invoked as both a problem to be addressed, indeed, *the* problem, and the solution to that very problem being proposed. In this context abstracted social capital theory provides serviceable discursive resources for contemporary governmentality through education policy. This has important implications for social justice in relation to individual and collective identity, particularly where identity and identity formation are simultaneously institutional (at the level of schools) and institutionalised (at the level of relations between schools). These issues and problems run to the heart of contemporary legitimation of social, economic and education policy, providing rationales for social regulation of the public sphere. In this context, abstracted social capital theory endorses hierarchy disguised as differentiation. In effect, we are identifying what may be another form of New Labour 'teflonism' which obscures the role of the state in the context of the non-fungibility of capitals and the unequal distribution of economic capital, life chances, etc.

This is possible, partly, because the discourses of liberal, progressive cultural ecology recommend diversity as a form of social cohesion or reinforcement, a mechanism for social strengthening by cultural enrichment and flexibility, encouraging new adaptive forms of organic solidarity for both intra- and inter-societal relations. The maximisation of mutual respect for diversity, for distinctive, discrete and claimed identities, becomes the progressive maxim of postmodernist cultural justice (Delanty 2000; Fraser 1997; Gewirtz 1998, 2000). It is a motif of New Labour for promoting the appearance of inclusive diversity while adapting largely neo-liberal mechanisms for realising this under a social capitalist umbrella.

Such social justice issues concerning social diversity and cultural justice have already edged onto the agendas for education policy in curriculum, pedagogy and designation of school types where marketisation takes policy in a neo-liberal direction. In this process, multi-cultural and anti-racist problematics (Gundara 2000) for identity politics of schooled knowledge, as well as for parallel concerns in relation to gender (Arnot and Dillabough 2000; Weiner 1994) and disability (Barnes *et al.* 2002) are familiar. However, the question of school types and schools as institutions within systems of identity-forming machinery in relation to social class and economic inequalities has lost much of its salience, as Old Labour's social democratic political perspective has given ground to neo-liberalism, and the 'old school tie' has become a non-issue. These traditional social class issues are now less directly addressed as *social* justice or identity concerns as such. Instead, New Labour (following neo-liberal leads) opts significantly for human capital formation thinly disguised as cultural justice (Phillips 1999) and proposes a politics of cultural inclusion while denying economic redistribution possibilities or measurable social convergence.

In part, this governmentalist strategy takes advantage of the fact that the issues are complex, so that, in social justice terms, the problems of relations of institutional identity are obscured and rendered ambiguous. Questions of social justice, redesigned as the identity-forming implications of the systems of educational institutions, mingle two principles of differentiation into an unresolveable antagonism, but ideologically delivered as the coherence of the specialisation/beaconisation duality. That is, parental school choice and school pupil selection processes may be seen as both a form of (a) respect for cultural differences (liberal identity politics of gender, ethnicity, faith, etc.) *and* (b) implicated in positional differences (class politics) for maintaining or enhancing intergenerational social location. In either case, choice of schools becomes problematic as rights, *either* to choose schooling that is conducive to cultural identity as legitimate identity reproduction (who am I/are we?) *or*, for credentials, positional goods in relation to who you want to be occupationally. Thus, claiming and labelling differentiated school identities has been repackaged. Its effect is a fudging, empowering/disempowering discursive strategy for both central government and school managers in local education markets. This possibility occurs because the antagonism becomes compounded where cultural identity choices operate as proxies for social advantage in the local education market, where the good school just happens to be the successful school in terms of relative positioning in the systems of credentialing of identities. Here the old social capitalism of the overtly class-based old boy network is obscured and displaced while the contemporary social capitalism of the class-based networking continues apace behind the facade of the specialisation/beaconisation model of apparently just allocations of educated identities, sensitive to individual talent and potential of each child, as Estelle Morris had put it. In this situation, social and cultural (in)justice become inextricably entangled, as the work of Bourdieu (and Passeron 1977) and Bernstein (1977) have amply illustrated, as did that of Young (1958) on the de-merits of meritocracy, in an earlier era, the 1950s.

Conclusion

In this chapter we have addressed New Labour policy on diversification in education and explored its implications for social justice. The social justice questions we have been addressing as New Labour's education policies unfold are: will specialisation/beaconisation succeed in helping the weak/poor up to the level of the strong, to equalise, at least, the parity of esteem of identity between the schools involved, and contribute to productive horizontal differentiation of institutional identities? Or, will specialisation/beaconisation rationalise the already existing system of educational hierarchy? Will specialisation/beaconisation support, and be seen to support, the identity/ies and interests of the least esteemed and least advantaged? Will we see convergence, relative stability, or divergence, in achievement, esteem of identities and status? Or, will the forces of distinction continue to do their work to secure social class consolidation and even polarisation as seems to be happening with income? We see little to be optimistic about concerning the social distribution of power in these respects. Our pessimism about the social justice outcomes is revealed through our ideology/critique of the obfuscatory role of social capital ideas in this policy of diversification, which we have identified as the complex and oscillating duality of specialisation/beaconisation. Here we have argued that institutionalised hierarchies of school status operate as, and through, horizontal diversity of institutionalised school identities in a system of schools managed by social capitalistic professional networks of teachers, mobilised around both exchanging specialised knowledge and skills, and improving the weak. It is difficult to envisage how such a system of stratified schools, located in education markets and articulated with the wider processes of power, can produce anything but unequal outcomes, disguised as organic diversity and specialisation, while in reality consolidating further the already existing social class and education hierarchy.

Notes

1 The Education Action Zone (EAZ) policy, started in 1998 and now integrated into the Excellence in Cities programme, is an area-based initiative to raise educational achievement and promote social inclusion in areas of social disadvantage. Its main features, which embody social capital ideas, are clusters of co-operating schools and the Education Action Forum, made up of local partnerships, which manages the EAZ.
2 Excellence in Cities, launched in 1999, is the second New Labour initiative to raise achievement and promote social inclusion. Here the social capital elements include networking between education and the Neighbourhood Renewal Strategy and New Deal for Communities, developing links with the community in recruiting governors and collaborative educational initiatives such as learning centres, learning mentors and mini-EAZs.
3 'Bog-standard' comprehensives emerged as an iconic epithet in the public debate following the announcement of the specialist education policy in the Green Paper (DfEE 2001), when Alastair Campbell, Blair's official spokesman, commented that 'The days of the bog-standard [non-specialist] comprehensive are over' (12 Feb. 2001). 'Bargepole' comprehensives, a similarly iconic condensation symbol, came from Estelle Morris's speech to the Social Market Foundation (Morris 2002), when she said, 'As a teacher, I go into some schools and think "I would like to work here" but there are some I wouldn't touch with a bargepole' (24 June 2002).

References

Arnot, M. and Dillabough, J. (eds) (2000) *Challenging Democracy: International Perspectives on Gender, Education and Citizenship*, London: RoutledgeFalmer

Ball, S. J., (1990) *Politics and policy making in education*, London: Routledge

Balloch, S. and Taylor, M. (eds) (2001) *Partnership Working: Policy and Practice*, Bristol: Policy Press

Barnes, C., Oliver, M. and Barton, L. (eds) (2002) *Disability Studies Today*, Cambridge: Polity Press

Baron, S., Field, J. and Schuller, T. (eds) (2000) *Social Capital: Critical Perspectives*, Oxford: Oxford University Press

Bernstein, B. (1977) *Class, Codes and Control*, vol. 3, 2nd edn, London: Routledge and Kegan Paul

Bernstein, B. (1996) *Pedagogy, Symbolic Control and Identity: Theory, Research and Critique*, Oxford: Rowman & Littlefield

Blair, T. (1998) *The Third Way: New Politics for the New Century*, Fabian Pamphlet 588, London: Fabian Society

Blair, T. (2002) Speech to Labour Party Conference, Tuesday, 1 October

Bourdieu, P. (1983) 'The forms of capital' in Halsey, A. H., Lauder, H., Brown, P. and Wells, A. S. (eds) (1997) *Education: Culture, Economy and Society*, Oxford: Oxford University Press

Bourdieu, P. and Passeron, J.-C. (1977) *Reproduction in Education, Culture and Society*, London: Sage

Castells, M. (1996) *The Rise of Network Society*, Oxford: Blackwell

Clarke, J., Gewirtz, S. and McLaughlin, E. (eds) (2000) *New Managerialism, New Welfare*, London: Sage

Coleman, J. S. (1988) 'Social capital in the creation of human capital' in Halsey, A. H., Lauder, H., Brown, P. and Wells, A. S. (eds) (1997) *Education: Culture, Economy and Society*, Oxford: Oxford University Press

Coleman, J. S. (1990) *Equality and Achievement in Education*, Boulder: Westview Press

Coleman, J. S. and Hoffer, T. (1987) *Public and Private High Schools: the Impact of Communities*, New York: Basic Books

Coleman, J. S., Hoffer, T. and Kilgore, S. (1982) *High School Achievement*, New York: Basic Books

Dean, M. (1999) *Governmentality: Power and Rule in Modern Society*, London: Sage

Delanty, G. (2000) *Citizenship in a Global Age: Society, Culture and Politics*, Buckingham: Open University Press

Department for Education (1992) *Choice and Diversity: a New Framework for Schools*, London: HMSO

Department for Education and Employment (1997) *Excellence in Schools*, London: Stationery Office

Department for Education and Employment (2001) *Schools: Building on Success*, Cm. 5050, London: Stationery Office

Department for Education and Skills (2001) *Schools: Achieving Success*, Cm. 5230, London: Stationery Office

Department for Education and Skills (2002) *Investment for Reform: Comprehensive Spending Review 2002*, London: Stationery Office

Driver, S. and Martell, L. (1998) *New Labour: Politics after Thatcherism*, Cambridge: Polity Press

Eagleton, T. (1991) *Ideology: an Introduction*, London: Verso

Fine, B. (1999) 'The developmental state is dead – long live social capital?' *Development and Change*, 30: 1–19

Foucault, M. (1980) 'The juridical apparatus' in Gordon, C. (ed.), *Power/Knowledge*, London: Pantheon Books 1980

Foucault, M. (1991) 'Governmentality' in Birchell, G., Gordon, C. and Miller, P. (eds) *The Foucault Effect: Studies in Governmentality*, London: Harvester Wheatsheaf

Fraser, N. (1997) 'From redistribution to recognition? Dilemmas of justice in a "post socialist" age' in Phillips, A. (ed.) (1998) *Feminism and Politics*, Oxford: Oxford University Press

Fukuyama, F. (1995) *Trust: the Social Virtues and the Creation of Prosperity*, London: Hamish Hamilton

Gamarnikow, E. and Green, A. (1999a) 'Developing social capital: dilemmas, possibilities and limitations in education' in Hayton, A. (ed.) *Tackling Disaffection and Social Exclusion: Education Perspectives and Policies*, London: Kogan Page

Gamarnikow, E. and Green, A. (1999b) 'The Third Way and social capital: Education Action Zones and a new agenda for education, parents and community', *International Studies in Sociology of Education*, 9, 1: 3–23

Gewirtz, S. (1998) 'Conceptualising justice in education: mapping the territory', *Journal of Education Policy*, 13, 4: 469–484

Gewirtz, S. (2000) 'Social justice, New Labour and school reform' in Lewis, G., Gewirtz, S. and Clarke, J. (eds) (2000) *Rethinking Social Policy*, London: Sage

Gewirtz, S. (2001) *The Managerial School: Post-welfarism and Social Justice in Education*, London: RoutledgeFalmer

Giddens, A. (1998) *The Third Way: the Renewal of Social Democracy*, Cambridge: Polity Press

Giddens, A. (ed.) (2001) *The Global Third Way Debate*, Cambridge: Polity Press

Gillborn, D. and Youdell, D. (2000) *Rationing Education: Policy Reform and School Inequality*, Buckingham: Open University Press

Glendinning, C., Powell, M. and Rummery, K. (eds) (2002) *Partnerships, New Labour and the Governance of Welfare*, Bristol: Policy Press

Gundara, J. S. (2000) *Interculturalism, Education and Inclusion*, London: Sage

Laborde, C. (2002) 'The reception of John Rawls in Europe', *European Journal of Political Theory*, 1, 2: 139–141

Leadbeater, C. (1997) *The Rise of the Social Entrepreneur*, London: Demos

Leadbeater, C. and Goss, S. (1998) *Civic Entrepreneurship*, London: Demos

Malesevic, S. and MacKenzie, I. (eds) (2002) *Ideology after Postmodernism*, London: Pluto Press

Marshall, T. H. (1950) 'Citizenship and social class' in Held, D. (ed.) (1983) *States and Societies*, Oxford: Martin Robertson

Morris, E. (2002) 'Reform of the Comprehensive System', speech given to the Social Market Foundation, London, 24 June, www.smf.co.uk/Morris_24_06.html

Morrow, V. (2001) *Networks and Neighbourhoods: Children's and Young People's Perspectives*, London: Health Development Agency

Office of National Statistics (2001) *Social Capital: a Literature Review*, www.statistics.gov.uk/socialcapital

Phillips, A. (1999) *Which Equalities Matter?*, Cambridge: Polity Press

Powell, M. (ed.) (1999) *New Labour, New Welfare State? The Third Way in British Social Policy*, Bristol: Policy Press

Putnam, R. D. (2000) *Bowling Alone: the Collapse and Revival of American Community*, New York: Simon and Shuster

Putnam, R. D. with Leonardi, R. and Nanetti, R. Y. (1994) *Making Democracy Work: Civic Traditions in Modern Italy*, Princeton, NJ: Princeton University Press

Rawls, J. (1973) *A Theory of Justice*, Oxford: Oxford University Press

Secretary of State for Social Security (1999) *Tackling Poverty and Social Exclusion: Providing Opportunities for all*, Cm. 4445, London: Stationery Office

Thompson, J. B. (1984) *Studies in the Theory of Ideology*, Cambridge: Polity Press

Thrupp, M. (1999) *Schools Making a Difference: Let's be Realistic!* Buckingham: Open University Press

Weiner, G. (1994) *Feminisms in Education*, Buckingham: Open University Press

Whitty, G., Edwards, T. and Gewirtz, S. (1993) *Specialisation and Choice in Urban Education: the City Technology College Experiment*, London: Routledge

Wolf, A. (2002) *Does Education Matter? Myths about Education and Economic Growth*, London: Penguin

World Bank, Social Capital Website: www.worldbank.org/poverty/scapital

World Bank (2000) *Attacking Poverty*, World Bank Development Report 2000–1, Oxford: Oxford University Press/World Bank

Young, I. M. (1990) *Justice and the Politics of Difference*, Princeton, NJ: Princeton University Press

Young, M. (1958) *The Rise of the Meritocracy*, Harmondsworth: Penguin

Index